D0877505

This book is dedicated to C programmers everywhere.

Contents

7. Memory Allocation   **114**

8. Characters and Strings   **135**

9. Boolean Expressions and Variables   **141**

10. C Preprocessor   **146**

11. ANSI/ISO Standard C   **167**

12. The Standard I/O Library   191

13. Library Functions   221

14. Floating Point   248

15. Variable-Length Argument Lists   257

Questions

1. Declarations and Initializations

Basic Types

1.1 How should I decide which integer type to use?
1.2 Why aren't the sizes of the standard types precisely defined?
1.3 Are typedefs like `int16` and `int32` a good idea?
1.4 What should the 64-bit type on new, 64-bit machines be?

Pointer Declarations

1.5 What's wrong with the declaration "`char* p1, p2;`"? I get errors when I try to use p2.
1.6 What's wrong with "`char *p; *p = malloc(10);`"?

Declaration Style

1.7 What's the best way to declare and define global variables?
1.8 What's the best way of implementing opaque (abstract) data types in C?
1.9 How can I make a sort of "semiglobal" variable, that is, one that's private to a few functions spread across a few source files?

Storage Classes

1.10 Do all declarations for the same `static` function or variable have to include the storage class `static`?
1.11 What does `extern` mean in a function declaration?
1.12 What's the `auto` keyword good for?

Typedefs

1.13 What's the difference between using a typedef or a preprocessor macro for a user-defined type?
1.14 I can't seem to define a linked list node that contains a pointer to itself.
1.15 How can I define a pair of mutually referential structures?
1.16 What's the difference between struct x1 { ... };
and typedef struct { ... } x2; ?
1.17 What does "`typedef int (*funcptr)();`" mean?

The const Qualifier

1.18 I have a typedef for char *, and it's not interacting with const the way I expect. Why not?

1.19 Why can't I use const values in initializers and array dimensions?

1.20 What's the difference between const char *p and char * const p?

Complex Declarations

1.21 How do I declare an array of N pointers to functions returning pointers to functions returning pointers to characters, or figure out what similarly complicated declarations mean?

1.22 How can I declare a function that returns a pointer to a function of its own type?

Array Sizes

1.23 Can I declare a local array (or parameter array) of a size matching a passed-in array, or set by another parameter?

1.24 Why doesn't sizeof work on arrays declared extern?

Declaration Problems

1.25 Why is my compiler complaining about an invalid redeclaration of a function that I define and call only once?

1.26 My compiler is complaining about mismatched function prototypes that look fine to me. Why?

1.27 I'm getting strange syntax errors on the very first declaration in a file, but it looks fine. Why?

1.28 Why isn't my compiler letting me declare a large array, such as double array[256][256] ?

Namespace

1.29 How can I determine which identifiers are safe for me to use and which are reserved?

Initialization

1.30 What can I safely assume about the initial values of variables that are not explicitly initialized?

1.31 Why can't I initialize a local array with a string?

1.32 What is the difference between char a[] = "string"; and char *p = "string"; ?

1.33 Is char a[3] = "abc"; legal?

1.34 How do I initialize a pointer to a function?

1.35 Can I initialize unions?

2. Structures, Unions, and Enumerations

Structure Declarations

Structure Operations

Structure Padding

Accessing Members

Miscellaneous Structure Questions

Unions

Enumerations

4. Pointers

Basic Pointer Use

Pointer Manipulations

Pointers as Function Parameters

Miscellaneous Pointer Use

5. Null Pointers

Null Pointers and Null Pointer Constants

The **NULL** Macro

9.   Boolean Expressions and Variables

10.   The C Preprocessor

Macro Definitions

Header Files

Conditional Compilation

11. ANSI/ISO Standard C

The const Qualifier

Using main()

Preprocessor Features

Other ANSI C Issues

Old or Nonstandard Compilers

19.   System Dependencies

20. Miscellaneous

20.27 What are the differences between C and C++? Can I use a C++ compiler to compile C code?

Algorithms

20.28 What's a good way to compare two strings for close, but not necessarily exact, equality?

20.29 What is hashing?

20.30 How can I generate random numbers with a normal, or Gaussian, distribution?

20.31 How can I find the day of the week given the date?

20.32 Will 2000 be a leap year?

20.33 Why can `tm_sec` in the `tm` structure range from 0 to 61?

Trivia

20.34 How do you write a program that produces its own source code as its output?

20.35 What is "Duff's Device"?

20.36 When will the next Obfuscated C Code Contest be held? How can I get a copy of previous winning entries?

20.37 What was the `entry` keyword mentioned in K&R1?

20.38 Where does the name "C" come from, anyway?

20.39 How do you pronounce `"char"`?

20.40 Where are the on-line versions of this book?

Preface

At some point in 1979, I heard a lot of people talking about this relatively new language, C, and the book that had just come out about it. I bought a copy of K&R, otherwise known as *The C Programming Language,* by Brian Kernighan and Dennis Ritchie, but it sat on my shelf for a while because I didn't have an immediate need for it (besides which I was busy being a college freshman at the time). It proved in the end to be an auspicious purchase, though, because when I finally did take it up, I never put it down: I've been programming in C ever since.

In 1983, I came across the Usenet newsgroup net.lang.c, which was (and its successor comp.lang.c still is) an excellent place to learn a lot more about C, to find out what questions everyone else is having about C, and to discover that you may not know all there is to know about C after all. It seems that C, despite its apparent simplicity, has a number of decidedly nonobvious aspects, and certain questions come up over and over again. This book is a collection of some of those questions, with answers, based on the Frequently Asked Questions ("FAQ") list I began posting to comp.lang.c in May 1990.

I hasten to add, however, that this book is not intended as a critique or "hatchet job" on the C language. It is all too easy to blame a language (or any tool) for the difficulties its users encounter with it or to claim that a properly designed tool "ought" to prevent its users from misusing it. It would therefore be easy to regard a book like this, with its long lists of misuses, as a litany of woes attempting to show that the language is hopelessly deficient. Nothing could be farther from the case.

I would never have learned enough about C to be able to write this book, and I would not be attempting to make C more pleasant for others to use by writing this book now, if I did not think that C is a great language or if I did not enjoy programming in it. I *do* like C, and one of the reasons I teach classes in it and spend time participating in discussion about it on the Internet is that I would like to discover which aspects of C (or of programming in general) are difficult to learn or keep people from being able to program efficiently and effectively. This book represents some of what I've learned: These questions are certainly some of the ones people have the most trouble with, and the answers have been refined over several years in an attempt to ensure that people don't have too much trouble with *them*.

A reader will certainly have trouble if there are any errors in these answers, and although the reviewers and I have worked hard to eliminate them, it can be as difficult to eradicate the last error from a large manuscript as it is to stamp out the last bug in a program. I will appreciate any corrections or suggestions sent to me in care of the publisher or at the e-mail address given, and I would like to offer the customary $1.00 reward to the first finder of any error. If you have access to the Internet, you can check for an errata list (and a scorecard of the finders) at the ftp and http addresses mentioned in question 20.40.

As I hope I've made clear, this book is not a critique of the C programming language, nor is it a critique of the book from which I first learned C or of that book's authors. I didn't just learn C from K&R; I also learned a lot about programming. As I contemplate my own contribution to the C programming literature, my only regret is that the present book does not live up to a nice observation made in the second edition of K&R, namely, that "C is not a big language, and it is not well served by a big book." I hope that those who most deeply appreciate C's brevity and precision (and that of K&R) will not be too offended by the fact that this book says some things over and over and over or in three slightly different ways.

Although my name is on the cover, there are a lot of people behind this book, and it's difficult to know where to start handing out acknowledgments. In a sense, every one of comp.lang.c's readers (today estimated at 320,000) is a contributor: The FAQ list behind this book was written for comp.lang.c first, and this book retains the flavor of a good comp.lang.c discussion.

This book also retains, I hope, the philosophy of correct C programming that I began learning when I started reading net.lang.c. Therefore, I shall first acknowledge the posters who stand out in my mind as having most clearly and consistently articulated that philosophy: Doug Gwyn, Guy Harris, Karl Heuer, Henry Spencer, and Chris Torek. These gentlemen have displayed remarkable patience over the years, answering endless questions with generosity and wisdom. I was the one who stuck his neck out and started writing the Frequent questions down, but I would hate to give the impression that the answers are somehow mine. I was once the student (I believe it was Guy who answered my post asking essentially the present volume's question 5.10), and I owe a real debt to the masters who went before me. This book is theirs as much as mine, though I retain title to any inadequacies or mistakes I've made in the presentation.

The former on-line FAQ list grew by a factor of three in the process of becoming this book, and its growth was a bit rapid and awkward at times.

Mark Brader, Vinit Carpenter, Stephen Clamage, Jutta Degener, Doug Gwyn, Karl Heuer, Joseph Kent, and George Leach read proposals or complete drafts and helped to exert some control over the process; I thank them for their many careful suggestions and corrections. Their efforts grew out of a shared wish to improve the overall understanding of C in the programming community. I appreciate their dedication.

Three of those reviewers have also been long-time contributors to the on-line FAQ list. I thank Jutta Degener and Karl Heuer for their help over the years, and I especially thank Mark Brader, who has been my most persistent critic ever since I first began posting the comp.lang.c FAQ list five years ago. I don't know how he has had the stamina to make as many suggestions and corrections as he has and to overcome my continuing stubborn refusal to agree with some of them, even though (as I eventually understood) they really *were* improvements. You can thank Mark for the form of many of this book's explanations and blame me for mangling any of them.

Additional assorted thanks: to Susan Cyr for the cover art; to Bob Dinse and Eskimo North for providing the network access that is particularly vital to a project like this; to Bob Holland for providing the computer on which I've done most of the writing; to Pete Keleher for the Alpha text editor; to the University of Washington Mathematics Research and Engineering libraries for access to their collections; and to the University of Washington Oceanography department for letting me borrow their tape drives to access my dusty old archives of Usenet postings.

Thanks to Tanmoy Bhattacharya for the example in question 11.10, to Arjan Kenter for the code in question 13.7, to Tomohiko Sakamoto for the code in question 20.31, and to Roger Miller for the line in question 11.35.

Thanks to all these people, all over the world, who have contributed to the FAQ list in various ways by offering suggestions, corrections, constructive criticism, or other support: Jamshid Afshar, David Anderson, Tanner Andrews, Sudheer Apte, Joseph Arceneaux, Randall Atkinson, Rick Beem, Peter Bennett, Wayne Berke, Dan Bernstein, John Bickers, Gary Blaine, Yuan Bo, Dave Boutcher, Michael Bresnahan, Vincent Broman, Stan Brown, Joe Buehler, Kimberley Burchett, Gordon Burditt, Burkhard Burow, Conor P. Cahill, D'Arcy J.M. Cain, Christopher Calabrese, Ian Cargill, Paul Carter, Mike Chambers, Billy Chambless, Franklin Chen, Jonathan Chen, Raymond Chen, Richard Cheung, Ken Corbin, Ian Cottam, Russ Cox, Jonathan Cox-head, Lee Crawford, Steve Dahmer, Andrew Daviel, James Davies, John E. Davis, Ken Delong, Norm Diamond, Jeff Dunlop, Ray Dunn, Stephen M. Dunn, Michael J. Eager, Scott Ehrlich, Arno Eigenwillig, Dave Eisen, Bjorn Engsig, David Evans, Clive D.W. Feather, Dominic Feeley, Simao Ferraz, Chris Flatters, Rod Flores, Alexander Forst, Steve Fosdick, Jeff Francis, Tom Gambill, Dave Gillespie, Samuel Goldstein, Tim Goodwin, Alasdair Grant,

Ron Guilmette, Michael Hafner, Tony Hansen, Elliotte Rusty Harold, Joe Harrington, Des Herriott, John Hascall, Ger Hobbelt, Dexter Holland & Co., Jos Horsmeier, Blair Houghton, James C. Hu, Chin Huang, David Hurt, Einar Indridason, Vladimir Ivanovic, Jon Jagger, Ke Jin, Kirk Johnson, Larry Jones, James Kew, Lawrence Kirby, Kin-ichi Kitano, the kittycat, Peter Klausler, Andrew Koenig, Tom Koenig, Adam Kolawa, Jukka Korpela, Ajoy Krishnan T, Markus Kuhn, Deepak Kulkarni, Oliver Laumann, John Lauro, Felix Lee, Mike Lee, Timothy J. Lee, Tony Lee, Marty Leisner, Don Libes, Brian Liedtke, Philip Lijnzaad, Keith Lindsay, Yen-Wei Liu, Paul Long, Christopher Lott, Tim Love, Tim McDaniel, Kevin McMahon, Stuart Mac-Martin, John R. MacMillan, Andrew Main, Bob Makowski, Evan Manning, Barry Margolin, George Matas, Brad Mears, Bill Mitchell, Mark Moraes, Darren Morby, Bernhard Muenzer, David Murphy, Walter Murray, Ralf Muschall, Ken Nakata, Todd Nathan, Landon Curt Noll, Tim Norman, Paul Nulsen, David O'Brien, Richard A. O'Keefe, Adam Kolawa, James Ojaste, Hans Olsson, Bob Peck, Andrew Phillips, Christopher Phillips, François Pinard, Nick Pitfield, Wayne Pollock, Dan Pop, Lutz Prechelt, Lynn Pye, Kevin D. Quitt, Pat Rankin, Arjun Ray, Eric S. Raymond, Peter W. Richards, Dennis Ritchie, Eric Roode, Manfred Rosenboom, J. M. Rosenstock, Rick Rowe, Erkki Ruohtula, John Rushford, Rutabaga, Kadda Sahnine, Matthew Saltzman, Rich Salz, Chip Salzenberg, Matthew Sams, Paul Sand, David W. Sanderson, Frank Sandy, Christopher Sawtell, Jonas Schlein, Paul Schlyter, Doug Schmidt, Rene Schmit, Russell Schulz, Dean Schulze, Chris Sears, Patricia Shanahan, Raymond Shwake, Peter da Silva, Joshua Simons, Ross Smith, Henri Socha, Leslie J. Somos, David Spuler, James Stern, Bob Stout, Steve Sullivan, my sweetie Melanie Summit, Erik Talvola, Dave Taylor, Clarke Thatcher, Wayne Throop, Steve Traugott, Ilya Tsindlekht, Andrew Tucker, Gøran Uddeborg, Rodrigo Vanegas, Jim Van Zandt, Wietse Venema, Tom Verhoeff, Ed Vielmetti, Larry Virden, Chris Volpe, Mark Warren, Alan Watson, Kurt Watzka, Larry Weiss, Martin Weitzel, Howard West, Tom White, Freek Wiedijk, Dik T. Winter, Lars Wirzenius, Dave Wolverton, Mitch Wright, Conway Yee, Ozan S. Yigit, and Zhuo Zang. I have tried to keep track of everyone whose suggestions I have used, but I fear I've probably overlooked a few; my apologies to anyone whose name should be on this list but isn't.

Finally, I'd like to thank my editor at Addison-Wesley, Debbie Lafferty, for tapping me on the electronic shoulder one day and asking if I might be interested in writing this book. I was, and you now hold it, and I hope that it may help to make C programming as pleasant for you as it is for me.

Steve Summit   Seattle, Washington
summit@aw.com   July, 1995

Introduction

You've probably had the experience, in a bar or at a party, of losing a bet on whether you could perform some seemingly simple task that turned out, based on idiosyncrasies of the human body or the laws of physics, to be impossible. The guy making the bet knew that the more people he challenged, the more likely he was to keep winning, because those idiosyncrasies and laws, even if obscure, are fairly constant and predictable.

In a similar way, if you take a large number of people and set them at some complex task, such as learning the C programming language, many of them will run into exactly the same problems and have exactly the same questions. The questions and problems may or may not have been predictable when the task was first designed, and the answers may seem obvious in hindsight, but people *will* keep having some of the same problems, and the same questions *will* keep coming up. These problems and questions don't necessarily indicate that the task was impossible, merely that it was difficult enough to be interesting.

Not surprisingly, these problems and questions are regularly asked on the Internet, particularly in the interactive discussion newsgroups known as Usenet. The reasonably obvious idea of collecting the frequent questions gave rise to a tradition of Frequently Asked Questions, or FAQ lists. FAQ lists don't always serve their intended purpose of reducing the incidence of frequently asked questions, but if the questions are in fact consistent, the fact that they were asked often enough to be selected for inclusion in an FAQ list suggests that they might match questions which you or some other readers of this book are asking, too.

About This Book

Most books (about C or any other topic) are written from the author's point of view. They discuss the topics the author thinks you should know, presented in a way that makes sense to the author. If that way doesn't make sense to you (and, at some level, it can't, because the author presumably knows the material already while you presumably don't), you may be left with deep, unanswered questions.

This book, however, is organized around some 400 of those questions, all based on real ones asked by real people attempting to learn or program in C. This book is not targeted at just those topics that the author thinks are important; it is targeted at the topics that real readers think are important, based on the questions they ask. The chances are good that if you are learning or using C and you have a question about C that isn't answered in any of the other books you've checked, you'll find it answered here.

This book can't promise to answer *every* question you'll have when you're programming in C, since many of the questions that will come up in your programming will have to do with your problem domain, and this book covers only the C language itself. Just as it can't cover every aspect of every problem anyone might try to solve in C, this book cannot cover every aspect of every operating system that anyone might try to write a C program for or every algorithm that anyone might try to implement in C. Specific problems, specific operating systems, and general-purpose algorithms are properly discussed in books or other materials devoted to those topics. Nevertheless, certain questions involving operating systems and algorithms are quite frequent, so Chapters 19 and 20 provide brief, introductory answers to a few of them, but please don't expect the treatment to be complete.

The questions in this book are those that people typically have after reading an introductory C textbook or taking a C programming class. Therefore, this book will *not* teach you C, nor does it discuss fundamental issues that any C textbook should cover. Furthermore, this book's answers are intended for the most part to be definitively correct and to avoid propagating any misconceptions. Therefore, a few answers are more elaborate than might at first seem necessary: They give you the *complete* picture rather than oversimplifying or leaving out important details. (It is, after all, oversimplifications or omitted details that are behind many of the misconceptions this book's questions and answers address.) Within the elaborate answers, you will find shortcuts and simplifications where necessary, and in the glossary you will find definitions of the precise terms that accurate explanations often demand. The shortcuts and simplifications are, of course, safe ones: They should not lead to later misunderstandings, and you can always come back to the more complete explanations or pursue some of the references, if you later desire the full story.

As we'll see particularly in Chapters 3 and 11, the standard definitions of C do not specify the behavior of every C program that can be written. Some programs fall into various gray areas: They may happen to work on some systems, and they may not be strictly illegal, but they are not guaranteed to work everywhere. This book is about portable C programming, so its answers advise against using nonportable constructs if at all possible.

The on-line FAQ list underlying this book was written as a dialog: When people didn't understand it, they said so. That feedback has been invaluable in refining the form of the answers. Although a printed book is obviously more static, such a dialog is still appropriate: Your comments, criticisms, and suggestions are welcome. If you have access to the Internet, you may send comments to summit@aw.com, or you may send them on paper in care of the publisher. A list of any errors that are discovered in this book will be maintained and available on the Internet; see question 20.40 for information.

Question Format

The bulk of this book consists of a series of question/answer pairs. Many answers also contain a list of references; a few also refer to footnotes, which you can skip if you find that they're too picky. Several respected references are cited repeatedly, under these abbreviations:

ANSI	The (original) ANSI C Standard, X3.159-1989
CT&P	*C Traps and Pitfalls* by Andrew Koenig
H&S	Harbison and Steele, *C: A Reference Manual,* Fourth Edition
ISO	The ISO C Standard, ISO 9899:1990
K&R1	Kernighan and Ritchie, *The C Programming Language,* First Edition
K&R2	Kernighan and Ritchie, *The C Programming Language,* Second Edition
PCS	*Portable C Software* by Mark Horton
Rationale	The Rationale for the ANSI C Standard, X3.159-1989

Other references are cited by their full titles; full citations for all references appear in the bibliography.

This `constant width` typeface is used to indicate C syntax (function and variable names, keywords, etc.) and also to indicate a few operating system commands (`cc`, etc.). An occasional notation of the form tty(4) indicates the section "tty" in chapter 4 of the *UNIX Programmer's Manual.*

Code Samples

This is a book about C, so many small pieces of it are necessarily written in C. The examples are written primarily for clarity of exposition. They are *not* always written in the most efficient way possible; making them "faster" would often make them less clear. (See question 20.13 for more information about code efficiency.) They are primarily written using modern, ANSI-style syntax; see question 11.29 for conversion tips if you're still using a "classic" compiler.

The author and publisher invite you to use and modify these code fragments in your own programs, but of course we would appreciate acknowledgment if you do so. (Some fragments are from other sources and are so attributed; please acknowledge those contributors if you use those codes.) The source code for the larger examples is available on the Internet via anonymous ftp from aw.com in directory cseng/authors/summit/cfaq (see also question 18.12).

To underscore certain points, it has unfortunately been necessary to include a few code fragments that are examples of things *not* to do. In the answers, such code fragments are marked with an explicit comment like /* WRONG */ to remind you not to emulate them. (Code fragments in questions are not usually so marked; it should be obvious that the code fragments in questions are suspect, as the question is usually "Why doesn't this work?")

Organization

As mentioned, this book's questions are based on real questions asked by real people, and real-world questions do not always fall into neat hierarchies. Many questions touch on several topics: What seems to be a memory allocation problem may in fact reflect an improper declaration. (Several questions that straddle chapter boundaries appear in both chapters, to make them easier to find.) In any case, this is not a book you have to read through sequentially: Use the table of contents, the list of questions that follows it, the index, and the cross-references between questions to find the topics that are of interest to you. (And, if you have some free time, you may find yourself reading through sequentially anyway; perhaps you'll encounter the answer to a question you hadn't thought to ask yet.)

Usually, you have to declare your data structures before you can start writing code, so Chapter 1 starts out by talking about declaration and initialization. C's structure, union, and enumeration types are complicated enough that they deserve a chapter of their own; Chapter 2 discusses how they are declared and used.

Most of the work of a program is carried out by expression statements, which are the subject of Chapter 3.

Chapters 4 through 7 discuss the bane of many a beginning C programmer: pointers. Chapter 4 covers pointers in general, Chapter 5 focuses on the special case of null pointers, Chapter 6 describes the relationship between pointers and arrays, and Chapter 7 explores what is often the *real* problem when pointers are misbehaving: the underlying memory allocation.

Almost all C programs manipulate characters and strings, but these types are implemented at a low level by the language. The programmer is often responsible for managing these types correctly; some questions that come up while doing so are collected in Chapter 8. Similarly, C does not have a formal Boolean type; Chapter 9 briefly discusses C's Boolean expressions and the appropriate ways of implementing a user-defined Boolean type, if desired.

The C preprocessor (the part of the compiler responsible for handling #include and #define directives, and in fact all lines beginning with #) is distinct enough that it almost represents a separate language and is covered in its own chapter, Chapter 10.

The ANSI C Standardization committee (X3J11), in the process of clarifying C's definition and making it palatable to the world, introduced a number of new features and made a few significant changes. Questions specific to ANSI/ISO Standard C are collected in Chapter 11. If you had experience with pre-ANSI C (also called "K&R" or "classic" C), you will find Chapter 11 to be a useful introduction to the differences. If you are comfortably using ANSI C, on the other hand, the distinction between pre-ANSI and ANSI features may not be interesting. In any case, all of the questions in Chapter 11 that also relate to other topics (declarations, the C preprocessor, library functions, etc.) also appear in or are otherwise cross-referenced from those other chapters.

C's definition is relatively spartan in part because many features are not built in to the language but are accessed via library functions. The most important of these are the "Standard I/O," or "stdio" functions, which are discussed in Chapter 12. Other library functions are covered in Chapter 13.

Chapters 14 and 15 discuss two more advanced topics: floating point and variable-length argument lists. Floating-point computations tend to be tricky no matter what system or language you're using; Chapter 14 outlines a few general floating-point issues and a few that are specific to C. The possibility that a function can accept a varying number of arguments, though perhaps arguably unnecessary or dangerous, is occasionally convenient and is central to C's printf function; techniques for dealing with variable-length argument lists are discussed in Chapter 15.

Hiding in Chapter 16 are some questions you may want to jump to first if you're already comfortable with most of the preceding material: They concern the occasional strange problems and mysterious bugs that crop up in a program and can be agonizingly frustrating to track down.

When there are two or more equally "correct" ways of writing a program (and there usually are), one may be preferable based on subjective criteria having to do with more than whether the code simply compiles and runs correctly. Chapter 17 discusses a few of these ephemeral issues of programming style.

You can't build C programs in isolation: You need a compiler, and you may need some additional documentation, source code, or tools. Chapter 18 discusses some available tools and resources, including lint, a nearly forgotten but once indispensable tool for checking certain aspects of program correctness and portability.

As mentioned, the C language does not specify everything you necessarily need to get a real program working. Questions such as "How do I read one character without waiting for the Return key?" and "How do I find the size of a file?" are extremely common, but C does not define the answers; these operations depend on the facilities provided by the underlying operating system. Chapter 19 presents a number of these questions, along with brief answers for popular operating systems.

Finally, Chapter 20 collects the miscellaneous questions that don't fit anywhere else: bit manipulation, efficiency, algorithms, C's relationship to other languages, and a few trivia questions. (The introduction to Chapter 20 contains a slightly more detailed breakdown of its disparate contents.)

To close this introduction, here are two preliminary questions not so much about C but more about this book:

Question: **Why should I buy this book, if it's available for free on the Internet?**

Answer: This book contains over three times as much material as does the version that's posted to comp.lang.c, and in spite of the advantages of electronic documentation, it really can be easier to deal with this amount of information in a printed form. (You'd spend a lot of time downloading this much information from the net and printing it, and the typography wouldn't be as pretty, either.)

Question: **How do you pronounce "FAQ"?**

Answer: I pronounce it "eff ay kyoo," and this was, I believe, the original pronunciation when FAQ lists were first "invented." Many people now pronounce it "fack," which is nicely evocative of the word "fact." I'd pronounce the plural, as in the title of this book, "eff ay kyooze," but many people pronounce it like "fax." None of these pronunciations are strictly right or wrong; "FAQ" is a new term, and popular usage plays a certain role in shaping any term's evolution.

(It's equally imponderable, by the way, whether "FAQ" refers to the question alone, to the question plus its answer, or to the whole list of questions and answers.)

But now, on with the real questions!

Declarations and Initializations

C's declaration syntax is practically a little programming language in itself. A declaration consists of several parts (though not all are required): a storage class, a base type, type qualifiers, and finally the declarators (which may also contain initializers). Each declarator not only declares a new identifier but may also indicate that the identifier is to be an array, a pointer, a function, or some arbitrarily complicated combination. The underlying idea is that the declaration mimics the eventual use of the identifier. (Question 1.21 discusses this "declaration mimics use" relationship in more detail.)

Basic Types

Some programmers are surprised to discover that even though C is a fairly low-level language, its type system is nevertheless mildly abstract; the sizes and representations of the basic types are not precisely defined by the language.

1.1

Question: How should I decide which integer type to use?

Answer: If you might need large values (above 32,767 or below −32,767), use `long`. Otherwise, if space is very important (i.e., if there are large arrays or many structures), use `short`. Otherwise, use `int`. If well-defined overflow characteristics are important and negative values are not, or if you want to steer clear of sign-extension problems when manipulating bits or bytes, use one of the corresponding `unsigned` types. (Beware when mixing signed and unsigned values in expressions, though; see question 3.19.)

Although character types (especially `unsigned char`) can be used as "tiny" integers, doing so is sometimes more trouble than it's worth. The compiler will have to emit extra code to convert between `char` and `int` (making the executable larger), and unexpected sign extension can be troublesome. (Using `unsigned char` can help; see question 12.1 for a related problem.)

A similar space/time tradeoff applies when deciding between `float` and `double`. (Many compilers still convert all `float` values to `double` during expression evaluation.) None of the above rules apply if the address of a variable is taken and must have a particular type.

It's often incorrectly assumed that C's types are defined to have certain, exact sizes. In fact, what's guaranteed is that:

- type `char` can hold values up to 127;
- types `short  int` and `int` can hold values up to 32,767;
- type `long  int` can hold values up to 2,147,483,647; and
- the sizes follow the obvious progression:

  ```
  sizeof(char) <= sizeof(short) <= sizeof(int) <= sizeof(long)
  ```

These values imply that `char` is at least 8 bits, `short  int` and `int` are at least 16 bits, and `long  int` is at least 32 bits. (The signed and unsigned versions of each type are guaranteed to have the same size.) Under ANSI C, the maximum and minimum values for a particular machine can be found in the header file `<limits.h>` and are summarized in the following table:

Base type	Minimum size (bits)	Minimum value (signed)	Maximum value (signed)	Maximum value (unsigned)
char	8	−127	127	255
short	16	−32,767	32,767	65,535
int	16	−32,767	32,767	65,535
long	32	−2,147,483,647	2,147,483,647	4,294,967,295

The values in the table are the minimums guaranteed by the standard. Many implementations allow larger values, but portable programs shouldn't depend on it.

If for some reason you need to declare something with an exact size, be sure to encapsulate the choice behind an appropriate typedef. Usually the only good reason for needing an exact size is when attempting to conform to some externally imposed storage layout. See also questions 1.3 and 20.5.

References: K&R1 §2.2 p. 34
  K&R2 §2.2 p. 36, §A4.2 pp. 195–6, §B11 p. 257
  ANSI §2.2.4.2.1, §3.1.2.5
  ISO §5.2.4.2.1, §6.1.2.5
  H&S §5.1, §5.2 pp. 110–4

1.2

Question: Why aren't the sizes of the standard types precisely defined?

Answer: Although C is considered relatively low level as high-level languages go, it does take the position that the exact size of an object (i.e., in bits) is an implementation detail. (The only place where C lets you specify a size in bits is in bitfields within structures; see questions 2.25 and 2.26.) Most programs do not need precise control over these sizes; many programs that do try to achieve this control would be better off if they didn't.

Type `int` is supposed to represent a machine's natural word size and is the right type to use for most integer variables. See question 1.1 for other guidelines; see also questions 12.42 and 20.5.

1.3

Question: Since C doesn't define sizes exactly, I've been using typedefs like `int16` and `int32`. I can then define these typedefs to be `int`, `short`, `long`, etc., depending on what machine I'm using. That should solve everything, right?

Answer: If you truly need control over exact type sizes, this is the right approach. However, you should remain aware of several things:

- An exact match might not be possible (on the occasional 36-bit machine, for example).

- A typedef like `int16` or `int32` accomplishes nothing if its intended meaning is "at least" the specified size, because types `int` and `long` are *already* essentially defined as being "at least 16 bits" and "at least 32 bits," respectively.

- Typedefs will never do anything about byte-order problems (e.g., if you're trying to interchange data or conform to externally imposed storage layouts).

See also questions 10.16 and 20.5.

1.4

Question: **What should the 64-bit type on new, 64-bit machines be?**

Answer: This is a sticky question. You can look at it in at least three ways:

1. On existing 16- and 32-bit systems, two of the three integer types (`short` and plain `int`, or plain `int` and `long`) are typically the same size. A 64-bit machine provides an opportunity to make all three types different sizes. Therefore, some vendors support 64-bit `long ints`.

2. Sadly, a lot of existing code is written to assume that `ints` and `longs` are the same size or that one or the other of them is exactly 32 bits. Rather than risk breaking such code, some vendors introduce a new, nonstandard, 64-bit `long long` (or `__longlong` or `__very long`) type instead.

3. Finally, it can be argued that plain `int` should be 64 bits on a 64-bit machine, since `int` traditionally reflects "the machine's natural word size."

Programmers interested in writing portable code should therefore insulate any use of a 64-bit type behind an appropriate typedef (and will also have to provide 64-bit support manually when porting such code to 16- or 32-bit environments.) Vendors feeling compelled to introduce a new, longer integral type should advertise it as being "at least 64 bits" (which is truly new, a type traditional C does not have) and not "exactly 64 bits."

References: ANSI §F.5.6
            ISO §G.5.6

Pointer Declarations

Although most questions about pointers come in Chapters 4 through 7, here are two that touch specifically on declarations.

Question: What's wrong with this declaration?

```
char* p1, p2;
```

I get errors when I try to use **p2**.

Answer: Nothing is wrong with the declaration—except that it doesn't do what you probably want. The * in a pointer declaration is not part of the base type; it is part of the *declarator* containing the name being declared (see question 1.21). In the declaration as written, no matter what the whitespace suggests, the first declarator is "* p1"; since it contains a *, it declares p1 as a pointer to char. The declarator for p2, however, contains nothing but p2, so p2 is declared as a plain char, probably not what was intended. To declare two pointers within the same declaration, use

```
char *p1, *p2;
```

Since the * is part of the declarator, it's best to use whitespace as shown; writing char* invites mistakes and confusion.

See also question 1.13.

Question: I'm trying to declare a pointer and allocate some space for it, but it's not working. What's wrong with this code?

```
char *p;
*p = malloc(10);
```

Answer: The pointer you declared is p, not *p. See question 4.2.

Declaration Style

Declaring functions and variables before using them is not done just to keep the compiler happy; it also injects useful order into a programming project. When declarations are arranged appropriately within a project, mismatches and other difficulties can be more easily avoided, and the compiler can more accurately catch any errors that do occur.

1.7

Question: What's the best way to declare and define global variables?

Answer: First, although a single "global" variable or function can have many *declarations* (and in many translation units), there must be exactly one *definition*. For global variables, the definition is the declaration that allocates space and provides an initialization value, if any. For functions, the definition is the "declaration" that provides the function body. For example, these are declarations:

```
extern int i;

extern int f();
```

(The keyword `extern` is optional in function declarations; see question 1.11.)
These are definitions:

```
int i = 0;

int f()
{
        return 1;
}
```

When you need to share variables or functions across several source files, you will of course want to ensure that all definitions and declarations are consistent. The best arrangement is to place each definition in a relevant .c file.

Then, put an external declaration in a header (".h") file and use `include` to bring the header and the declaration in wherever needed. The .c file containing the definition should also include that same header file, so that the compiler can check that the definition matches the declarations.

This rule promotes a high degree of portability: It is consistent with the requirements of the ANSI/ISO C Standard and is also consistent with most pre-ANSI compilers and linkers. (UNIX compilers and linkers typically use a "common model," which allows multiple definitions as long as at most one is initialized; this behavior is mentioned as a "common extension" by the standard, no pun intended. A few old, nonstandard systems may require an explicit initializer to distinguish a definition from an external declaration.)

It is possible to use preprocessor tricks to arrange that a line such as

```
DEFINE(int, i);
```

need be entered only once in one header file and turned into a definition or a declaration, depending on the setting of some macro. It's not clear though, whether this is worth the trouble, especially since it's usually a better idea to keep global variables to a minimum.

It's more than a good idea to put global declarations in header files: If you want the compiler to be able to catch inconsistent declarations for you, you *must* place them in header files. In particular, never place a prototype for an external function in a .c file; if the definition of the function ever changes, it would be too easy to forget to change the prototype, and an incompatible prototype is worse than useless.

See also questions 1.24, 10.6, 17.2, and 18.8.

References: K&R1 §4.5 pp. 76–7
K&R2 §4.4 pp. 80–1
ANSI §3.1.2.2, §3.7, §3.7.2, §F.5.11
ISO §6.1.2.2, §6.7, §6.7.2, §G.5.11
Rationale §3.1.2.2
H&S §4.8 pp. 101–4, §9.2.3 p. 267
CT&P §4.2 pp. 54–6

1.8

Question: What's the best way of implementing opaque (abstract) data types in C?

Answer: See question 2.4.

1.9

Question: How can I make a sort of "semiglobal" variable, that is, one that's private to a few functions spread across a few source files?

Answer: You can't do this in C. If it's impossible or inconvenient to put all the functions in the same source file, use one of these traditional workarounds:

1. Pick a unique prefix for the names of all functions and global variables in a library or package of related functions, and warn users of the package not to define or use any symbols with names matching that prefix other than those documented as being for public consumption. (In other words, an undocumented but otherwise global symbol with a name matching that prefix is, by convention, "private.")

2. Use a name beginning with an underscore, since such names shouldn't be used by ordinary code. (See question 1.29 for more information and for a description of the "no man's land" between the user and implementation namespaces.)

It may also be possible to use special linker invocations to adjust the visibility of names, but any such techniques are outside of the scope of the C language.

Storage Classes

We've covered two parts of declarations: base types and declarators. The next few questions discuss the storage class, which determines visibility and lifetime (also called "scope" and "duration") of the objects or functions declared.

1.10

Question: Do all declarations for the same **static** function or variable have to include the storage class **static**?

Answer: The language in the standard does not quite require this (what's most important is that the *first* declaration contain **static**), but the rules are rather intricate and differ slightly for functions and for data objects. (Furthermore, existing practice has varied widely in this area.) Therefore, it's safest if `static` appears consistently in the definition and all declarations.

References: ANSI §3.1.2.2
            ISO §6.1.2.2
            Rationale §3.1.2.2
            H&S §4.3 p. 75

1.11

Question: What does **extern** mean in a function declaration?

Answer: The storage class `extern` is significant only with data declarations. In function declarations, it can be used as a stylistic hint to indicate that the function's definition is probably in another source file, but there is no formal difference between

```
extern int f();
```
and
```
int f();
```

See also question 1.10.

References: ANSI §3.1.2.2, §3.5.1
            ISO §6.1.2.2, §6.5.1
            Rationale §3.1.2.2
            H&S §4.3, §4.3.1 pp. 75–6

1.12

Question: What's the **auto** keyword good for?

Answer: Nothing; it's archaic. (It's a holdover from C's typeless predecessor language B, which lacked keywords such as `int` and which required that every declaration have a storage class.) See also question 20.37.

References: K&R1 §A8.1 p. 193
            ANSI §3.1.2.4, §3.5.1
            ISO §6.1.2.4, §6.5.1
            H&S §4.3 p. 75, §4.3.1 p. 76

Typedefs

Although it is syntactically a storage class, the `typedef` keyword is, as its name suggests, involved in defining new type names, not new functions or variables.

1.13

Question: What's the difference between using a typedef or a preprocessor macro for a user-defined type?

Answer: In general, typedefs are preferred, in part because they can correctly encode pointer types. For example, consider these declarations:

```
typedef char *String_t;
#define String_d char *
String_t s1, s2;
String_d s3, s4;
```

In these declarations, `s1`, `s2`, and `s3` are all declared as `char *`, but `s4` is declared as a `char`, which is probably not the intention. (See also question 1.5.)

Preprocessor macros do have the advantage that `#ifdef` works on them (see also question 10.15). On the other hand, typedefs have the advantage that they obey scope rules (that is, they can be declared local to a function or a block).

See also questions 1.17, 2.22, 11.11, and 15.11.

References: K&R1 §6.9 p. 141
         K&R2 §6.7 pp. 146–7
         CT&P §6.4 pp. 83–4

1.14

Question: I can't seem to declare a linked list successfully. I tried this declaration, but the compiler gave me error messages.

```
typedef struct {
        char *item;
        NODEPTR next;
} *NODEPTR;
```

Can't a structure in C contain a pointer to itself?

Answer: Structures in C can certainly contain pointers to themselves; the discussion and example in section 6.5 of K&R make this clear.

The problem with this example is the typedef. A typedef defines a new name for a type, and in simpler cases* you can define a new structure type and a typedef for it at the same time, but not in this case. A typedef declaration cannot be used until it is defined, and in the fragment given, it is not yet defined at the point where the `next` field is declared.

To fix this code, first give the structure a tag ("`struct node`"). Then declare the `next` field as a simple `struct node *`, or disentangle the typedef declaration from the structure definition, or both. One corrected version is:

```
typedef struct node {
        char *item;
        struct node *next;
} *NODEPTR;
```

You could also precede the structure declaration with the typedef, in which case you could use the NODEPTR typedef when declaring the `next` field, after all:

```
typedef struct node *NODEPTR;

struct node {
        char *item;
        NODEPTR next;
};
```

In this case, you declare a new typedef name involving `struct node` even though `struct node` has not been completely defined yet; this you're allowed to do.

---

*In the simple example `typedef struct { int i; } simplestruct;` both the structure and its typedef name ("`simplestruct`") are defined at the same time; note that there is no structure tag.

Finally, here is a rearrangement incorporating both suggestions:

```
struct node {
        char *item;
        struct node *next;
};
typedef struct node *NODEPTR;
```

It's a matter of style which method to prefer; see Chapter 17. See also questions 1.15 and 2.1.

References: K&R1 §6.5 p. 101
          K&R2 §6.5 p. 139
          ANSI §3.5.2, §3.5.2.3, esp. examples
          ISO §6.5.2, §6.5.2.3
          H&S §5.6.1 pp. 132–3

1.15

Question: **How can I define a pair of mutually referential structures? I tried**

```
typedef struct {
        int afield;
        BPTR bpointer;
} *APTR;

typedef struct {
        int bfield;
        APTR apointer;
} *BPTR;
```

but the compiler doesn't know about BPTR when it is used in the first structure declaration.

Answer: As in question 1.14, the problem lies not in the structures or the pointers but in the typedefs. First, give the two structures tags, and define the link pointers without using typedefs:

```
struct a {
      int afield;
      struct b *bpointer;
};

struct b {
      int bfield;
      struct a *apointer;
};
```

The compiler can accept the field declaration `struct b *bpointer` within `struct a`, even though it has not yet heard of `struct b` (which is "incomplete" at that point). Occasionally, it is necessary to precede this couplet with the line

```
struct b;
```

This empty declaration masks the pair of structure declarations (if in an inner scope) from a different `struct b` in an outer scope.

After declaring the two structures with structure tags, you can then declare the typedefs separately:

```
typedef struct a *APTR;
typedef struct b *BPTR;
```

Alternatively, you can define the typedefs before the structure definitions, in which case you can use them when declaring the link pointer fields:

```
typedef struct a *APTR;
typedef struct b *BPTR;
struct a {
      int afield;
      BPTR bpointer;
};
struct b {
      int bfield;
      APTR apointer;
};
```

See also question 1.14.

References: K&R2 §6.5 p. 140
          ANSI §3.5.2.3
          ISO §6.5.2.3
          H&S §5.6.1 p. 132

1.16

Question: What's the difference between these two declarations?

```
struct x1 { ... };
typedef struct { ... } x2;
```

Answer: See question 2.1.

1.17

Question: What does "`typedef int (*funcptr)();`" mean?

Answer: It defines a typedef, `funcptr`, for a pointer to a function (taking unspecified arguments) returning an `int`. It can be used to declare one or more pointers to functions:

```
funcptr pf1, pf2;
```

This declaration is equivalent to the more verbose and perhaps harder to understand

```
int (*pf1)(), (*pf2)();
```

See also questions 1.21, 4.12, and 15.11.

References: K&R1 §6.9 p. 141
          K&R2 §6.7 p. 147

The const Qualifier

Another aspect of a C declaration is the type qualifier, which is new in ANSI C. Questions about qualifiers are collected in Chapter 11.

1.18

Question: I've got the declarations

```
typedef char *charp;
const charp p;
```

Why is **p** turning out **const** instead of the characters pointed to?

Answer: See question 11.11.

1.19

Question: Why can't I use **const** values in initializers and array dimensions, like this?

```
const int n = 5;
int a[n];
```

Answer: See question 11.8.

1.20

Question: How do **const char *p, char const *p,** and **char * const p** differ?

Answer: See questions 11.9 and 1.21.

Complex Declarations

C's declarations can be arbitrarily complex. Once you're used to deciphering them, you can make sense of even the most complicated ones, although truly bewildering declarations should rarely be necessary in the first place. If you

don't feel like cluttering your program with arcane declarators such as
`*(*(*a[N])())()`, you can always use a few typedefs to clarify things, as
described in question 1.21, option 2.

1.21

Question: How do I declare an array of *N* pointers to functions returning
pointers to functions returning pointers to characters, or figure out what similarly complicated declarations mean?

Answer: The first part of this question can be answered in at least three
ways:

1. `char *(*(*a[N])())();`

2. Build the declaration up incrementally, using typedefs:

   ```
   typedef char *pc;        /* pointer to char */
   typedef pc fpc();        /* fcn returning ptr to char */
   typedef fpc *pfpc;       /* pointer to above */
   typedef pfpc fpfpc();    /* function returning... */
   typedef fpfpc *pfpfpc;   /* pointer to... */
   pfpfpc a[N];             /* array of... */
   ```

3. Use `cdecl`, which turns English into C and vice versa. You provide a
   longhand description of the type you want, and `cdecl` responds with the
   equivalent C declaration:

   ```
   cdecl> declare a as array of pointer to function returning
          pointer to function returning pointer to char

   char *(*(*a[])())()
   ```

   The `cdecl` program can also explain complicated declarations (you give
   it a complicated declaration and it responds with an English description),
   help with casts, and indicate which set of parentheses the arguments go in
   (for complicated function definitions, like the one here). Versions of
   `cdecl` are in volume 14 of comp.sources.unix (see question 18.16) and
   K&R2.

C's declarations can be confusing because they come in two parts: a base type and a *declarator*, which contains the identifier, or name, being declared. The declarator may also contain the characters *, [ ], and ( ), saying whether the name is a pointer to, array of, or function returning the base type, or some combination.* For example, in

```
char *pc;
```

the base type is char, the identifier is pc, and the declarator is *pc; this tells us that *pc is a char (this is what "declaration mimics use" means).

One way to make sense of complicated C declarations is by reading them "inside out," remembering that [ ] and ( ) bind more tightly than *. For example, given

```
char *(*pfpc)();
```

we can see that pfpc is a pointer (the inner *) to a function (the ( )) to a pointer (the outer *) to char. When we later use pfpc, the expression *(*pfpc)() (the value pointed to by the return value of a function pointed to by pfpc) will be a char.

Another way of analyzing these declarations is to decompose the declarator while composing the description, maintaining the "declaration mimics use" relationship:

*(*pfpc)()	is a	char
(*pfpc)()	is a	pointer to char
(*pfpc)	is a	function returning pointer to char
pfpc	is a	pointer to function returning pointer to char

If you'd like to make things clearer when declaring complicated types like these, you can make the analysis explicit by using a chain of typedefs, as in the preceding option 2.

The pointer-to-function declarations in these examples have not included information about parameter type. When the parameters have complicated types, declarations can *really* get messy. (Modern versions of cdecl can help here, too.)

References: K&R2 §5.12 p. 122
           ANSI §3.5ff (esp. §3.5.4)
           ISO §6.5ff (esp. §6.5.4)
           H&S §4.5 pp. 85–92, §5.10.1 pp. 149–50

---

*Furthermore, a storage class (static, register, etc.) may appear along with the base type, and type qualifiers (const, volatile) may be interspersed with both the type and the declarator. See also question 11.9.

1.22

Question: How can I declare a function that returns a pointer to a function of its own type? I'm building a state machine with one function for each state, each of which returns a pointer to the function for the next state. But I can't find a way to declare the functions—I seem to need a function returning a pointer to a function returning a pointer to a function returning a pointer to a function ..., *ad infinitum.*

Answer: You can't quite do it directly. One way is to have the function return a generic function pointer (see question 4.13), with some judicious casts to adjust the types as the pointers are passed around:

```
typedef int (*funcptr)();          /* generic fcn ptr */
typedef funcptr (*ptrfuncptr)();
               /* ptr to fcn returning g.f.p. */

funcptr start(), stop();
funcptr state1(), state2(), state3();

statemachine()
{
     ptrfuncptr state = start;

     while(state != stop)
          state = (ptrfuncptr)(*state)();

     return 0;
}

funcptr start()
{
     return (funcptr)state1;
}
```

(The second `ptrfuncptr` typedef hides some particularly dark syntax; without it, the `state` variable would have to be declared as `funcptr (*state)()`, and the call would contain a bewildering cast of the form `(funcptr (*)())(*state)()`.)

Another way (suggested by Paul Eggert, Eugene Ressler, Chris Volpe, and perhaps others) is to have each function return a structure containing only a pointer to a function returning that structure:

```
struct functhunk {
        struct functhunk (*func)();
};

struct functhunk start(), stop();
struct functhunk state1(), state2(), state3();

statemachine()
{
        struct functhunk state = {start};

        while(state.func != stop)
                state = (*state.func)();
}

struct functhunk start()
{
        struct functhunk ret;
        ret.func = state1;
        return ret;
}
```

Note that these examples use the older, explicit style of calling via function pointers; see question 4.12. See also question 1.17.

Array Sizes

1.23

Question: Can I declare a local array (or parameter array) of a size matching a passed-in array or set by another parameter?

Answer: Unfortunately, you can't. See questions 6.15 and 6.19.

1.24

Question: I have an **extern** array defined in one file and used in another:

file1.c: file2.c:

```
int array[] = {1, 2, 3};        extern int array[];
```

Why doesn't sizeof work on array in file2.c?

Answer: An extern array of unspecified size is an incomplete type; you cannot apply sizeof to it, because sizeof operates at compile time and is not able to learn the size of an array that is defined in another file.

   You have three options:

1. Declare a companion variable, containing the size of the array, defined and initialized (with sizeof) in the same source file where the array is defined:

   file1.c: file2.c:

   ```
   int array[] = {1, 2, 3};        extern int array[];
   int arraysz = sizeof(array);    extern int arraysz;
   ```

   See also question 6.23.

2. Define a manifest constant for the size so that it can be used consistently in the definition and the **extern** declaration:

   file1.h:

   ```
   #define ARRAYSZ 3
   ```

   file1.c: file2.c:

   ```
   #include "file1.h"              #include "file1.h"
   int array[ARRAYSZ];             extern int array[ARRAYSZ];
   ```

3. Use a sentinel value (typically, 0, -1, or NULL) in the array's last element, so that code can determine the end without an explicit size indication:

   file1.c: file2.c:

   ```
   int array[] = {1, 2, 3, -1};    extern int array[];
   ```

Obviously, the choice will depend to some extent on whether the array was already being initialized; if it was, option 2 is poor. See also question 6.21.

References: H&S §7.5.2 p. 195

Declaration Problems

Sometimes the compiler insists on complaining about your declarations no matter how carefully constructed you thought they were. These questions uncover some of the reasons why. (Chapter 16 is a similar collection of baffling run-time problems.)

1.25

Question: Why is my compiler complaining about an invalid redeclaration of a function that I define and call only once?

Answer: Functions that are called without a declaration in scope (perhaps because the first call precedes the function's definition) are assumed to be declared as if by:

```
extern int f();
```

That is, an undeclared function is assumed to return int and to accept an unspecified number of arguments, although there must be a fixed number of them and none may be "narrow." If the function is later defined otherwise, the compiler complains about the discrepancy. Functions returning other than int or accepting any "narrow" arguments or a variable number of arguments must all be declared before they are called. (It's safest to declare all functions, so that function prototypes can check that arguments are passed correctly.)

Another possible source of this problem is that the function has the same name as another one declared in a header file.

See also questions 11.3 and 15.1.

References: K&R1 §4.2 p. 70
K&R2 §4.2 p. 72
ANSI §3.3.2.2
ISO §6.3.2.2
H&S §4.7 p. 101

1.26

Question: My compiler is complaining about mismatched function proto-types that look fine to me. Why?

Answer: See question 11.3.

1.27

Question: I'm getting strange syntax errors on the very first declaration in a file, but it looks fine. Why?

Answer: See question 10.9.

1.28

Question: Why isn't my compiler letting me declare a large array, such as:

```
double array[256][256];
```

Answer: See question 19.23 and maybe question 7.16.

Namespace

Naming never seems as though it should be that much of a problem, but of course it can be. Coming up with names for functions and variables isn't quite as difficult as coming up with names for books, buildings, or babies—you don't have to worry whether the public will *like* the names in your pro-grams—but you do have to be more sure that the names aren't already taken.

1.29

Question: How can I determine which identifiers are safe for me to use and which are reserved?

Answer: Namespace management can be a sticky issue. The problem—which isn't always obvious—is that you don't want to pick identifiers already in use by the implementation and therefore get "multiply defined" errors or—even worse—quietly replace one of the implementation's symbols and break everything. You also want some guarantee that later releases won't usurp names you're legitimately using.* (Few things are more frustrating than taking a debugged, working, production program; recompiling it under a new release of a compiler; and having the build fail due to namespace or other problems.) Therefore, the ANSI/ISO C Standard contains rather elaborate definitions carving out distinct namespace subsets for the user and the implementation.

To make sense of ANSI's rules, and before we can say whether a given identifier is reserved, we must understand three attributes of the identifier: its scope, namespace, and linkage.

- C has four kinds of scope (regions over which an identifier's declaration is in effect): function, file, block, and prototype. (The fourth one exists only in the parameter lists of function prototype declarations; see also question 11.5.)

- C has four kinds of namespaces: labels (i.e., `goto` targets); tags (names of structures, unions, and enumerations; these three aren't separate even though they theoretically could be); structure/union members (one namespace per structure or union); and everything else termed "ordinary identifiers" by the standard (functions, variables, typedef names, and enumeration constants). Another set of names (though not termed a "namespace" by the standard) consists of preprocessor macros; these are all expanded before the compiler gets around to considering the four formal namespaces.

- The standard defines three kinds of "linkage": external, internal, and none. For our purposes, external linkage means global, non-static variables and functions (across all source files); internal linkage means static variables and functions with file scope; and "no linkage" refers to local variables, and also things like typedef names and enumeration constants.

---

*These concerns apply not only to public symbols but also to the names of the implementation's various internal, private functions.

The rules, paraphrased from ANSI §4.1.2.1 (ISO §7.1.3), are as follows:

- Rule 1. All identifiers beginning with an underscore followed by an upper-case letter or another underscore are always reserved (all scopes, all namespaces).
- Rule 2. All identifiers beginning with an underscore are reserved for ordinary identifiers (functions, variables, typedefs, enumeration constants) with file scope.
- Rule 3. A macro name defined in a standard header is reserved for any use if the header that defines it is included.
- Rule 4. All standard library identifiers with external linkage (i.e., function names) are always reserved as identifiers with external linkage.
- Rule 5. Typedef and tag names, with file scope, defined in standard headers, are reserved at file scope (in the same namespace) if the corresponding header is included. (The standard really says "each identifier with file scope," but the only standard identifiers not covered by rule 4 are typedef and tag names.)

Rules 3 and 4 are further complicated by the fact that several sets of macro names and standard library identifiers are reserved for "future directions"; that is, later revisions of the standard may define new names matching certain patterns. This table lists the patterns reserved for "future directions" whenever a given standard header is included:

Header	Future directions patterns
`<ctype.h>`	`is[a-z]*`, `to[a-z]*` (functions)
`<errno.h>`	`E[0-9]*`, `E[A-Z]*` (macros)
`<locale.h>`	`LC_[A-Z]*` (macros)
`<math.h>`	`cosf`, `sinf`, `sqrtf`, etc.
	`cosl`, `sinl`, `sqrtl`, etc. (all functions)
`<signal.h>`	`SIG[A-Z]*`, `SIG_[A-Z]*` (macros)
`<stdlib.h>`	`str[a-z]*` (functions)
`<string.h>`	`mem[a-z]*`, `str[a-z]*`, `wcs[a-z]*` (functions)

The notation `[A-Z]` means "any uppercase letter"; similarly, `[a-z]` and `[0-9]` indicate lowercase letters and digits. The notation `*` means "anything." For example, if you include `<stdlib.h>`, all external identifiers beginning with the letters `str` followed by a lowercase letter are reserved.

What do these five rules really mean? If you want to be on the safe side:

1, 2. Don't name anything with a leading underscore.

3. Don't name anything matching a standard macro (including the "future directions" patterns).

4. Don't give any functions or global variables names that are already taken by functions or variables in the standard library or that match any of the "future directions" patterns. (Strictly speaking, "matching" means matching in the first six characters, without regard to case; see question 11.27.)

5. Don't redefine standard typedef or tag names.

In fact, the preceding list is overly conservative. If you wish, you may remember the following exceptions:

1, 2. You may use identifiers consisting of an underscore followed by a digit or a lowercase letter for labels and structure/union members and at function, block, or prototype scope.

3. You may use names matching standard macro names if you don't include the header files that define them.

4. You may use names of standard library functions as static or local variables (strictly speaking, as identifiers with internal or no linkage).

5. You may use standard typedef and tag names if you don't include the header files that declare them.

However, before relying on any of these exceptions, recognize that some of them are pretty risky (especially exceptions 3 and 5, since you could accidentally include the relevant header file at a later time, perhaps through a chain of nested #include files). Others, especially the one labeled 1, 2, represent a "no man's land" between the user namespaces and the namespaces reserved to the implementation.

One reason for providing these exceptions is to allow the implementors of various add-in libraries a way to declare their own internal, or "hidden," identifiers. If you make use of any of the exceptions, you won't clash with any identifiers defined by the standard, but you might clash with something defined by a third-party library you're using. (If, on the other hand, you're the one who's implementing an add-on library, you're welcome to make use of them, if necessary, and if you're careful.)

It *is* generally safe to make use of exception 4 to give function parameters or local variables names matching standard library functions or "future directions" patterns. For example, "string" is a common—and legal—name for a parameter or local variable.

References: ANSI §3.1.2.1, §3.1.2.2, §3.1.2.3, §4.1.2.1, §4.13
                    ISO §6.1.2.1, §6.1.2.2, §6.1.2.3, §7.1.3, §7.13
                    Rationale §4.1.2.1
                    H&S §2.5 pp. 21–3, §4.2.1 p. 67, §4.2.4 pp. 69–70, §4.2.7 p. 78, §10.1 p. 284

Initialization

A declaration of a variable can, of course, also contain an initial value for that variable, although in the absence of an explicit initializer, certain default initializations may be performed.

1.30

Question: What can I safely assume about the initial values of variables that are not explicitly initialized? If global variables start out as "zero," is that good enough for null pointers and floating-point zeroes?

Answer: Variables, including arrays and structures, with *static* duration—those declared outside of functions and those declared with the storage class static—are guaranteed initialized (just once, at program startup) to zero, as if the programmer had typed "= 0" or "= {0}". Therefore, such variables are initialized to the null pointer (of the correct type; see also Chapter 5) if they are pointers and to 0.0 if they are floating point.*

Variables with *automatic* duration (that is, local variables without the static storage class) start out containing garbage unless they are explicitly initialized. (Nothing useful can be predicted about the garbage.) If they do have initializers, they are initialized each time the function is called (or, for variables local to inner blocks, each time the block is entered at the top†). When an automatic array or structure (an "aggregate") has a partial initializer, the remainder is initialized to 0, just as for statics.‡ See also question 1.31.

---

*This requirement means that compilers and linkers on machines that use nonzero internal representations for null pointers or floating-point zeroes cannot necessarily make use of uninitialized, 0-filled memory but must emit explicit initializers for these values (rather as if the programmer had).

†Initializers are not effective if you jump into the middle of a block with either a goto or a switch. Initializers are therefore never effective on variables declared in the main block of a switch statement.

‡Early printings of K&R2 incorrectly stated that partially initialized automatic aggregates were filled out with garbage.

Finally, dynamically allocated memory that is obtained with `malloc` and `realloc` is also likely to contain garbage and must be initialized by the calling program, as appropriate. Memory obtained with `calloc` is all-bits-0, but this is not necessarily useful for pointer or floating-point values (see question 7.31 and Chapter 5).

References: K&R1 §4.9 pp. 82–4
K&R2 §4.9 pp. 85–6
ANSI §3.5.7, §4.10.3.1, §4.10.5.3
ISO §6.5.7, §7.10.3.1, §7.10.5.3
H&S §4.2.8 pp. 72–3, §4.6 pp. 92–3, §4.6.2 pp. 94–5, §4.6.3 p. 96, §16.1 p. 386

1.31

Question: **Why is this code, straight out of a book, not compiling?**

```
f()
{
        char a[] = "Hello, world!";
}
```

Answer: Perhaps you have a pre-ANSI compiler, which doesn't allow initialization of "automatic aggregates" (non-`static` local arrays, structures, and unions). You have four possible workarounds:

1. If the array won't be written to or if you won't need a fresh copy during any subsequent calls, you can declare it `static` (or perhaps make it global).

2. If the array won't be written to, you could replace it with a pointer:

```
f()
{
        char *a = "Hello, world!";
}
```

You can always initialize local `char *` variables to point to string literals (but see question 1.32).

3. If neither of the preceding conditions holds, you'll have to initialize the array by hand with `strcpy` when the function is called:

```
f()
{
        char a[14];
        strcpy(a, "Hello, world!");
}
```

4. Get an ANSI-compatible compiler.

See also question 11.29.

1.32

Question: **What is the difference between these initializations?**

```
char a[] = "string literal";
char *p  = "string literal";
```

My program crashes if I try to assign a new value to `p[i]`.

Answer: A string literal—the formal term for a double-quoted string in C source—can be used in two slightly different ways:

1. As the initializer for an array of `char`, as in the declaration of `char a[]`, it specifies the initial values of the characters in that array and, if necessary, its size.

2. Anywhere else, it turns into an unnamed, static array of characters, and this unnamed array may be stored in read-only memory, which is why you can't safely modify it. In an expression context, the array is converted at once to a pointer, as usual (see Chapter 6), so the second declaration initializes p to point to the unnamed array's first element.

Some compilers have a switch controlling whether strings are writable (for compiling old code), and some may have options to cause string literals to be formally treated as arrays of `const char` (for better error catching).

See also questions 1.31, 6.1, 6.2, and 6.8.

References: K&R2 §5.5 p. 104
ANSI §3.1.4, §3.5.7
ISO §6.1.4, §6.5.7
Rationale §3.1.4
H&S §2.7.4 pp. 31–2

1.33

Question: Is **char a[3] = "abc";** legal?

Answer: Yes. See question 11.22.

1.34

Question: I finally figured out the syntax for declaring pointers to functions, but now how do I initialize one?

Answer: Use something like this:

```
extern int func();
int (*fp)() = func;
```

When the name of a function appears in an expression like this, it "decays" into a pointer (that is, it has its address implicitly taken), much as an array name does. An explicit declaration for the function is normally needed, as shown, since implicit external function declaration does not happen in this case (because the function name in the initialization is not part of a function call).

See also question 4.12.

1.35

Question: Can I initialize unions?

Answer: See question 2.20.

2

Structures, Unions, and Enumerations

Structures, unions, and enumerations are all similar in that they let you define new data types. First, you define the new type by declaring the members or fields of structures and unions or the constants making up an enumeration. At the same time, you may optionally give the new type a *tag* by which it can be referred to later. Having defined a new type, you can declare instances of it, either at the same time the type is defined or later (using the tag).

To complicate matters, you can also use `typedef` to define new type names for user-defined types, just as you can for all types. If you do, though, you'll need to realize that the typedef name has nothing to do with the tag name (if any).

The questions in this chapter are arranged as follows: Questions 2.1 through 2.18 cover structures, 2.19 and 2.20 cover unions, 2.22 through 2.24 cover enumerations, and 2.25 and 2.26 cover bitfields.

Structure Declarations

2.1

Question: What's the difference between these two declarations?

```
struct x1 { ... };
typedef struct { ... } x2;
```

Answer: The first form declares a *structure tag;* the second declares a *type-def.* The main difference is that the second declaration is of a slightly more abstract type—its users don't necessarily know that it is a structure, and the keyword `struct` is not used when declaring instances of it:

```
x2 b;
```

Structures declared with tags, on the other hand, must be defined with the

```
struct x1 a;
```

form.*

(It's also possible to play it both ways:

```
typedef struct x3 { ... } x3;
```

It's legal, if potentially obscure, to use the same name for both the tag and the typedef, since they live in separate namespaces. See question 1.29.)

2.2

Question: Why doesn't this work?

```
struct x { ... };
x thestruct;
```

Answer: C is not C++. Typedef names are not automatically generated for structure tags. Actual structures are declared in C with the `struct` keyword:

```
struct x thestruct;
```

---

*It may be worth mentioning that this entire distinction is absent in C++ and perhaps in some C++ compilers masquerading as C compilers. In C++, structure tags are essentially declared as typedefs automatically.

If you wish, you can declare a typedef when you declare a structure and use the typedef name to declare actual structures:

```
typedef struct { … } tx;
```

```
tx thestruct;
```

See also question 2.1.

2.3

Question: Can a structure contain a pointer to itself?

Answer: Most certainly. A problem can arise if you try to use typedefs; see questions 1.14 and 1.15.

2.4

Question: What's the best way of implementing opaque (abstract) data types in C?

Answer: One good way is for clients to use structure pointers (perhaps additionally hidden behind typedefs) that point to structure types that are not publicly defined. In other words, a client uses structure pointers (and calls functions accepting and returning structure pointers) without knowing anything about what the fields of the structure are. As long as the details of the structure aren't needed—i.e., as long as the -> and `sizeof` operators are not used—C can in fact handle pointers to structures of incomplete type. Only within the source files implementing the abstract data type are complete declarations for the structures actually in scope.

See also question 11.5.

2.5

Question: Why does the declaration

```
extern f(struct x *p);
```

give me an obscure warning message ("struct x introduced in prototype scope" or "struct x declared inside parameter list")?

Answer: See question 11.5.

Question: I came across some code that declared a structure like this:

```
struct name {
        int namelen;
        char namestr[1];
};
```

and then did some tricky allocation to make the **namestr** array act as if it had several elements, with the number recorded by **namelen.** How does this work? Is it legal or portable?

Answer: It's not clear if it's legal or portable, but it is rather popular. An implementation of the technique might look something like this:

```
#include <stdlib.h>
#include <string.h>

struct name *makename(char *newname)
{
        struct name *ret =
                malloc(sizeof(struct name)-1 + strlen(newname)+1);
                              /* -1 for initial [1]; +1 for \0 */
        if(ret != NULL) {
                ret->namelen = strlen(newname);
                strcpy(ret->namestr, newname);
        }

        return ret;
}
```

This function allocates an instance of the name structure with the size adjusted so that the namestr field can hold the requested name (not just one character, as the structure declaration would suggest).

Despite its popularity, the technique is also somewhat notorious: Dennis Ritchie has called it "unwarranted chumminess with the C implementation," and an official interpretation has deemed that it is not strictly conforming with the C standard. (A thorough treatment of the arguments surrounding the legality of the technique is beyond the scope of this book.) It does seem to be portable to all known implementations. (Compilers that check array bounds carefully might issue warnings.)

Another possibility is to declare the variable-size element very large rather than very small. The preceding example could be rewritten like this:

```
#include <stdlib.h>
#include <string.h>

#define MAX 100

struct name {
    int namelen;
    char namestr[MAX];
};

struct name *makename(char *newname)
{
    struct name *ret =
        malloc(sizeof(struct name)-MAX+strlen(newname)+1);
                                        /* +1 for \0 */
    if(ret != NULL) {
        ret->namelen = strlen(newname);
        strcpy(ret->namestr, newname);
    }

    return ret;
}
```

Here MAX should of course be larger than any name that will be stored. However, it looks as though this technique is disallowed by a strict interpretation of the standard as well.

Of course, the right thing to do to be truly safe is use a character pointer instead of an array:

```
#include <stdlib.h>
#include <string.h>

struct name {
        int namelen;
        char *namep;
};

struct name *makename(char *newname)
{
        struct name *ret = malloc(sizeof(struct name));
        if(ret != NULL) {
                ret->namelen = strlen(newname);
                ret->namep = malloc(ret->namelen + 1);
                if(ret->namep == NULL) {
                        free(ret);
                        return NULL;
                }
                strcpy(ret->namep, newname);
        }

        return ret;
}
```

Obviously, the "convenience" of having the length and the string stored in the same block of memory has now been lost, and freeing instances of this structure will require two calls to `free`; see question 7.23.

When the data type being stored is characters, as in the preceding examples, it is straightforward to coalesce the two calls to `malloc` into one, to preserve contiguity (and therefore rescue the ability to use a single call to `free`):

```
struct name *makename(char *newname)
{
        char *buf = malloc(sizeof(struct name) +
                            strlen(newname) + 1);
        struct name *ret = (struct name *)buf;
        ret->namelen = strlen(newname);
        ret->namep = buf + sizeof(struct name);
        strcpy(ret->namep, newname);

        return ret;
}
```

However, piggybacking a second region onto a single `malloc` call like this is portable only if the second region is to be treated as an array of `char`. For any larger type, alignment (see questions 2.12 and 16.7) becomes significant and would have to be preserved.

References: Rationale §3.5.4.2

Structure Operations

2.7

Question: I heard that structures could be assigned to variables and passed to and from functions. Why does K&R1 explicitly say that they can't be?

Answer: K&R1 also said that the restrictions on structure operations would be lifted in a forthcoming version of the compiler, and in fact the operations of assigning structures, passing structures as function arguments, and returning structures from functions were fully functional in Ritchie's compiler even as K&R1 was being published. Although a few early C compilers lacked these operations, all modern compilers support them, and they are part of the standard, so there should be no reluctance to use them.*

(Note that when a structure is assigned, passed, or returned, the copying is done monolithically. This means that the copies of any pointer fields will point to the same place as the original. In other words, anything pointed to is *not* copied.)

See the code fragments in question 14.11 for an example of structure operations in action.

References: K&R1 §6.2 p. 121
K&R2 §6.2 p. 129
ANSI §3.1.2.5, §3.2.2.1, §3.3.16
ISO §6.1.2.5, §6.2.2.1, §6.3.16
H&S §5.6.2 p. 133

---

*However, passing large structures to and from functions can be expensive (see question 2.9), so you may want to consider using pointers instead (as long as you don't need pass-by-value semantics, of course).

2.8

Question: Why can't structures be compared using the built-in == and != operators?

Answer: There is no single, good way for a compiler to implement structure comparison that is consistent with C's low-level flavor. A simple byte-by-byte comparison could founder on random bits present in unused "holes" in the structure (such padding is used to keep the alignment of later fields correct; see question 2.12). A field-by-field comparison might require unacceptable amounts of repetitive code for large structures. Any compiler-generated comparison could not be expected to compare pointer fields appropriately in all cases; for example, it's often appropriate to compare char * fields with strcmp rather than with == (see also question 8.2).

If you need to compare two structures, you'll have to write your own function to do so, field by field.

References: K&R2 §6.2 p. 129
ANSI §4.11.4.1 footnote 136
Rationale §3.3.9
H&S §5.6.2 p. 133

2.9

Question: How are structure passing and returning implemented?

Answer: When structures are passed as arguments to functions, the entire structure is typically pushed on the stack, using as many words as are required. (Programmers often choose to use pointers to structures instead, precisely to avoid this overhead.) Some compilers merely pass a pointer to the structure, although they may have to make a local copy to preserve pass-by-value semantics.

Structures are often returned from functions in a location pointed to by an extra, compiler-supplied "hidden" argument to the function. Some older compilers used a special, static location for structure returns, although this made structure-valued functions nonreentrant, which ANSI C disallows.

References: ANSI §2.2.3
ISO §5.2.3

2.10

Question: How can I pass constant values to functions that accept structure arguments? How can I create nameless, immediate, constant structure values?

Answer: C has no way of generating anonymous structure values. You will have to use a temporary structure variable or a little structure-building function; see question 14.11 for an example. (The GNU C compiler provides structure constants as an extension, and the mechanism will probably be added to a future revision of the C standard.) See also question 4.10.

2.11

Question: How can I read/write structures from/to data files?

Answer: It is relatively straightforward to write a structure out using `fwrite`:

```
fwrite(&somestruct, sizeof somestruct, 1, fp);
```

and a corresponding `fread` invocation can read it back in. What happens here is that `fwrite` receives a pointer to the structure and writes (or `fread` correspondingly reads) the memory image of the structure as a stream of bytes. The `sizeof` operator determines how many bytes the structure occupies.

This call to `fwrite` is correct under an ANSI compiler as long as a prototype for `fwrite` is in scope, usually because `<stdio.h>` is included. Under pre-ANSI C, a cast on the first argument is required:

```
fwrite((char *)&somestruct, sizeof somestruct, 1, fp);
```

What's important is that `fwrite` receive a byte pointer, not a structure pointer.

Data files written as memory images with `fwrite`, however, will *not* be portable, particularly if they contain floating-point fields or pointers. The memory layout of structures is machine and compiler dependent. Different compilers may use different amounts of padding, and the sizes and byte orders of fundamental types vary across machines. Therefore, structures written as memory images cannot necessarily be read back in by programs running on other machines (or even compiled by other compilers), and this is an important concern if the data files you're writing will ever be interchanged between machines. See also questions 2.12 and 20.5.

Note also that if the structure contains any pointers (`char *` strings or pointers to other data structures), only the pointer values will be written, and they are most unlikely to be valid when read back in. Finally, note that for widespread portability, you must use the `"b"` flag when opening the files; see question 12.38.

A more portable solution, although it's a bit more work initially, is to write a pair of functions for writing and reading a structure, field by field, in a portable (perhaps even human-readable) way.

References: H&S §15.13 p. 381

Structure Padding

2.12

Question: Why is my compiler leaving holes in structures, wasting space and preventing "binary" I/O to external data files? Can I turn off the padding or otherwise control the alignment of structure fields?

Answer: Many machines access values in memory most efficiently when the values are appropriately aligned. For example, on a byte-addressed machine, `short ints` of size 2 might best be placed at even addresses, and `long ints` of size 4 at addresses that are multiples of 4. Some machines cannot perform unaligned accesses at all and *require* that all data be appropriately aligned.

Suppose that you declare this structure

```
struct {
        char c;
        int i;
};
```

The compiler will usually leave an unnamed, unused hole between the `char` and `int` fields to ensure that the `int` field is properly aligned. (This incremental alignment of the second field based on the first relies on the fact that the structure itself is always properly aligned, with the most conservative alignment requirement. The compiler guarantees this alignment for structures it allocates, as does `malloc`.)

Your compiler may provide an extension to give you control over the packing of structures (i.e., whether they are padded), perhaps with a #pragma (see question 11.20), but there is no standard method.

If you're worried about wasted space, you can minimize the effects of padding by ordering the members of a structure from largest to smallest. You can sometimes get more control over size and alignment by using bitfields, although they have their own drawbacks (see question 2.26).

See also questions 16.7 and 20.5.

References: K&R2 §6.4 p. 138
          H&S §5.6.4 p. 135

2.13

Question: Why does **sizeof** report a larger size than I expect for a structure type, as if there were padding at the end?

Answer: Structures may have this padding (as well as internal padding), if necessary, to ensure that alignment properties will be preserved when an array of contiguous structures is allocated. Even when the structure is not part of an array, the end padding remains, so that sizeof can always return a consistent size. See question 2.12.

References: H&S §5.6.7 pp. 139–40

Accessing Members

2.14

Question: How can I determine the byte offset of a field within a structure?

Answer: ANSI C defines the offsetof() macro, which should be used if available; see <stddef.h>. If your compiler doesn't define this macro, one possible implementation is:

```
#define offsetof(type, mem) ((size_t) \
    ((char *)&((type *)0)->mem - (char *)(type *)0))
```

This implementation is not 100% portable; some compilers may legitimately refuse to accept it.

(The complexities of the definition bear a bit of explanation. The subtraction of a carefully converted null pointer is supposed to guarantee that a simple offset is computed even if the internal representation of the null pointer is not 0. The casts to (char *) arrange that the offset so computed is a byte offset. The nonportability is in pretending, if only for the purposes of address calculation, that there is an instance of the type sitting at address 0. Note, however, that since the pretend instance is not referenced, an access violation is unlikely.)

See question 2.15 for a usage hint.

References: ANSI §4.1.5
ISO §7.1.6
Rationale §3.5.4.2
H&S §11.1 pp. 292–3

2.15

Question: **How can I access structure fields by name at run time?**

Answer: Build a table of names and offsets, using the offsetof() macro. The offset of field b in struct a is:

```
offsetb = offsetof(struct a, b)
```

If structp is a pointer to an instance of this structure and if field b is an int (with offset as computed here), b's value can be set indirectly with:

```
*(int *)((char *)structp + offsetb) = value;
```

2.16

Question: **Does C have an equivalent to Pascal's with statement?**

Answer: See question 20.23.

Miscellaneous Structure Questions

2.17

Question: If an array name acts like a pointer to the base of an array, why isn't the same thing true of a structure?

Answer: The rule (see question 6.3) that causes array references to "decay" into pointers is a special case that applies only to arrays and that reflects their "second-class" status in C. (An analogous rule applies to functions.) Structures, however, are first-class objects: When you mention a structure, you get the entire structure.

2.18

Question: This program works correctly, but it dumps core after it finishes. Why?

```
struct list {
        char *item;
        struct list *next;
}

/* Here is the main program. */

main(argc, argv)
{ ... }
```

Answer: A missing semicolon at the end of the structure declaration causes `main` to be declared as returning a structure. (The connection is difficult to see because of the intervening comment.) Since structure-valued functions are usually implemented by adding a hidden return pointer (see question 2.9), the generated code for `main()` tries to accept three arguments, although only two are passed (in this case, by the C startup code). See also questions 10.9 and 16.4.

Reference: CT&P §2.3 pp. 21–2

Unions

2.19

Question: What's the difference between a structure and a union?

Answer: A union is essentially a structure in which all of the fields overlay each other; you can use only one field at a time. (You can also cheat, by writing to one field and reading from another, to inspect a type's bit patterns or interpret them differently, but that's obviously pretty machine dependent.) The size of a union is the maximum of the sizes of its individual members, whereas the size of a structure is the sum of the sizes of its members. (In both cases, the size may be increased by padding; see questions 2.12 and 2.13.)

References: ANSI §3.5.2.1
ISO §6.5.2.1
H&S §5.7 pp. 140–5 esp. §5.7.4

2.20

Question: Is there a way to initialize unions?

Answer: The ANSI/SIO C Standard allows an initializer for the first member of a union. There is no standard way of initializing any other member. (Under a pre-ANSI compiler, there is generally no way of initializing a union at all.)

Many proposals have been advanced to allow more flexible union initialization, but none has been adopted yet. (The GNU C compiler provides initialization of any union member as an extension, and this feature is likely to make it into a future revision of the C standard.) If you're really desperate, you can sometimes define several variant copies of a union, with the members in different orders, so that you can declare and initialize the one having the appropriate first member. (These variants are guaranteed to be implemented compatibly, so it's okay to "pun" them by initializing one and then using the other.)

References: K&R2 §6.8 pp. 148–9
ANSI §3.5.7
ISO §6.5.7
H&S §4.6.7 p. 100

2.21

Question: Is there an automatic way to keep track of which field of a union is in use?

Answer: No. You can implement an explicitly "tagged" union yourself:

```
struct taggedunion {
        enum {UNKNOWN, INT, LONG, DOUBLE, POINTER} code;
        union {
                int i;
                long l;
                double d;
                void *p;
        } u;
};
```

You will have to make sure that the code field is always set appropriately when the union is written to; the compiler won't do any of this for you automatically. (C unions are not like Pascal variant records.)

Reference: H&S §5.7.3 p. 143

Enumerations

2.22

Question: What is the difference between an enumeration and a set of preprocessor **#defines**?

Answer: At the present time, there is little difference. The C standard says that enumerations have integral type and that enumeration constants are of type int, so both may be freely intermixed with other integral types, without errors. (If such intermixing were disallowed without explicit casts, judicious use of enumerations could catch certain programming errors.)

Some advantages of enumerations are that the numeric values are automatically assigned, that a debugger may be able to display the symbolic values when enumeration variables are examined, and that they obey block scope. (A compiler may also generate nonfatal warnings when enumerations and integers are indiscriminately mixed, since doing so can still be considered bad style even though it is not strictly illegal.) A disadvantage is that the programmer has little control over those nonfatal warnings; some programmers also resent not having control over the sizes of enumeration variables.

References: K&R2 §2.3 p. 39, §A4.2 p. 196
        ANSI §3.1.2.5, §3.5.2, §3.5.2.2, Appendix E
        ISO §6.1.2.5, §6.5.2, §6.5.2.2, Annex F
        H&S §5.5 pp. 127–9, §5.11.2 p. 153

2.23

Question: Are enumerations portable?

Answer: Enumerations were a mildly late addition to the language (they were not in K&R1), but they are definitely part of the language now; they're in the C standard, and all modern compilers support them. They're quite portable, although historical uncertainty about their precise definition led to their specification in the Standard being rather weak (see question 2.22).

2.24

Question: Is there an easy way to print enumeration values symbolically?

Answer: No. You can write a small function (one per enumeration) to map an enumeration constant to a string, either by using a `switch` statement or by searching an array. (If you're worried only about debugging, a good debugger should automatically print enumeration constants symbolically.)

Bitfields

2.25

Question: What do these colons and numbers mean in some structure declarations?

```
struct record {
        char *name;
        int refcount : 4;
        unsigned dirty : 1;
};
```

Answer: Those are *bitfields;* the number gives the exact size of the field, in bits. (See any complete book on C for the details.) Bitfields can be used to save space in structures having several binary flags or other small fields. They can also be used in an attempt to conform to externally imposed storage layouts. (Their success at the latter task is mitigated by the fact that bitfields are assigned left to right on some machines and right to left on others.)

Note that the colon notation for specifying the size of a field in bits is valid *only* in structures (and in unions); you cannot use this mechanism to specify the size of arbitrary variables. (See questions 1.2 and 1.3.)

References: K&R1 §6.7 pp. 136–8
K&R2 §6.9 pp. 149–50
ANSI §3.5.2.1
ISO §6.5.2.1
H&S §5.6.5 pp. 136–8

2.26

Question: Why do people use explicit masks and bit-twiddling code so much instead of declaring bitfields?

Answer: Bitfields are thought to be nonportable, although they are no less portable than other parts of the language. You don't know how large they can be, but that's equally true for values of type `int`. You don't know by default whether they're signed, but that's equally true of type `char`. You don't know whether they're laid out from left to right or right to left in memory, but that's equally true of the bytes of *all* types and matters only if you're trying to conform to externally imposed storage layouts. (Doing so is always nonportable; see also questions 2.12 and 20.5.)

Bitfields are inconvenient when you also want to be able to manipulate some collection of bits as a whole (perhaps to copy a set of flags). You can't have arrays of bitfields; see also question 20.8. Many programmers suspect that the compiler won't generate good code for bitfields; historically, this was sometimes true.

Straightforward code using bitfields is certainly clearer than the equivalent explicit masking instructions; it's too bad that bitfields can't be used more often.

Expressions

One of C's design goals is efficient implementation—for C compilers to be reasonably small and easy to write and for good code to be reasonably easy to generate. This dual goal has significant impacts on the language specification, although the implications are not always appreciated by users, particularly if they are used to languages that are more tightly specified or that try to do more for them (such as protecting them from their own mistakes).

Evaluation Order

A compiler is given relatively free rein in choosing the evaluation order of the various subexpressions within a complicated expression; this order is not as constrained by operator precedence and associativity as you might think. The order chosen by the compiler is immaterial unless there are multiple visible side effects or if several parallel side effects involve a single variable, in which case the behavior may be undefined.

3.1

Question: Why doesn't this code work?

```
a[i] = i++;
```

Answer: The subexpression i++ causes a side effect—it modifies i's value—which leads to undefined behavior, since i is also referenced elsewhere in the same expression. There is no way of knowing whether the reference will happen before or after the side effect—in fact, *neither* obvious interpretation might hold; see question 3.9. (Note that although the language in K&R suggests that the behavior of this expression is unspecified, the C standard makes the stronger statement that it is undefined—see question 11.33.)

References: K&R1 §2.12 p. 50
           K&R2 §2.12 pp. 53–4
           ANSI §3.3
           ISO §6.3

3.2

Question: Under my compiler, this code prints 49:

```
int i = 7;
printf("%d\n", i++ * i++);
```

Regardless of the order of evaluation, shouldn't it print 56?

Answer: It's true that the postincrement and postdecrement operators ++ and -- perform their operations after yielding the former value. What's often misunderstood are the implications and precise definition of "after." An increment or decrement operation is *not* guaranteed to be performed immediately after giving up the previous value and before any other part of the expression is evaluated. The only guarantee is that the update will be performed sometime before the expression is considered "finished" (before the next "sequence point," in ANSI C's terminology; see question 3.8). In the example, the compiler chose to multiply the previous value by itself and to perform both increments afterward.

The behavior of code that contains multiple, ambiguous side effects has always been undefined. A single expression should not cause the same object to be modified twice or to be modified and then inspected. Don't even try to find out how your compiler implements such things, let alone write code that depends on them (contrary to the ill-advised exercises in many C textbooks); as Kernighan and Ritchie wisely point out, "if you don't know *how* they are done on various machines, that innocence may help to protect you." See also questions 3.8, 3.11, and 11.33.

References: K&R1 §2.12 p. 50
K&R2 §2.12 p. 54
ANSI §3.3
ISO §6.3
CT&P §3.7 p. 47
PCS §9.5 pp. 120–1

3.3

Question: I've experimented with this code on several compilers:

```
int i = 3;
i = i++;
```

Some gave **i** the value 3, some gave 4, but one gave 7. I know that the behavior is undefined, but how could it give 7?

Answer: Undefined behavior means that *anything* can happen. See questions 3.9 and 11.33. (Also, note that neither i++ nor ++i is the same as i+1. If you want to increment i, use i=i+1 or i++ or ++i, not some combination. See also question 3.12.)

3.4

Question: Can I use explicit parentheses to force the order of evaluation I want and control these side effects? Even if I don't, doesn't precedence dictate it?

Answer: Not in general. Operator precedence and explicit parentheses impose only a partial ordering on the evaluation of an expression. In the expression f() + g() * h() we know that the multiplication will happen before the addition, but we don't know which of the three functions will be called first. In other words, precedence specifies order of evaluation only partially, where "partially" emphatically does *not* cover evaluation of operands.

Parentheses tell the compiler which operands go with which operators but do *not* force the compiler to evaluate everything within the parentheses first. Adding explicit parentheses to the preceding expression to make it

```
f() + (g() * h())
```

would make no difference in the order of the function calls. Similarly, adding explicit parentheses to the expression from question 3.2 accomplishes nothing, since ++ already has higher precedence than *):

```
(i++) * (i++)          /* WRONG */
```

The expression remains undefined with or without the parentheses.

When you need to ensure the order of subexpression evaluation, you may need to use explicit temporary variables and separate statements.

References: K&R1 §2.12 p. 49, §A.7 p. 185
          K&R2 §2.12 pp. 52–3, §A.7 p. 200

3.5

Question: But what about the `&&` and `||` operators? I see code like "`while((c = getchar()) != EOF && c != '\n')`".

Answer: Those operators, as well as the `? :` operator, receive a special exception: Left-to-right evaluation is guaranteed.* See also questions 3.6 and 3.8.

References: K&R1 §2.6 p. 38, §§A7.11–12 pp. 190–1
          K&R2 §2.6 p. 41, §§A7.14–5 pp. 207–8
          ANSI §3.3.13, §3.3.14, §3.3.15
          ISO §6.3.13, §6.3.14, §6.3.15
          H&S §7.7 pp. 217–8, §7.8 pp. 218–20, §7.12.1 p. 229
          CT&P §3.7 pp. 46–7

---

*The comma operator also guarantees left-to-right evaluation and an intermediate sequence point; see also question 3.7.

3.6

Question: Is it safe to assume that the right-hand side of the `&&` and `||` operators won't be evaluated if the left-hand side determines the outcome?

Answer: Yes. Idioms such as

```
if(d != 0 && n / d > 0)
        { /* average is greater than 0 */ }
```

and

```
if(p == NULL || *p == '\0')
        { /* no string */ }
```

are quite common in C and depend on this so-called short-circuiting behavior. In the first example, in the absence of short-circuiting behavior, the right-hand side would divide by 0—and perhaps crash—if d were equal to 0. In the second example, the right-hand side would attempt to reference nonexistent memory—and perhaps crash—if p were a null pointer.)

References: ANSI §3.3.13, §3.3.14
        ISO §6.3.13, §6.3.14
        H&S §7.7 pp. 217–8

3.7

Question: Why did

```
printf("%d %d", f1(), f2());
```

call **f2** first? I thought that the comma operator guaranteed left-to-right evaluation.

Answer: The comma operator does guarantee left-to-right evaluation, but the commas separating the arguments in a function call are not comma operators.* The order of evaluation of the arguments to a function call is *unspecified*. (See question 11.33.)

---

*If the commas separating the arguments in a function call were comma operators, no function could receive more than one argument!

References: K&R1 §3.5 p. 59
K&R2 §3.5 p. 63
ANSI §3.3.2.2
ISO §6.3.2.2
H&S §7.10 p. 224

3.8

Question: How can I understand complex expressions like the ones in this chapter and avoid writing undefined ones? What's a "sequence point"?

Answer: A sequence point is a point at which the dust has settled and all side effects that have been seen so far are guaranteed to be complete. The sequence points listed in the C standard are:

- at the end of a *full expression* (an expression statement or any other expression that is not a subexpression within any larger expression);
- at the | |, &&, ?:, and comma operators; and
- at a function call (after the evaluation of all the arguments, just before the actual call).

The standard states:

> Between the previous and next sequence point an object shall have its stored value modified at most once by the evaluation of an expression. Furthermore, the prior value shall be accessed only to determine the value to be stored.

These two rather opaque sentences say several things. First, they talk about operations bounded by the "previous and next sequence points"; such operations usually correspond to full expressions. (In an expression statement, the "next sequence point" is usually at the terminating semicolon, and the "previous sequence point" is at the end of the previous statement. An expression may also contain intermediate sequence points, as listed previously.)

The first sentence rules out both the examples i++ * i++ and i = i++ from questions 3.2 and 3.3—in both cases, i has its value modified twice within the expression, i.e., between sequence points. (If we were to write a similar expression that did have an internal sequence point, such as i++ && i++, it *would* be well defined, if questionably useful.)

The second sentence can be quite difficult to understand. It turns out that it disallows code like a[i] = i++ from question 3.1. (In fact, the other expressions we've been discussing also violate the second sentence.) To see why, let's first look more carefully at what the standard is trying to allow and disallow.

Clearly, expressions like a = b and c = d + e that read some values and use them to write others, are well defined and legal. Clearly,* expressions like i = i++ that modify the same value twice are abominations that needn't be allowed (or in any case, needn't be well defined, i.e., we don't have to figure out a way to say what they do, and compilers don't have to support them). Expressions like these are disallowed by the first sentence.

It's also clear* that we'd like to disallow expressions like a[i] = i++ that modify i *and* use it along the way, but not disallow expressions like i = i + 1 that use and modify i but only modify it later when it's reasonably easy to ensure that the final store of the final value (into i, in this case) doesn't interfere with the earlier accesses.

And that's what the second sentence says: If an object is written to within a full expression, any and all accesses to it within the same expression must be for the purposes of computing the value to be written. This rule effectively constrains legal expressions to those in which the accesses demonstrably precede the modification. The old standby i = i + 1 is allowed because the access of i is used to determine i's final value. The example a[i] = i++ is disallowed because one of the accesses of i (the one in a[i]) has nothing to do with the value that ends up being stored in i (which happens over in i++), and so there's no good way to define—for either our understanding or the compiler's—whether the access should take place before or after the incremented value is stored. Since there's no good way to define it, the standard declares that it is undefined and that portable programs simply must not use such constructs.

See also questions 3.9 and 3.11.

References: ANSI §2.1.2.3, §3.3, Appendix B
             ISO §5.1.2.3, §6.3, Annex C
             Rationale §2.1.2.3
             H&S §7.12.1 pp. 228–9

---

*Well, you may disagree, but it was clear to the people who wrote the standard.

3.9

Question: So if I write

```
a[i] = i++;
```

and I don't care which cell of **a[]** gets written to, the code is fine, and **i** gets incremented by 1, right?

Answer: No. For one thing, if you don't care which cell of a[] gets written to, why write code that seems to write to a[] at all? More significantly, once an expression or a program becomes undefined, *all* aspects of it become undefined. When an undefined expression has (apparently) two plausible interpretations, do not mislead yourself by imagining that the compiler will choose one or the other. The standard does not require that a compiler make an obvious choice, and some compilers don't. In this case, not only do we not know whether a[i] or a[i+1] is written to, it is possible that a completely unrelated cell of the array (or any random part of memory) may be written to, and it is also not possible to predict what final value i will receive. See questions 3.2, 3.3, 11.33, and 11.35.

3.10

Question: People keep saying that the behavior of **i = i++** is undefined, but I just tried it on an ANSI-conforming compiler and got the results I expected.

Answer: See question 11.35.

3.11

Question: How can I avoid these undefined evaluation-order difficulties if I don't feel like learning the complicated rules?

Answer: The easiest answer is that if you steer clear of expressions that don't have reasonably obvious interpretations, you'll generally steer clear of the undefined ones, too. (Of course, "reasonably obvious" means different things to different people. This answer works as long as you agree that a[i] = i++ and i = i++ are not "reasonably obvious.")

To be a bit more precise, here are some simpler rules that are slightly more conservative than the ones in the standard but that will help to make sure that your code is "reasonably obvious" and equally understandable to both the compiler *and* your fellow programmers:

1. Make sure that each expression modifies at most one object: a simple variable, a cell of an array, or the location pointed to by a pointer (e.g., *p). A "modification" is a simple assignment with the = operator; a compound assignment with an operator like +=, -=, or *=; or an increment or decrement with ++ or -- (in either pre or post forms).

2. If an object (as just defined) appears more than once in an expression and is the object modified in the expression, make sure that *all* appearances of the object that fetch its value participate in the computation of the new value which is stored. This rule allows the expression i = i + 1 because although the object i appears twice and is modified, the appearance (on the right-hand side) that fetches i's old value is used to compute i's new value.

3. If you want to break rule 1, make sure that the several objects being modified are distinctly different. Also, try to limit yourself to two or at most three modifications and of a style matching those of the following examples. (Make sure that you continue to follow rule 2 for each object modified.)

   The expression c = *p++ is allowed under this rule, because the two objects modified (c and p) are distinct. The expression *p++ = c is also allowed, because p and *p (i.e., p itself and what it points to) are both modified but are almost certainly distinct. Similarly, both c = a[i++] and a[i++] = c are allowed, because c, i, and a[i] are presumably all distinct. Finally, expressions in which three or more things are modified—e.g., p, q, and *p in *p++ = *q++, and i, j, and a[i] in a[i++] = b[j++]—are allowed *if* all three objects are distinct, i.e., only if two *different* pointers p and q or two *different* array indices i and j are used.

4. You may also break the first two rules if you interpose a defined sequence-point operator between the two modifications or between the modification and the access. This expression (commonly seen in a while loop while

reading a line) is legal because the second access of the variable c occurs after the sequence point implied by &&:

```
(c = getchar()) != EOF && c != '\n'
```

Without the sequence point, the expression would be illegal because the access of c while comparing it to '\n' on the right does not "determine the value to be stored" on the left.

Other Expression Questions

C has a reasonably simple set of rules for promoting operands of different types that appear in the same expression. Usually, these rules are just simple enough, but questions 3.14 and 3.15 describe two situations in which they can lead to unexpected results. Besides conversion surprises, the questions in this section concern the autoincrement operator and the conditional (or "ternary") ?: operator.

3.12

Question: **If I'm not using the value of the expression, should I use i++ or ++i to increment a variable?**

Answer: It doesn't matter. The only difference between i++ and ++i is the value that is passed on to the containing expression. When there is no containing expression (that is, when they stand alone as *full expressions*), both forms are equivalent in that they simply increment i. (It doesn't matter whether they give up the previous or incremented value, since the value is not used.)

It may be worth noting that as full expressions, the forms i += 1 and i = i + 1 are also equivalent, both to each other and to i++ and ++i.

See also question 3.3.

References: K&R1 §2.8 p. 43
K&R2 §2.8 p. 47
ANSI §3.3.2.4, §3.3.3.1
ISO §6.3.2.4, §6.3.3.1
H&S §7.4.4 pp. 192–3, §7.5.8 pp. 199–200

3.13

Question: I need to check whether one number lies between two others. Why doesn't **if(a < b < c)** work?

Answer: The relational operators, such as <, are all binary; they compare two operands and return a true or false (1 or 0) result. Therefore, the expression a < b < c compares a to b and then checks whether the resulting 1 or 0 is less than c. (To see it more clearly, imagine that it had been written as (a < b) < c, because that's how the compiler interprets it.) To check whether one number lies between two others, use code like this:

```
if(a < b && b < c)
```

References: K&R1 §2.6 p. 38
            K&R2 §2.6 pp. 41–2
            ANSI §3.3.8, §3.3.9
            ISO §6.3.8, §6.3.9
            H&S §§7.6.4,7.6.5 pp. 207–10

3.14

Question: Why doesn't this code work?

```
int a = 1000, b = 1000;
long int c = a * b;
```

Answer: Under C's integral promotion rules, the multiplication is carried out using int arithmetic, and the result may overflow or be truncated before being promoted and assigned to the long int left-hand side. Use an explicit cast on at least one of the operands to force long arithmetic:

```
long int c = (long int)a * b;
```

An alternative, equivalent form would be:

```
long int c = (long int)a * (long int)b;
```

Note that the expression (long int)(a * b) would *not* have the desired effect. An explicit cast of this form (i.e., applied to the result of the multiplication) is equivalent to the implicit conversion that would occur anyway when the value is assigned to the long int left-hand side; like the implicit conversion, it happens too late, after the damage has been done.

See also question 3.15.

References: K&R1 §2.7 p. 41
K&R2 §2.7 p. 44
ANSI §3.2.1.5
ISO §6.2.1.5
H&S §6.3.4 p. 176
CT&P §3.9 pp. 49–50

3.15

Question: Why does this code keep giving me 0?

```
double degC, degF;
degC = 5 / 9 * (degF - 32);
```

Answer: If both operands of a binary operator are integers, C performs an integer operation, regardless of the type of the rest of the expression. In this case, the integer operation is truncating division, yielding 5 / 9 = 0. (Note, however, that the problem of having subexpressions evaluated in an unexpected type is not restricted to division or, for that matter, to type int.) The operation will work as you expect if you cast one of the operands to float or double or if you use a floating-point constant, i.e.:

```
degC = (double)5 / 9 * (degF - 32);
```

or

```
degC = 5.0 / 9 * (degF - 32);
```

Note that the cast must be on one of the operands; casting the result (as in (double)(5 / 9) * (degF - 32)) would not help.

See also question 3.14.

References: K&R1 §1.2 p. 10, §2.7 p. 41
K&R2 §1.2 p. 10, §2.7 p. 44
ANSI §3.2.1.5
ISO §6.2.1.5
H&S §6.3.4 p. 176

3.16

Question: I need to assign a complicated expression to one of two variables, depending on a condition. Can I use code like this?

```
((condition) ? a : b) = complicated_expression;
```

Answer: No. The ?: operator, like most operators, yields a value, and you can't assign to a value. (In other words, ?: does not yield an *lvalue*.) If you really want to, you can try something like this:

```
*((condition) ? &a : &b) = complicated_expression;
```

(This is admittedly not as pretty.)

References: ANSI §3.3.15 esp. footnote 50
            ISO §6.3.15
            H&S §7.1 pp. 179–80

3.17

Question: I have some code containing expressions like

```
a ? b = c : d
```

Some compilers are accepting it but some are not. Why?

Answer: In the original definition of the language, = was of lower precedence than ?:, so early compilers tended to trip up on an expression like that one, attempting to parse it as if it had been written:

```
(a ? b) = (c : d)
```

Since it has no other sensible meaning, however, later compilers have allowed the expression and interpret it as if an inner set of parentheses were implied:

```
a ? (b = c) : d
```

Here, the left-hand operand of the = is simply b, not the invalid a ? b. In fact, the grammar specified in the ANSI/ISO C Standard effectively requires this interpretation. (The grammar in the standard is not precedence based and says that any expression may appear between the ? and : symbols.)

An expression like the one in the question is perfectly acceptable to an ANSI compiler, but if you ever have to compile it under an older compiler, you can always add the explicit, inner parentheses.

References: K&R1 §2.12 p. 49
ANSI §3.3.15
ISO §6.3.15
Rationale §3.3.15

Preserving Rules

The "reasonably simple set of rules for promoting operands of different types" changed slightly between classic and ANSI/ISO C; these questions discuss that change.

3.18

Question: **What does the warning "semantics of '>' change in ANSI C" mean?**

Answer: This message represents an attempt by certain (perhaps overzealous) compilers to warn you that some code may perform differently under the ANSI C "value preserving" rules than under the older "unsigned preserving" rules.

The wording of this message is rather confusing, because what has changed is not really the semantics of the > operator (in fact, almost any C operator can appear in the message) but rather the semantics of the implicit conversions that always occur when two dissimilar types meet across a binary operator or when a narrow integral type must be promoted.

(If you didn't think that you were using any unsigned values in your expression, the most likely culprit is strlen. In standard C, strlen returns size_t, which is an unsigned type.)

See question 3.19.

3.19

Question: What's the difference between the "unsigned preserving" and "value preserving" rules?

Answer: These rules concern the behavior when an unsigned type must be promoted to a "larger" type. Should it be promoted to a larger signed or unsigned type? (To foreshadow the answer, it may depend on whether the larger type is truly larger.)

Under the unsigned preserving (also called "sign preserving") rules, the promoted type is always unsigned. This rule has the virtue of simplicity, but it can lead to surprises (see the first example that follows).

Under the value preserving rules, the conversion depends on the actual sizes of the original and promoted types. If the promoted type is truly larger—which means that it can represent all the values of the original, unsigned type as signed values—the promoted type is signed. If the two types are actually the same size, the promoted type is unsigned (as for the unsigned preserving rules).

Since the *actual* sizes of the types are used in making the determination, the results will vary from machine to machine. On some machines, short int is smaller than int, but on other machines, they're the same size. On some machines, int is smaller than long int, but on others, they're the same size.

In practice, the difference between the unsigned and value preserving rules matters most often when one operand of a binary operator is (or promotes to) int and the other one might, depending on the promotion rules, be either int or unsigned int. If one operand is unsigned int, the other will be converted to that type—almost certainly causing an undesired result if its value was negative (again, see the first example that follows). When the ANSI C standard was established, the value preserving rules were chosen, to reduce the number of cases where these surprising results occur. (On the other hand, the value preserving rules also reduce the number of *predictable* cases, because portable programs cannot depend on a machine's type sizes and hence cannot know which way the value preserving rules will fall.)

Here is a contrived example showing the sort of surprise that can occur under the unsigned preserving rules:

```
unsigned short us = 10;
int i = -5;
if(i > us)
        printf("whoops!\n");
```

The important issue is how the expression i > us is evaluated. Under the unsigned preserving rules (and under the value preserving rules on a machine for which short integers and plain integers are the same size), us is promoted to unsigned int. The usual integral conversions say that when types unsigned int and int meet across a binary operator, both operands are converted to unsigned, so i is converted to unsigned int, as well. The old value of i, −5, is converted to some large unsigned value (65,531 on a 16-bit machine). This converted value is greater than 10, so the code prints "whoops!"

Under the value preserving rules, on a machine for which plain integers are larger than short integers, us is converted to a plain int (and retains its value, 10), and i remains a plain int. The expression is not true, and the code prints nothing. (To see why the values can be preserved only when the signed type is larger, remember that a value like 40,000 can be represented as an unsigned 16-bit integer but not as a signed one.)

Unfortunately, the value preserving rules do not prevent all surprises. The example just presented still prints "whoops" on a machine for which short and plain integers are the same size. The value preserving rules may also inject a few surprises of their own—consider the code:

```
unsigned char uc = 0x80;
unsigned long ul = 0;
ul |= uc << 8;
printf("0x%lx\n", ul);
```

Before being shifted left, uc is promoted. Under the unsigned preserving rules, it is promoted to an unsigned int, and the code goes on to print 0x8000, as expected. Under the value preserving rules, however, uc is promoted to a *signed* int (as long as an int is larger than a char, which is usually the case). The intermediate result uc << 8 goes on to meet ul, which is unsigned long. The signed, intermediate result must therefore be promoted as well, and if int is smaller than long, the intermediate result is sign extended, becoming `0xffff8000` on a machine with 32-bit `long`s. On such a machine, the code prints `0xffff8000`, which is probably not what was expected. (On machines for which `int` and `long` are the same size, the code prints `0x8000` under either set of rules.)

To avoid surprises (under either set of rules or due to an unexpected change of rules), it's best to avoid mixing signed and unsigned types in the same expression, although as the second example shows, this rule is not always sufficient. You can always use explicit casts to indicate, unambiguously, exactly where and how you want conversions performed; see questions 12.42 and 16.7 for examples. (Some compilers attempt to warn you when they detect ambiguous cases or expressions that would have behaved differently under the unsigned preserving rules, although sometimes these warnings fire too often; see also question 3.18.)

References: K&R2 §2.7 p. 44, §A6.5 p. 198, Appendix C p. 260
           ANSI §3.2.1.1, §3.2.1.2, §3.2.1.5
           ISO §6.2.1.1, §6.2.1.2, §6.2.1.5
           Rationale §3.2.1.1
           H&S §§6.3.3, 6.3.4 pp. 174–7

4   Pointers

Pointers, though certainly one of the most powerful and popular features of C, are nonetheless the bane of many a beginning programmer. When pointers don't point where they should, the possibilities for mayhem are endless. (Actually, many of the apparent problems with pointers have more to do with memory allocation; see Chapter 7.)

Basic Pointer Use

4.1

Question: What are pointers really good for, anyway?

Answer: They're good for lots of things, including:

- dynamically allocated arrays (see questions 6.14 and 6.16)
- generic access to several similar variables
- (simulated) by-reference function parameters (see questions 4.8 and 20.1)

- dynamically allocated data structures of all kinds, especially trees and linked lists
- walking over arrays (for example, while parsing strings)
- efficient, by-reference "copies" of arrays and structures, especially as function parameters

(Note that this is hardly a comprehensive list!)

See also question 6.8.

4.2

Question: **I'm trying to declare a pointer and allocate some space for it, but it's not working. What's wrong with this code?**

```
char *p;
*p = malloc(10);
```

Answer: The pointer you declared is `p`, not `*p`. To make a pointer point somewhere, you just use the name of the pointer:

```
p = malloc(10);
```

It's when you're manipulating the pointed-to memory that you use `*` as an indirection operator:

```
*p = 'H';
```

It's easy to make the mistake shown in the question, though, because if you had used the `malloc` call as an initializer in the declaration of a local variable, it would have looked like this:

```
char *p = malloc(10);
```

When you break an initialized pointer declaration up into a declaration and a later assignment, you have to remember to remove the `*`.

In summary, in an expression, `p` is the pointer, and `*p` is what it points to (a `char`, in this example).

See also questions 1.21, 7.1, and 8.3.

References: CT&P §3.1 p. 28

4.3

Question: What does ***p++** increment: **p** or what it points to?

Answer: Unary operators, such as *, ++, and --, all associate (group) from right to left. Therefore, *p++ increments p (and returns the value pointed to by p before the increment). To increment the value pointed to by p, use (*p)++ (or perhaps ++*p, if the order of the side effect doesn't matter).

References: K&R1 §5.1 p. 91
        K&R2 §5.1 p. 95
        ANSI §3.3.2, §3.3.3
        ISO §6.3.2, §6.3.3
        H&S §7.4.4 pp. 192–3, §7.5 p. 193, §§7.5.7,7.5.8 pp. 199–200

Pointer Manipulations

4.4

Question: I'm trying to use pointers to manipulate an array of **ints**. What's wrong with this code?

```
int array[5], i, *ip;
for(i = 0; i < 5; i++) array[i] = i;
ip = array;
printf("%d\n", *(ip + 3 * sizeof(int)));
```

I expected the last line to print 3, but it printed garbage.

Answer: You're doing a bit more work than you have to or should. Pointer arithmetic in C is always automatically scaled by the size of the objects pointed to. What you want to say is simply:

```
printf("%d\n", *(ip + 3));     /* or ip[3] — see Q 6.3 */
```

This will print the third element of the array. In code like this, you don't need to worry about scaling by the size of the pointed-to elements; by attempting to do so explicitly, you inadvertently tried to access a nonexistent element past the end of the array (probably `array[6]` or `array[12]`, depending on `sizeof(int)` on your machine).

References: K&R1 §5.3 p. 94
K&R2 §5.4 p. 103
ANSI §3.3.6
ISO §6.3.6
H&S §7.6.2 p. 204

4.5

Question: I have a **char *** pointer that happens to point to some **ints**, and I want to step it over them. Why doesn't this code work?

```
((int *)p)++;
```

Answer: In C, a cast operator does not mean "pretend that these bits have a different type and treat them accordingly"; it is a conversion operator, and by definition it yields an *rvalue,* which cannot be assigned to or incremented with ++. (It is an anomaly in older compilers and an extension in gcc that such expressions are ever accepted.) Say what you mean; use

```
p = (char *)((int *)p + 1);
```

Or, since p is a char *, simply use

```
p += sizeof(int);
```

To be *really* explicit, you could use

```
int *ip = (int *)p;
p = (char *)(ip + 1);
```

Whenever possible, you should choose appropriate pointer types in the first place instead of trying to treat one type as another.

See also question 16.7.

References: K&R2 §A7.5 p. 205
ANSI §3.3.4 (esp. footnote 14)
ISO §6.3.4
Rationale §3.3.2.4
H&S §7.1 pp. 179–80

4.6

Question: Why can't I perform arithmetic on a **void *** pointer?

Answer: See question 11.24.

4.7

Question: I've got some code that's trying to unpack external structures, but it's crashing with a message about an "unaligned access." What does this mean?

Answer: See question 16.7.

Pointers as Function Parameters

4.8

Question: I have a function that accepts, and is supposed to initialize, a pointer:

```
void f(ip)
int *ip;
{
        static int dummy = 5;
        ip = &dummy;
}
```

But when I call it like this:

```
int *ip;
f(ip);
```

the pointer in the caller remains unchanged.

Answer: Are you sure that the function initialized what you thought it did? Remember, arguments in C are passed by value. In the preceding code the called function alters only the passed copy of the pointer. To make it work as you expect, you can pass the address of the pointer; the function ends up accepting a pointer to a pointer:

```
void f(ipp)
int **ipp;
{
        static int dummy = 5;
        *ipp = &dummy;
}

    ...

        int *ip;
        f(&ip);
```

In this case, we're essentially simulating pass by reference.

Another solution is to have the function return the pointer:

```
int *f()
{
        static int dummy = 5;
        return &dummy;
}

    ...

        int *ip = f();
```

See also questions 4.9 and 4.11.

4.9

Question: If I want to write a function that takes a generic pointer as an argument and I want to simulate passing it by reference, can I give the formal parameter type **void** ** and do something like this?

```
void f(void **);
double *dp;
f((void **)&dp);
```

Answer: Not portably. Code like this may work and is sometimes recommended, but it relies on all pointer types having the same internal representation (which is common but not universal; see question 5.17).

C has no generic pointer-to-pointer type. Values of type void * act as generic pointers only because conversions are applied automatically when other pointer types are assigned to and from void *; such conversions cannot be performed if an attempt is made to indirect on a void ** value that points at something other than a void *. When you use a void ** pointer value (for instance, when you use the * operator to access the void * value to which the void ** points), the compiler has no way of knowing whether that void * value was once converted from another pointer type. Rather, the compiler must assume that it is nothing more than a void *; it cannot perform any implicit conversions.

In other words, any void ** value you play with must be the address of an actual void * value somewhere. Casts like (void **) &dp, although they may shut the compiler up, are nonportable and may not even do what you want; see also question 13.9. If the pointer that the void ** points to is not a void * and if it has a different size or representation than a void *, the compiler isn't going to be able to access it correctly.

To make the previous code fragment work, you'd have to use an intermediate void * variable:

```
double *dp;
void *vp = dp;
f(&vp);
dp = vp;
```

The assignments to and from vp give the compiler the opportunity to perform any conversions, if necessary.

Again, the discussion so far assumes that different pointer types might have different sizes or representations, which is rare today but not unheard of. To appreciate the problem with void ** more clearly, compare the situation to an analogous one involving, say, types int and double, which probably have different sizes and certainly have different representations. Suppose that we have a function:

```
void incme(double *p)
{
        *p += 1;
}
```

We can then do something like this:

```
int i = 1;
double d = i;
incme(&d);
i = d;
```

The obvious result is that i is incremented by 1. (This is analogous to the correct void ** code involving the auxiliary vp.) Suppose, on the other hand, that we were to attempt something like this:

```
int i = 1;
incme((double *)&i);       /* WRONG */
```

This code is analogous to the fragment in the question and would almost certainly not work.

4.10

Question: I have a function

```
extern int f(int *);
```

that accepts a pointer to an **int**. How can I pass a constant by reference? A call like

```
f(&5);
```

doesn't seem to work.

Answer: You can't do this directly. You will have to declare a temporary variable and then pass its address to the function:

```
int five = 5;
f(&five);
```

In C, a function that accepts a pointer to a value rather than simply accepting the value probably intends to modify the pointed-to value, so it may be a bad idea to pass pointers to constants. Indeed, if f is in fact declared as accepting an int *, a diagnostic is required if you attempt to pass it a pointer to a const int. (The function could be declared as accepting a const int * if it promises not to modify the pointed-to value.)

See also questions 2.10, 4.8, and 20.1.

4.11

Question: Does C even have "pass by reference"?

Answer: Not really. Strictly speaking, C always uses pass by value. C seems to have something like pass by reference in two situations: You can simulate pass by reference yourself by defining functions that accept pointers and then using the & operator when calling, and the compiler will essentially simulate it for you when you pass an array to a function (by passing a pointer instead, see question 6.4 and others). Formally, though, C has nothing truly equivalent to pass by reference or C++ reference parameters. (However, function-like preprocessor macros do provide a form of "call by name.") See also questions 4.8, 7.9, 12.27, and 20.1.

References: K&R1 §1.8 pp. 24–5, §5.2 pp. 91–3
K&R2 §1.8 pp. 27–8, §5.2 pp. 91–3
ANSI §3.3.2.2, esp. footnote 39
ISO §6.3.2.2
H&S §9.5 pp. 273–4

Miscellaneous Pointer Use

4.12

Question: I've seen different methods used for calling functions via pointers. What's the story?

Answer: Originally, a pointer to a function had to be "turned into" a "real" function, with the * operator, before calling:

```
int r, (*fp)(), func();
fp = func;
r = (*fp)();
```

The interpretation of the last line is clear: fp is a pointer to a function, so *fp is the function. Append an argument list in parentheses (and extra parentheses around *fp to get the precedence right), and you've got a function call.

It can also be argued that functions are always called via pointers and that "real" function names always decay implicitly into pointers in expressions, as they do in initializations; see question 1.34. This reasoning, made widespread through pcc and adopted in the ANSI standard, means that r = fp(); is legal and works correctly, whether fp is the name of a function or a pointer to one. (The usage has always been unambiguous; there is nothing you ever could have done with a function pointer followed by an argument list except call the function pointed to.) An explicit * is still allowed and recommended if portability to older compilers is important.

See also question 1.34.

References: K&R1 §5.12 p. 116
K&R2 §5.11 p. 120
ANSI §3.3.2.2
ISO §6.3.2.2
Rationale §3.3.2.2
H&S §5.8 p. 147, §7.4.3 p. 190

4.13

Question: What's the total generic pointer type? My compiler complained when I tried to stuff function pointers into a **void** *.

Answer: There is no "total generic pointer type." A void * is guaranteed to hold only object (i.e., data) pointers; converting a function pointer to type void * is not portable. (On some machines, function addresses can be very large—larger than any data pointers.)

It is guaranteed, however, that all function pointers can interconverted, as long as they are converted back to an appropriate type before calling. Therefore, you can pick any function type (usually int (*) () or void (*) (), that is, pointer to function of unspecified arguments returning int or void) as a generic function pointer. When you need a place to hold object and function pointers interchangeably, the portable solution is to use a union of a void * and a generic function pointer (of whichever type you choose).

See also questions 1.22 and 5.8.

References: ANSI §3.1.2.5, §3.2.2.3, §3.3.4
          ISO §6.1.2.5, §6.2.2.3, §6.3.4
          Rationale §3.2.2.3
          H&S §5.3.3 p. 123

4.14

Question: How are integers converted to and from pointers? Can I temporarily stuff an integer into a pointer, or vice versa?

Answer: Once upon a time, it was guaranteed that a pointer could be converted to an integer (although one never knew whether an int or a long might be required), that an integer could be converted to a pointer, that a pointer remained unchanged when converted to a (large enough) integer and back again, and that the conversions (and any mapping) were intended to be "unsurprising to those who know the addressing structure of the machine." In other words, there is some precedent and support for integer/pointer conversions, but they have always been machine dependent and hence nonportable. Explicit casts have always been required (although early compilers rarely complained if you left them out).

The ANSI/ISO C Standard, in order to ensure that C is widely implementable, has weakened those earlier guarantees. Pointer-to-integer and integer-to-pointer conversions are implementation-defined (see question 11.33), and there is no longer a guarantee that pointers can be converted to integers and back, without change.

Forcing pointers into integers or integers into pointers has never been good practice. When you need a generic slot that can hold either kind of data, a union is a much better idea.

See also questions 5.18 and 19.25.

References: K&R1 §A14.4 p. 210
        K&R2 §A6.6 p. 199
        ANSI §3.3.4
        ISO §6.3.4
        Rationale §3.3.4
        H&S §6.2.3 p. 170, §6.2.7 pp. 171–2

5 Null Pointers

For each pointer type, C defines a special pointer value, the null pointer, that is guaranteed not to point to any object or function of that type. (The null pointer is analogous to the nil pointer in Pascal and LISP.) C programmers are often confused about the proper use of null pointers and about their internal representation (even though the internal representation should not matter to most programmers). The *null pointer constant* used for representing null pointers in source code involves the integer 0, and many machines represent null pointers internally as a word with all bits zero, but the second fact is *not* guaranteed by the language.

Because confusion about null pointers is so common, this chapter discusses them rather exhaustively. (Questions 5.13–5.17 are a retrospective on the confusion itself.) If you are fortunate enough not to share the many misunderstandings covered or find the discussion too exhausting, you can skip to question 5.15 for a quick summary.

Null Pointers and Null Pointer Constants

These first three questions cover the fundamental definitions of null pointers in the language.

5.1

Question: What is this infamous null pointer, anyway?

Answer: The language definition states that for each pointer type, there is a special value—the "null pointer"—that is distinguishable from all other pointer values and that is "guaranteed to compare unequal to a pointer to any object or function." That is, a null pointer points definitively nowhere; it is not the address of any object or function. The address-of operator & will never yield a null pointer, nor will a successful call to `malloc`.* (A null pointer is returned when `malloc` fails, and this is a typical use of null pointers: as a "special" pointer value with another meaning, usually "not allocated" or "not pointing anywhere yet.")

A null pointer is conceptually different from an uninitialized pointer. A null pointer is known not to point to any object or function; an uninitialized pointer might point anywhere. See also questions 1.30, 7.1, and 7.31.

Each pointer type has a null pointer, and the internal values of null pointers for different types may differ. Although programmers need not know the internal values, the compiler must always be informed which type of null pointer is required, so that it can make the distinction if necessary (see question 5.2).

References: K&R1 §5.4 pp. 97–8
K&R2 §5.4 p. 102
ANSI §3.2.2.3
ISO §6.2.2.3
Rationale §3.2.2.3
H&S §5.3.2 pp. 121–3

---

*A "successful" call to `malloc(0)` can yield a null pointer; see question 11.26.

5.2

Question: **How do I get a null pointer in my programs?**

Answer: With a *null pointer constant.* According to the language definition, an "integral constant expression with the value 0" in a pointer context is converted into a null pointer at compile time. That is, when one side of an initialization, assignment, or comparison is a variable or expression of pointer type, the compiler can tell that a constant 0 on the other side requests a null pointer and can generate the correctly typed null pointer value. Therefore, the following fragments are perfectly legal:

```
char *p = 0;
if(p != 0)
```

See also question 5.3.

However, an argument being passed to a function is not necessarily recognizable as a pointer context, and the compiler may not be able to tell that an unadorned 0 "means" a null pointer. To generate a null pointer in a function call context, an explicit cast may be required, to force the 0 to be recognized as a pointer. For example, the UNIX system call `execl` takes a variable-length, null pointer–terminated list of character pointer arguments and is correctly called like this:

```
execl("/bin/sh", "sh", "-c", "date", (char *)0);
```

If the `(char *)` cast on the last argument were omitted, the compiler would not know to pass a null pointer and would pass an integer 0 instead. (Note that many UNIX manuals get this example wrong; see also question 5.11.)

When function prototypes are in scope, argument passing becomes an "assignment context," and most casts may safely be omitted, since the prototype tells the compiler that a pointer is required and of which type, enabling it to correctly convert an unadorned 0. Function prototypes cannot provide the types for variable arguments in variable-length argument lists, however, so explicit casts are still required for those arguments. (See also question 15.3.) It can be considered safest to properly cast all null pointer constants in function calls: to guard against varargs functions or those without prototypes, to allow interim use of non-ANSI compilers, and to demonstrate that you know what you are doing. (Incidentally, it's also a simpler rule to remember.)

Here is a summary of the rules for when null pointer constants may be used by themselves and when they require explicit casts:

Unadorned **0** okay	Explicit cast required
Initialization	
Assignment	
Comparison	
Function call, prototype in scope, fixed argument	Function call, no prototype in scope
	Variable argument in varargs function call

References: K&R1 §A7.7 p. 190, §A7.14 p. 192
K&R2 §A7.10 p. 207, §A7.17 p. 209
ANSI §3.2.2.3
ISO §6.2.2.3
H&S §4.6.3 p. 95, §6.2.7 p. 171

5.3

Question: Is the abbreviated pointer comparison "**if(p)**" to test for non-null pointers valid? What if the internal representation for null pointers is nonzero?

Answer: It is always valid. When C requires the Boolean value of an expression (in the if, while, for, and do statements and with the &&, ||, !, and ?: operators), a false value is inferred when the expression compares equal to zero and a true value otherwise. That is, whenever one writes

    if(expr)

where "expr" is any expression at all, the compiler essentially acts as if it had been written as

    if((expr) != 0)

Substituting the trivial pointer expression "p" for "expr," we have

    if(p)

is equivalent to

    if(p != 0)

This is a comparison context, so the compiler can tell that the (implicit) 0 is a null pointer constant and use the correct null pointer value. No trickery is involved here; compilers do work this way and generate identical code for both constructs. The internal representation of a null pointer does *not* matter.

The Boolean negation operator, !, can be described as follows:

```
!expr
```

is essentially equivalent to

```
(expr)?0:1
```

or to

```
((expr) == 0)
```

This leads to the conclusion that

```
if(!p)
```

is equivalent to

```
if(p == 0)
```

"Abbreviations," such as if(p), are perfectly legal but are considered by some to be bad style (and by others to be good style; see question 17.10).

See also question 9.2.

References: K&R2 §A7.4.7 p. 204
        ANSI §3.3.3.3, §3.3.9, §3.3.13, §3.3.14, §3.3.15, §3.6.4.1, §3.6.5
        ISO §6.3.3.3, §6.3.9, §6.3.13, §6.3.14, §6.3.15, §6.6.4.1, §6.6.5
        H&S §5.3.2 p. 122

The NULL Macro

So that a program's use of null pointers can be made a bit more explicit, a standard preprocessor macro, NULL, is defined, having as its value a null pointer constant. Unfortunately, although it is supposed to clarify things, this extra level of abstraction sometimes introduces extra levels of confusion.

5.4

Question: What is **NULL** and how is it defined?

Answer: As a matter of style, many programmers prefer not to have unadorned 0s—some representing numbers and some representing pointers— scattered through their programs. Therefore, the preprocessor macro NULL is defined by several headers, including <stdio.h> and <stddef.h>, with the value 0, possibly cast to (void *) (see also question 5.6). A programmer who wishes to make explicit the distinction between 0 the integer and 0 the null pointer constant can then use NULL whenever a null pointer is required.

Using NULL is a stylistic convention only; the preprocessor turns NULL back into 0, which is then recognized by the compiler, in pointer contexts, as before. In particular, a cast may still be necessary before NULL (as before 0) in a function call argument. The table in question 5.2 applies for both NULL and 0 (an unadorned NULL is equivalent to an unadorned 0).

NULL should be used *only* for pointers; see question 5.9.

References: K&R1 §5.4 pp. 97–8
           K&R2 §5.4 p. 102
           ANSI §4.1.5, §3.2.2.3
           ISO §7.1.6, §6.2.2.3
           Rationale §4.1.5
           H&S §5.3.2 p. 122, §11.1 p. 292

5.5

Question: How should **NULL** be defined on a machine that uses a nonzero bit pattern as the internal representation of a null pointer?

Answer: The same as on any other machine: as 0 or ((void *)0).

Whenever a programmer requests a null pointer, by writing either "0" or "NULL," it is the compiler's responsibility to generate whatever bit pattern the machine uses for that null pointer. (Again, the compiler can tell that an unadorned 0 requests a null pointer when the 0 is in a pointer context; see question 5.2.) Therefore, defining NULL as 0 on a machine for which internal null pointers are nonzero is as valid as on any other: The compiler must always be able to generate the machine's correct null pointers in response to unadorned 0s seen in pointer contexts. A constant 0 is a null pointer constant; NULL is just a convenient name for it (see also question 5.13).

Section 4.1.5 of the C standard states that NULL "expands to an implementation-defined null pointer constant," which means that the implementation gets to choose which form of 0 to use and whether to use a void * cast; see questions 5.6 and 5.7. "Implementation-defined" here does *not* mean that NULL might be defined to match an implementation-specific nonzero internal null pointer value.

See also questions 5.2, 5.10, and 5.17.

References: ANSI §4.1.5
 ISO §7.1.6
 Rationale §4.1.5

5.6

Question: **If NULL were defined as follows:**

```
#define NULL ((char *)0)
```

wouldn't that make function calls that pass an uncast NULL work?

Answer: Not in general. The problem is that some machines use different internal representations for pointers to different types of data. The suggested definition would make uncast NULL arguments to functions expecting pointers to characters work correctly, but pointer arguments of other types would still require explicit casts. Furthermore, such legal constructions as FILE *fp = NULL; could fail.

Nevertheless, ANSI C allows this alternative definition for NULL:*

```
#define NULL ((void *)0)
```

Besides potentially helping incorrect programs to work (but only on machines with homogeneous pointers, thus questionably valid assistance), this definition may catch programs that use NULL incorrectly (e.g., when the ASCII NUL character was really intended; see question 5.9). See also question 5.7.

Programmers who are accustomed to modern, "flat" memory architectures may find the idea of "different kinds of pointers" very difficult to accept. See question 5.17 for some examples.

Reference: Rationale §4.1.5

---

*Because of the special assignment properties of void * pointers, the initialization FILE *fp = NULL; *is* valid if NULL is defined as ((void *)0).

5.7

Question: My vendor provides header files that define **NULL** as **0L**. Why?

Answer: Some programs carelessly attempt to generate null pointers by using the NULL macro, without casts, in nonpointer contexts. (Doing so is not guaranteed to work; see questions 5.2 and 5.11.) On machines that have pointers larger than integers (such as PC compatibles in "large" model; see also question 5.17), a particular definition of NULL, such as 0L, can help these incorrect programs to work. (0L is a perfectly valid definition of NULL; it is an "integral constant expression with value 0.") Whether it is wise to coddle incorrect programs is debatable; see also question 5.6 and Chapter 17.

References: Rationale §4.1.5
        H&S §5.3.2 pp. 121–2

5.8

Question: Is **NULL** valid for pointers to functions?

Answer: Yes, (but see question 4.13).

References: ANSI §3.2.2.3
        ISO §6.2.2.3

5.9

Question: If **NULL** and **0** are equivalent as null pointer constants, which should I use?

Answer: Many programmers believe that NULL should be used in all pointer contexts, as a reminder that the value is to be thought of as a pointer. Others feel that the confusion surrounding NULL and 0 is only compounded by hiding 0 behind a macro and prefer to use unadorned 0 instead. There is no one right answer. (See also questions 9.4 and 17.10.) C programmers must understand that NULL and 0 are interchangeable in pointer contexts and that an uncast 0 is perfectly acceptable. Any usage of NULL (as opposed to 0) should be considered a gentle reminder that a pointer is involved; programmers should not depend on it (for either their own understanding or the compiler's) for distinguishing pointer 0s from integer 0s.

Only in pointer contexts are NULL and 0 equivalent. NULL should *not* be used when another kind of 0 is required, even though it might work, because doing so sends the wrong stylistic message. Furthermore, ANSI allows the definition of NULL to be ((void *)0), which will not work at all in nonpointer contexts. In particular, do not use NULL when the ASCII null character (NUL) is desired. If you'd like a symbolic constant for the null character, provide your own definition:

```
#define NUL '\0'
```

References: K&R1 §5.4 pp. 97–8
            K&R2 §5.4 p. 102

5.10

Question: But wouldn't it be better to use **NULL** rather than **0** in case the value of **NULL** changes, perhaps on a machine with nonzero internal null pointers?

Answer: No. (Using NULL may be preferable but not for this reason.) Although symbolic constants are often used in place of numbers because the numbers might change, this is *not* the reason that NULL is used in place of 0. Once again, the language guarantees that source-code 0s (in pointer contexts) generate null pointers. NULL is used only as a stylistic convention. See questions 5.5 and 9.4.

5.11

Question: I once used a compiler that wouldn't work unless **NULL** was used.

Answer: Unless the code being compiled was nonportable, that compiler was probably broken. Perhaps the code used something like this nonportable version of an example from question 5.2:

```
execl("/bin/sh", "sh", "-c", "date", NULL);     /* WRONG */
```

Under a compiler that defines NULL to ((void *)0) (see question 5.6), this code will happen to work.* However, if pointers and integers have different sizes or representations, the following (equally incorrect) code may not work:

```
execl("/bin/sh", "sh", "-c", "date", 0);        /* WRONG */
```

Correct, portable code uses an explicit cast:

```
execl("/bin/sh", "sh", "-c", "date", (char *)NULL);
```

With the cast, the code works correctly no matter what the machine's integer and pointer representations are and no matter which form of null pointer constant the compiler has chosen as the definition of NULL. (The code fragment in question 5.2, which used 0 instead of NULL, is equally correct; see also question 5.9.)

5.12

Question: I use the preprocessor macro

```
#define Nullptr(type) (type *)0
```

to help me build null pointers of the correct type.

Answer: This trick, though popular and superficially attractive, does not buy much. It is not needed in assignments and comparisons; see question 5.2. It does not even save keystrokes. Its use may suggest to the reader that the program's author is shaky on the subject of null pointers, requiring that the definition of the macro, its invocations, and *all* other pointer usages be checked. See also questions 9.1 and 10.2.

Retrospective

In some circles, misunderstandings about null pointers run rampant. These five questions explore some of the reasons why.

---

*Using (void *)0, in the guise of NULL, instead of (char *)0 happens to work only because of a special guarantee about the representations of void * and char * pointers.

5.13

Question: This is strange: **NULL** is guaranteed to be **0**, but the null pointer is not?

Answer: When the term "null" or "NULL" is casually used, one of several things may be meant:

1. The conceptual null pointer, the abstract language concept defined in question 5.1. It is implemented with ...

2. The internal, or run-time, representation of a null pointer, which may or may not be all bits 0 and which may be different for different pointer types. The actual values should be of concern only to compiler writers. Authors of C programs never see them, since they use ...

3. The null pointer constant, which is a constant integer 0* (see question 5.2). It is often hidden behind ...

4. The NULL macro, which is defined to be 0 or ((void *) 0) (see question 5.4). Finally, as red herrings, we have ...

5. The ASCII null character (NUL), which does have all bits zero but has no necessary relation to the null pointer except in name and ...

6. The "null string," which is another name for the empty string (""). Using the term "null string" can be confusing in C, because an empty string involves a null ('\0') character but *not* a null pointer, which brings us full circle.

In other words, to paraphrase the White Knight's description of his song in *Through the Looking-Glass*, the name of the null pointer is "0", but the name of the null pointer is called "NULL" (and we're not sure what the null pointer *is*).

This book uses the phrase "null pointer" (in lowercase) for sense 1, the character "0" or the phrase "null pointer constant" for sense 3, and the capitalized word "NULL" for sense 4.[†]

References: H&S §1.3 p. 325
       Through the Looking-Glass, chapter VIII.

---

*More precisely, a null pointer constant is an integer constant expression with the value 0, possibly cast to void *.

[†]To be very, very precise, the word "null" as a noun means only sense 5, and "NULL" means only sense 4; the other usages all use "null" as an adjective, as does the (unrelated) term "null statement." These are admittedly fine points.

5.14

Question: Why is there so much confusion surrounding null pointers? Why do these questions come up so often?

Answers: C programmers traditionally like to know more than they need to about the underlying machine implementation. The fact that null pointers are represented as zero in both source code and internally to most machines invites unwarranted assumptions. The use of a preprocessor macro (NULL) may seem to suggest that the value could change some day or on some weird machine. The construct "if (p == 0)" is easily misread as calling for conversion of p to an integral type rather than 0 to a pointer type, before the comparison. Finally, the distinction among the several uses of the term "null" (listed in question 5.13) is often overlooked.

One good way to wade out of the confusion is to imagine that C used a keyword (perhaps nil, like Pascal) as a null pointer constant. The compiler could either turn nil into the correct type of null pointer when it could determine the type from the source code or complain when it could not. In C, in fact, the keyword for a null pointer constant is not nil but 0, which works almost as well, except that an uncast 0 in a nonpointer context generates an integer zero instead of an error message; and if that uncast 0 was supposed to be a null pointer constant, the code may not work.

5.15

Question: Is there an easier way to understand all this null pointer stuff?

Answer: Follow these two simple rules:

1. When you want a null pointer constant in source code, use "0" or "NULL".

2. If the usage of "0" or "NULL" is an argument in a function call, cast it to the pointer type expected by the function being called.

The rest of this chapter has to do with other people's misunderstandings, with the internal representation of null pointers (which you shouldn't need to know), and with ANSI C refinements. If you understand questions 5.1, 5.2, and 5.4, and consider 5.3, 5.9, 5.13, and 5.14, you'll do fine.

5.16

Question: Given all the confusion surrounding null pointers, wouldn't it be easier simply to require them to be represented internally by zeroes?

Answer: Some implementations naturally represent null pointers by special, nonzero bit patterns, particularly when it can be arranged that inadvertently using those values triggers automatic hardware traps. Requiring null pointers to be represented internally as 0—and therefore disallowing use of the special, nonzero values—would be an unfortunate step backward, because catching errors that result in invalid accesses is a Good Thing.

Besides, what would such a requirement really accomplish? Proper understanding of null pointers does not require knowledge of the internal representation, whether zero or nonzero. Assuming that null pointers are internally zero does not make any code easier to write (except for a certain ill-advised usage of `calloc`; see question 7.31). Known-zero internal pointers would not reduce the need for casts in function calls, because the *size* of the pointer might still be different from that of an int. (If "nil" were used to request null pointers, as mentioned in question 5.14, the urge to assume an internal-zero representation would not even arise.)

5.17

Question: Seriously, have any actual machines really used nonzero null pointers or different representations for pointers to different types?

Answer: The Prime 50 series used segment 07777, offset 0 for the null pointer, at least for PL/I. Later models used segment 0, offset 0 for null pointers in C, necessitating new instructions, such as TCNP (Test C Null Pointer), evidently as a sop to all the extant poorly written C code that made incorrect assumptions. Older, word-addressed Prime machines were also notorious for requiring larger byte pointers (`char *`'s) than word pointers (`int *`'s).

The Eclipse MV series from Data General has three architecturally supported pointer formats (word, byte, and bit pointers), two of which are used by C compilers: byte pointers for `char *` and `void *`, and word pointers for everything else.

Some Honeywell-Bull mainframes use the bit pattern 06000 for (internal) null pointers.

The CDC Cyber 180 Series has 48-bit pointers consisting of a ring, segment, and offset. Most users (in ring 11) have null pointers of 0xB00000000000. It was common on old CDC ones-complement machines to use an all-one-bits word as a special flag for all kinds of data, including invalid addresses.

The old HP 3000 series uses different addressing schemes for byte addresses and for word addresses; like several of the previous machines, it therefore uses different representations for char * and void * pointers than for other pointers.

The Symbolics Lisp Machine, a tagged architecture, does not even have conventional numeric pointers; it uses the pair <NIL, 0> (basically a nonexistent <object, offset> handle) as a C null pointer.

Depending on the "memory model" in use, 8086-family processors (PC compatibles) may use 16-bit data pointers and 32-bit function pointers, or vice versa.

Some 64-bit Cray machines represent int * in the lower 48 bits of a word; char * additionally uses the upper 16 bits to indicate a byte address within a word.

Reference: K&R1 §A14.4 p. 211

What's Really at Address 0?

A null pointer should not be thought of as pointing at address 0, but if you find yourself accessing address 0 (either accidentally or deliberately), null pointers may seem to be involved.

5.18

Question: Is a run-time integral value of 0, cast to a pointer, guaranteed to be a null pointer?

Answer: No. Only *constant* integral expressions with value 0 are guaranteed to indicate null pointers. See also questions 4.14, 5.2, and 5.19.

5.19

Question: How can I access an interrupt vector located at the machine's location 0? If I set a pointer to 0, the compiler might translate it to a nonzero internal null pointer value.

Answer: Since whatever is at location 0 is obviously machine dependent, you're free to use whatever machine-dependent trick will work to get there. Read your vendor's documentation (and see Chapter 19). It's likely that if it's at all meaningful for you to be accessing location 0, the system will be set up to make it reasonably easy to do so. Some possibilities are:

- Simply set a pointer to 0. (This is the way that doesn't have to work, but if it's meaningful, it probably will.)

- Assign the integer 0 to an `int` variable and convert that `int` to a pointer. (This is also not guaranteed to work, but it probably will.)

- Use a union to set the bits of a pointer variable to 0:

  ```
  union {
          int *u_p;
          int u_i;   /* assumes sizeof(int) >= sizeof(int *) */
  } p;

  p.u_i = 0;
  ```

- Use `memset` to set the bits of a pointer variable to 0:

  ```
  memset((void *)&p, 0, sizeof(p));
  ```

- Declare an external variable or array:

  ```
  extern int location0;
  ```

  Then use an assembly language file or a special linker invocation to arrange that this symbol refers to (i.e., the variable is placed at) address 0.

See also questions 4.14 and 19.25.

References: K&R1 §A14.4 p. 210
K&R2 §A6.6 p. 199
ANSI §3.3.4
ISO §6.3.4
Rationale §3.3.4
H&S §6.2.7 pp. 171–2

5.20

Question: What does a run-time "null pointer assignment" error mean? How do I track it down?

Answer: This message, which typically occurs with MS-DOS compilers (see, therefore, Chapter 19) means that you've written to location 0 via a null (perhaps because uninitialized) pointer. (See also question 16.8.)

A debugger may let you set a data breakpoint or watchpoint or something on location 0. Alternatively, you could write a bit of code to stash away a copy of 20 or so bytes from location 0 and periodically check that the memory at location 0 hasn't changed.

6 Arrays and Pointers

A strength of C is its unification of arrays and pointers. Pointers can be conveniently used to access arrays and to simulate dynamically allocated arrays. The so-called equivalence between arrays and pointers is so close, however, that programmers sometimes lose sight of the remaining essential differences between the two, imagining either that they are identical or that various nonsensical similarities or identities can be assumed between them.

The cornerstone of the "equivalence" of arrays and pointers in C is the fact that most array references *decay* into pointers to the array's first element, as described in question 6.3. Therefore, arrays are "second-class citizens" in C: You can never manipulate an array in its entirety (i.e., to copy it or pass it to a function), because whenever you mention its name, you're left with a pointer rather than the entire array. Because arrays decay to pointers, the array subscripting operator `[]` always finds itself, deep down, operating on a pointer. In fact, the subscripting expression `a[i]` is defined in terms of the equivalent pointer expression `*((a)+(i))`.

Parts of this chapter (especially the "retrospective" questions 6.8–6.10) may seem redundant—people have many confusing ways of thinking about arrays and pointers, and this chapter tries to clear them up as best it can. If you find yourself bored by the repetition, stop reading and move on. But if you're confused or if things don't make sense, keep reading until they fall into place.

Basic Relationship of Arrays and Pointers

6.1

Question: I had the definition `char a[6]` in one source file, and in another I declared `extern char *a`. Why didn't it work?

Answer: The declaration `extern char *a` does not declare an array and therefore does not match the actual definition. The type pointer to type T is not the same as array of type T. Use `extern char a[]`.

References: ANSI §3.5.4.2
ISO §6.5.4.2
CT&P §3.3 pp. 33–4, §4.5 pp. 64–5

6.2

Question: But I heard that `char a[]` is identical to `char *a`. Is that true?

Answer: Not at all. (What you heard has to do with formal parameters to functions; see question 6.4.) Arrays are not pointers, although they are closely related (see question 6.3) and can be used similarly (see questions 4.1, 6.8, 6.10, and 6.14).

The array declaration `char a[6]` requests that space for six characters be set aside, to be known by the name a. That is, there is a location named a at which six characters can sit. The pointer declaration `char *p`, on the other hand, requests a place that holds a pointer, to be known by the name p. This pointer can point almost anywhere: to any `char`, to any contiguous array of chars, or nowhere*(see also questions 1.30 and 5.1).

As usual, a picture is worth a thousand words. The declarations

```
char a[] = "hello";
char *p = "world";
```

would initialize data structures that could be represented like this:

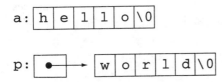

It is important to realize that a reference like `x[3]` generates different code, depending on whether x is an array or a pointer. Given those two declarations, when the compiler sees the expression `a[3]`, it emits code to start at the location `a`, move three past it, and fetch the character there. When it sees the expression `p[3]`, it emits code to start at the location `p`, fetch the pointer value there, add three to the pointer, and finally fetch the character pointed to. In other words, `a[3]` is three places past the start of the object *named* `a`, whereas `p[3]` is three places past the object *pointed to* by `p`. In our example, both `a[3]` and `p[3]` happen to be the character `'l'`, but the compiler gets there differently.

References: K&R2 §5.5 p. 104
CT&P §4.5 pp. 64–5

6.3

Question: So what is meant by the "equivalence of pointers and arrays" in C?

Answer: Much of the confusion surrounding arrays and pointers in C can be traced to a misunderstanding of this statement. Saying that arrays and pointers are "equivalent" means neither that they are identical nor even that they are interchangeable. Rather, "equivalence" refers to the following key definition: A reference to an object of type array of T that appears in an

---

*Don't interpret "anywhere" and "nowhere" too broadly. To be valid, a pointer must point to properly allocated memory (see questions 7.1, 7.2, and 7.3); to point definitively nowhere, a pointer must be a null pointer (see question 5.1).

expression decays (with three exceptions) into a pointer to its first element; the type of the resultant pointer is pointer to T. (The exceptions are when the array is the operand of a `sizeof` or an & operator or is a string literal initializer for a character array.* See questions 6.23, 6.12, and 1.32, respectively.)

As a consequence of this definition, and in spite of the fact that the underlying arrays and pointers are quite different, the compiler doesn't apply the array subscripting operator [] that differently to arrays and pointers, after all.† Given an array `a` and pointer `p`, an expression of the form `a[i]` causes the array to decay into a pointer, following the preceding rule, and then to be subscripted just as would be a pointer variable in the expression `p[i]` (although the eventual memory accesses will be different, as explained in question 6.2). If you were to assign the array's address to the pointer:

```
p = a;
```

`p[3]` and `a[3]` would access the same element.

This harmony of access explains how pointers can access arrays, serve in their stead as function parameters (see question 6.4), and simulate dynamic arrays (see question 6.14).

See also questions 6.8 and 6.10.

References: K&R1 §5.3 pp. 93–6
K&R2 §5.3 p. 99
ANSI §3.2.2.1, §3.3.2.1, §3.3.6
ISO §6.2.2.1, §6.3.2.1, §6.3.6
H&S §5.4.1 p. 124

6.4

Question: **If they're so different, why are array and pointer declarations interchangeable as function formal parameters?**

Answer: It's supposed to be a convenience.

Since arrays decay immediately into pointers, an array is never actually passed to a function. You can pretend that a function receives an array as a

---

*By "string literal initializer for a character array," we include also wide string literals for arrays of `wchar_t`.
†Strictly speaking, the [] operator is always applied to a pointer; see question 6.10 item 2.

parameter and illustrate it by declaring the corresponding parameter as an array:

```
f(char a[])
{ ... }
```

Interpreted literally, this declaration would have no use, so the compiler turns around and pretends that you'd written a pointer declaration, since that's what the function will in fact receive:

```
f(char *a)
{ ... }
```

There's nothing particularly wrong with talking about a function as if it "receives" an array if the function is traditionally used to operate on arrays or if the parameter is naturally treated within the function as an array.

This rewriting of array declarators into pointers holds only within function formal parameter declarations, nowhere else. If rewritten array parameter declarations bother you, you're under no compulsion to use them; many people have concluded that the confusion they cause outweighs the small advantage of having the declaration "look like" the call or the uses within the function. (Note that the conversion happens only once; something like char a2[][] won't work. See questions 6.18 and 6.19.)

See also question 6.21.

References: K&R1 §5.3 p. 95, §A10.1 p. 205
K&R2 §5.3 p. 100, §A8.6.3 p. 218, §A10.1 p. 226
ANSI §3.5.4.3, §3.7.1, §3.9.6
ISO §6.5.4.3, §6.7.1, §6.9.6
H&S §9.3 p. 271
CT&P §3.3 pp. 33–4
Ritchie, "The Development of the C Language"

Arrays Can't Be Assigned

If an array appears on the right-hand side of an assignment, only the pointer it decays to is copied, not the entire array. Furthermore, an array may not appear on the left-hand side of an assignment (in part because, by the previous sentence, there would never be an entire array for it to receive).

6.5

Question: Why can't I do something like this?

```
extern char *getpass();
char str[10];
str = getpass("Enter password: ");
```

Answer: Arrays are "second-class citizens" in C; one consequence is that you cannot assign to them (see also question 6.7). When you need to copy the contents of one array to another, you must do so explicitly. In the case of char arrays, the strcpy function is usually appropriate:

```
strcpy(str, getpass("Enter password: "));
```

When you want to pass arrays around without copying them, you can use pointers and simple assignment. See also questions 4.1 and 8.2.

References: ANSI §3.2.2.1
  ISO §6.2.2.1
  H&S §7.9.1 pp. 221–2

6.6

Question: If I can't assign to arrays, then how can this code work?

```
int f(char str[])
{
        if(str[0] == '\0')
                str = "none";
        ...
}
```

Answer: In this code, str is a function parameter, so its declaration is rewritten by the compiler as described in question 6.4. In other words, str *is* a pointer (of type char *), and it is legal to assign to it.

6.7

Question: How can an array be an lvalue if I can't assign to it?

Answer: The term *lvalue* doesn't quite mean "something you can assign to"; a better definition is "something that has a location (in memory)."* The ANSI/ISO C Standard goes on to define a "modifiable lvalue"; an array is not a modifiable lvalue. See also question 6.5.

References: ANSI §3.2.2.1
               ISO §6.2.2.1
               Rationale §3.2.2.1
               H&S §7.1 p. 179

Retrospective

Because the basic relationship between arrays and pointers occasionally generates so much confusion, here are a few questions about that confusion.

6.8

Question: Practically speaking, what is the difference between arrays and pointers?

Answer: An array is a single, preallocated chunk of contiguous elements (all of the same type), fixed in size and location. A pointer is a reference to any data element (of a particular type) anywhere. A pointer must be assigned to point to space allocated elsewhere, but it can be reassigned (and the space, if derived from malloc, can be resized) at any time. A pointer can point to an array and can simulate (along with malloc) a dynamically allocated array, but a pointer is a much more general data structure (see also question 4.1).

   Due to the so-called equivalence of arrays and pointers (see question 6.3), arrays and pointers often seem interchangeable; in particular, a pointer to a block of memory assigned by malloc is frequently treated (and can be

---

*The original definition of "lvalue" did have to do with the left-hand side of assignment statements.

referenced using [ ]) exactly as if it were a true array. See questions 6.14 and 6.16. (Be careful with `sizeof`; see question 7.28.)

See also questions 1.32, 6.10, and 20.14.

6.9

Question: Someone explained to me that arrays are really just constant pointers. Is this accurate?

Answer: That explanation is a bit of an oversimplification. An array name is "constant" in that it cannot be assigned to, but an array is *not* a pointer, as the discussion and pictures in question 6.2 should make clear. See also questions 6.3, 6.8, and 6.10.

6.10

Question: I'm still mystified. Is a pointer a kind of array, or is an array a kind of pointer?

Answer: An array is *not* a pointer, and vice versa. An array *reference* (that is, any mention of an array in a value context) *turns into* a pointer (see questions 6.2 and 6.3).

There are perhaps three ways to think about the situation:

1. Pointers can simulate arrays (though that's not all; see question 4.1).
2. There's hardly such a thing as an array (it is, after all, a "second-class citizen"); the subscripting operator [ ] is in fact a pointer operator.
3. At a higher level of abstraction, a pointer to a block of memory is effectively the same as an array (although this says nothing about other uses of pointers).

But to reiterate, here are two ways *not* to think about it:

4. "They're completely the same." (False; see question 6.2.)
5. "Arrays are constant pointers." (False; see question 6.9.)

See also question 6.8.

6.11

Question: I came across some "joke" code containing the "expression" `5["abcdef"]`. How can this be legal C?

Answer: Believe it or not, array subscripting is commutative in C.* This curious fact follows from the pointer definition of array subscripting, namely, that `a[e]` is identical to `*((a)+(e))` for *any* two expressions a and e, as long as one of them is a pointer expression and one is integral. The "proof" looks like this:

```
a[e]
*((a) + (e))        (by definition)
*((e) + (a))        (by commutativity of addition)
e[a]                (by definition)
```

This unsuspected commutativity is often mentioned in C texts as if it were something to be proud of, but it finds no useful application outside of the Obfuscated C Contest (see question 20.36).

Since strings in C are arrays of `char`, the expression `"abcdef"[5]` is perfectly legal and evaluates to the character `'f'`. You can think of it as a shorthand for:

```
char *tmpptr = "abcdef";

… tmpptr[5] …
```

See question 20.10 for a realistic example.

References: Rationale §3.3.2.1
           H&S §5.4.1 p. 124, §7.4.1 pp. 186–7

Pointers to Arrays

Since arrays usually decay into pointers, it's particularly easy to get confused when dealing with the occasional pointer to an entire array (as opposed to a pointer to its first element).

---

*The commutativity is of the array-subscripting operator `[]` itself; obviously, `a[i][j]` is in general different from `a[j][i]`.

6.12

Question: Since array references decay into pointers, what's the difference—if **array** is an array—between **array** and **&array**?

Answer: The type.

In standard C, **&array** yields a pointer, of type pointer to array of T, to the entire array. (In pre-ANSI C, the **&** in **&array** generally elicited a warning and was generally ignored.) Under all C compilers, a simple reference (without an explicit **&**) to an array yields a pointer, of type pointer to T, to the array's first element.

For a simple array, such as

```
int a[10];
```

a reference to a has type "pointer to **int**," and **&a** is "pointer to array of 10 **int**s." For a two-dimensional array such as

```
int array[NROWS][NCOLUMNS];
```

a reference to **array** has type "pointer to array of NCOLUMNS **int**s," whereas **&array** has type "pointer to array of NROWS arrays of NCOLUMNS **int**s."

See also questions 6.3, 6.13, and 6.18.

References: ANSI §3.2.2.1, §3.3.3.2
ISO §6.2.2.1, §6.3.3.2
Rationale §3.3.3.2
H&S §7.5.6 p. 198

6.13

Question: How do I declare a pointer to an array?

Answer: Usually, you don't want to. When people speak casually of a pointer to an array, they usually mean a pointer to its first element.

Instead of a pointer to an array, consider using a pointer to one of the array's elements. Arrays of type T decay into pointers to type T (see question 6.3), which is convenient; subscripting or incrementing the resultant pointer will access the individual members of the array. True pointers to arrays, when subscripted or incremented, step over entire arrays and are generally useful only when operating on arrays of arrays,* if at all. (See also question 6.18.)

If you really need to declare a pointer to an entire array, use something like "int (*ap) [N] ; " where N is the size of the array. (See also question 1.21.) If the size of the array is unknown, N can in principle be omitted, but the resulting type, "pointer to array of unknown size," is useless.

Here is an example showing the difference between simple pointers and pointers to arrays. Given the declarations

```
int a1[3] = {0, 1, 2};
int a2[2][3] = {{3, 4, 5}, {6, 7, 8}};
int *ip;                /* pointer to int */
int (*ap)[3];           /* pointer to array [3] of int */
```

you could use the simple pointer to int, ip, to access the one-dimensional array a1:

```
ip = a1;
printf("%d ", *ip);
ip++;
printf("%d\n", *ip);
```

This fragment would print

```
0 1
```

An attempt to use a pointer to array, ap, on a1:

```
ap = &a1;
printf("%d\n", **ap);
ap++;                        /* WRONG */
printf("%d\n", **ap);        /* undefined */
```

would print 0 on the first line and something undefined on the second (and might crash). The pointer to array would be useful only in accessing an array of arrays, such as a2:

```
ap = a2;
printf("%d %d\n", (*ap)[0], (*ap)[1]);
ap++;                        /* steps over entire (sub)array */
printf("%d %d\n", (*ap)[0], (*ap)[1]);
```

---

*This discussion also applies to three- or more dimensional arrays.

This last fragment would print

    3 4
    6 7

See also question 6.12.

References: ANSI §3.2.2.1
           ISO §6.2.2.1

Dynamic Array Allocation

The close relationship between arrays and pointers makes it easy to use a pointer to dynamically allocated memory to simulate an array, of size determined at run time.

6.14

Question: How can I set an array's size at run time? How can I avoid fixed-sized arrays?

Answer: The equivalence between arrays and pointers (see question 6.3) allows a pointer to memory obtained from `malloc` to simulate an array quite effectively. After executing

```
#include <stdlib.h>
int *dynarray = (int *)malloc(10 * sizeof(int));
```

(and if the call to `malloc` succeeds), you can reference `dynarray[i]` (for i from 0 to 9) just as if `dynarray` were a conventional, statically allocated array (`int a[10]`). See also questions 6.16, 7.28, and 7.29.

6.15

Question: How can I declare local arrays of a size matching a passed-in array?

Answer: You can't, in C. Array dimensions must be compile-time constants. (The GNU C compiler provides parameterized arrays as an extension.) You'll have to use `malloc`, and remember to call `free` before the function returns. See also questions 6.14, 6.16, 6.19, 7.22, and maybe 7.32.

References: ANSI §3.4, §3.5.4.2
ISO §6.4, §6.5.4.2

6.16

Question: How can I dynamically allocate a multidimensional array?

Answer: It is usually best to allocate an array* of pointers to pointers and then initialize each pointer to a dynamically allocated "row." Here is a two-dimensional example:

```
#include <stdlib.h>

int **array1 = (int **)malloc(nrows * sizeof(int *));
for(i = 0; i < nrows; i++)
        array1[i] = (int *)malloc(ncolumns * sizeof(int));
```

In real code, of course, all of `malloc`'s return values would be checked.

You can keep the array's contents contiguous, while making later reallocation of individual rows difficult, with a bit of explicit pointer arithmetic:

```
int **array2 = (int **)malloc(nrows * sizeof(int *));
array2[0] = (int *)malloc(nrows * ncolumns * sizeof(int));
for(i = 1; i < nrows; i++)
        array2[i] = array2[0] + i * ncolumns;
```

In either case (i.e., for `array1` or `array2`), the elements of the dynamic array can be accessed with normal-looking array subscripts: `array`x`[i][j]` (for $0 \le i <$ NROWS and $0 \le j <$ NCOLUMNS). The schematic illustration on page 106 shows the layout of `array1` and `array2`.

---

*Strictly speaking, these aren't arrays but rather objects to be *used* like arrays; see also question 6.14.

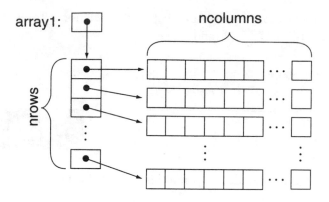

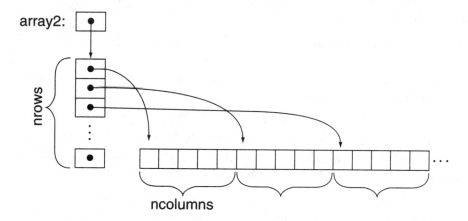

If the double indirection implied by the above schemes is for some reason unacceptable,* you can simulate a two-dimensional array with a single, dynamically-allocated one-dimensional array:

```
int *array3 = (int *)malloc(nrows * ncolumns * sizeof(int));
```

However, you must now perform subscript calculations manually, accessing the i,jth element with the expression `array3[i * ncolumns + j]`,† and this array cannot necessarily be passed to functions which expect multidimensional arrays. See also question 6.19.

---

*Note, however, that double indirection is not necessarily any less efficient than multiplicative indexing.

†A macro such as `#define Arrayaccess(a, i, j) ((a)[(i) * ncolumns + (j)])` could hide the explicit calculation. Invoking that macro, however, would require parentheses and commas that wouldn't look exactly like conventional C multidimensional array syntax, and the macro would need access to at least one of the dimensions, as well.

Finally, you could use pointers to arrays:

```
int (*array4)[NCOLUMNS] =
        (int (*)[NCOLUMNS])malloc(nrows * sizeof(*array4));
```

or even

```
int (*array5)[NROWS][NCOLUMNS] =
        (int (*)[NROWS][NCOLUMNS])malloc(sizeof(*array5));
```

Here, however, the syntax starts getting horrific (accesses to `array5` look like `(*array5)[i][j]`), and at most one dimension may be specified at run time.

With all of these techniques, you may of course need to remember to free the arrays when they are no longer needed; this takes several steps in the case of `array1` and `array2` (see also question 7.23):

```
for(i = 0; i < nrows; i++)
        free((void *)array1[i]);
free((void *)array1);
free((void *)array2[0]);
free((void *)array2);
```

Also, you cannot necessarily intermix dynamically allocated arrays with conventional, statically allocated ones (see question 6.20, and also question 6.18).

All of these techniques can also be extended to three or more dimensions. Here is a three-dimensional version of the first technique:

```
int ***a3d = (int ***)malloc(xdim * sizeof(int **));
for(i = 0; i < xdim; i++) {
        a3d[i] = (int **)malloc(ydim * sizeof(int *));
        for(j = 0; j < ydim; j++)
                a3d[i][j] = (int *)malloc(zdim * sizeof(int));
}
```

See also question 20.2.

6.17

Question: Here's a neat trick: If I write

```
int realarray[10];
int *array = &realarray[-1];
```

I can treat **array** as if it were a 1-based array. Is this legal?

Answer: Although this technique is attractive (and was used in old editions of the book *Numerical Recipes in C*), it does not conform to the C standards. Pointer arithmetic is defined only as long as the pointer points within the same allocated block of memory or to the imaginary "terminating" element one past it; otherwise, the behavior is undefined, *even if the pointer is not dereferenced.* The code in the question computes a pointer to memory before the beginning of `realarray` and could fail if, while subtracting the offset, an illegal address were generated (perhaps because the address tried to "wrap around" past the beginning of some memory segment).

References: K&R2 §5.3 p. 100, §5.4 pp. 102–3, §A7.7 pp. 205–6
    ANSI §3.3.6
    ISO §6.3.6
    Rationale §3.2.2.3

Functions and Multidimensional Arrays

It's difficult to pass multidimensional arrays to functions with full generality. The rewriting of array parameters as pointers (as discussed in question 6.4) means that functions that accept simple arrays seem to accept arrays of arbitrary length, which is convenient. However, the parameter rewriting occurs only on the "outermost" array, so the "width" and higher dimensions of multidimensional arrays cannot be similarly variable. This problem arises in part because in standard C, array dimensions must always be compile-time constants; they cannot, for instance, be specified by other parameters of a function.

6.18

Question: My compiler complained when I passed a two-dimensional array to a function expecting a pointer to a pointer. Why?

Answer: The rule (see question 6.3) by which arrays decay into pointers is not applied recursively. An array of arrays (i.e., a two-dimensional array in C) decays into a pointer to an array, not a pointer to a pointer. Pointers to arrays can be confusing and must be treated carefully; see also question 6.13. (The confusion is heightened by the existence of incorrect compilers, including some old versions of pcc and pcc-derived lints, which improperly accept assignments of multidimensional arrays to multilevel pointers.)

If you are passing a two-dimensional array to a function:

```
int array[NROWS][NCOLUMNS];
f(array);
```

the function's declaration must match:

```
f(int a[][NCOLUMNS])
{ ... }
```

or

```
f(int (*ap)[NCOLUMNS])    /* ap is a pointer to an array */
{ ... }
```

In the first declaration, the compiler performs the usual implicit parameter rewriting of "array of array" to "pointer to array" (see questions 6.3 and 6.4); in the second form, the pointer declaration is explicit. Since the called function does not allocate space for the array, it does not need to know the overall size, so the number of rows, NROWS, can be omitted. The "shape" of the array is still important, so the column dimension NCOLUMNS (and, for three- or more dimensional arrays, the intervening ones) must be retained.

If a function is already declared as accepting a pointer to a pointer, it is probably meaningless to pass a two-dimensional array directly to it. An intermediate pointer would have to be used when attempting to call it with a two-dimensional array:

```
extern g(int **ipp);

int *ip = &array[0][0];
g(&ip);             /* PROBABLY WRONG */
```

This usage, however, is misleading and almost certainly incorrect, since the array has been "flattened" (its shape has been lost).

See also questions 6.12 and 6.15.

References: K&R1 §5.10 p. 110
           K&R2 §5.9 p. 113
           H&S §5.4.3 p. 126

6.19

Question: How do I write functions that accept two-dimensional arrays when the "width" is not known at compile time?

Answer: It's not easy. One way is to pass in a pointer to the [0][0] element along with the two dimensions and to simulate array subscripting "by hand":

```
f2(aryp, nrows, ncolumns)
int *aryp;
int nrows, ncolumns;
{ ... array[i][j] is accessed as aryp[i * ncolumns + j] ... }
```

Note that the correct expression for manual subscripting involves ncolumns (the "width" of each row), not nrows (the *number* of rows); it's easy to get this backward.

This function could be called with the array from question 6.18 as

```
f2(&array[0][0], NROWS, NCOLUMNS);
```

It must be noted, however, that a program that performs multidimensional array subscripting "by hand" in this way is not in strict conformance with the ANSI C standard; according to an official interpretation, the behavior of accessing (&array[0][0])[x] is not defined for x >= NCOLUMNS.

The GNU C compiler allows local arrays to be declared having sizes that are specified by a function's arguments, but this is a nonstandard extension.

When you want to be able to use a function on multidimensional arrays of various sizes, one solution is to simulate all the arrays dynamically, as in question 6.16.

See also questions 6.15, 6.18, and 6.20.

References: ANSI §3.3.6
           ISO §6.3.6

6.20

Question: How can I use statically and dynamically allocated multidimensional arrays interchangeably when passing them to functions?

Answer: There is no single perfect method. Given the declarations

```
int array[NROWS][NCOLUMNS];
int **array1;                   /* ragged */
int **array2;                   /* contiguous */
int *array3;                    /* "flattened" */
int (*array4)[NCOLUMNS];
int (*array5)[NROWS][NCOLUMNS];
```

with the pointers initialized as in the code fragments in question 6.16 and functions declared as

```
f1(int a[][NCOLUMNS], int nrows, int ncolumns);
f2(int *aryp, int nrows, int ncolumns);
f3(int **pp, int nrows, int ncolumns);
```

where f1 accepts a conventional two-dimensional array, f2 accepts a "flattened" two-dimensional array, and f3 accepts a pointer-to-pointer, simulated array (see also questions 6.18 and 6.19), the following calls should work as expected:

```
f1(array, NROWS, NCOLUMNS);
f1(array4, nrows, NCOLUMNS);
f1(*array5, NROWS, NCOLUMNS);
f2(&array[0][0], NROWS, NCOLUMNS);
f2(*array, NROWS, NCOLUMNS);
f2(*array2, nrows, ncolumns);
f2(array3, nrows, ncolumns);
f2(*array4, nrows, NCOLUMNS);
f2(**array5, NROWS, NCOLUMNS);
f3(array1, nrows, ncolumns);
f3(array2, nrows, ncolumns);
```

The following two calls would probably work on most systems but involve questionable casts and work only if the dynamic ncolumns matches the static NCOLUMNS:

```
f1((int (*)[NCOLUMNS])(*array2), nrows, ncolumns);
f1((int (*)[NCOLUMNS])array3, nrows, ncolumns);
```

Only f2, as shown, can conveniently be made to work with both statically and dynamically allocated arrays, although it will *not* work with the traditional "ragged" array implementation, array1. However, note that passing &array[0][0] (or, equivalently, *array) to f2 is not strictly conforming; see question 6.19.

If you can understand why all of the preceding calls work and are written as they are and if you understand why the combinations that are not listed would not work, you have a *very* good understanding of arrays and pointers in C.

Rather than worrying about all of this, one approach to using multidimensional arrays of various sizes is to make them *all* dynamic, as in question 6.16. If there are no static multidimensional arrays—if all arrays are allocated like array1 or array2 in question 6.16—all functions can be written like f3.

Sizes of Arrays

The sizeof operator will tell you the size of an array if it can, but it's not able to if the size is not known or if the array has already decayed to a pointer.

6.21

Question: Why doesn't **sizeof** properly report the size of an array when the array is a parameter to a function? I have this test function and it prints 4, not 10:

```
f(char a[10])
{
        int i = sizeof(a);
        printf("%d\n", i);
}
```

Answer: The compiler pretends that the array parameter was declared as a pointer (that is, in the example, as char *a; see question 6.4), and sizeof reports the size of the pointer. See also questions 1.24 and 7.28.

References: H&S §7.5.2 p. 195

6.22

Question: How can code in a file where an array is declared as **extern** (i.e. it is defined and its size determined in another file) determine the size of the array? The **sizeof** operator doesn't seem to work.

Answer: See question 1.24.

6.23

Question: How can I determine how many elements are in an array, when **sizeof** yields the size in bytes?

Answer: Simply divide the size of the entire array by the size of one element:

```
int array[] = {1, 2, 3};
int narray = sizeof(array) / sizeof(array[0]);
```

References: ANSI §3.3.3.4
        ISO §6.3.3.4

7 Memory Allocation

Many people assume that pointers are the most difficult aspect of C to learn. Often, however, the problem is not so much managing the pointers as managing the memory to which they point. In keeping with C's low-level flavor, programmers are often responsible for explicitly allocating memory, yet it is easy to overlook the allocation of pointed-to objects. Using pointers that do not point to properly allocated memory is a never-ending source of serious bugs.

Basic Allocation Problems

Even if you're not calling `malloc`, you have to be sure that the memory you're trying to use (in particular, that pointed to by pointers) is properly allocated.

7.1

Question: **Why doesn't this fragment work?**

```
char *answer;
printf("Type something:\n");
gets(answer);
printf("You typed \"%s\"\n", answer);
```

Answer: The pointer variable `answer`, which is handed to `gets()` as the location into which the response should be stored, has not been set to point to any valid storage. It is an uninitialized variable, just as is the variable `i` in

```
int i;
printf("i = %d\n", i);
```

That is, in the first piece of code, we cannot say where the pointer `answer` points, just as we cannot say what value `i` will have in the second. (Since local variables are not initialized and typically contain garbage, it is not even guaranteed that `answer` starts out as a null pointer. See questions 1.30 and 5.1.)

The simplest way to correct the question-asking program is to use a local array instead of a pointer and to let the compiler worry about allocation:

```
#include <stdio.h>
#include <string.h>

char answer[100], *p;
printf("Type something:\n");
fgets(answer, sizeof answer, stdin);
if((p = strchr(answer, '\n')) != NULL)
    *p = '\0';
printf("You typed \"%s\"\n", answer);
```

This example also uses `fgets()` instead of `gets()`, so that the end of the array cannot be overwritten. (See question 12.23. Unfortunately for this example, `fgets()` does not automatically delete the trailing `\n`, as `gets()` would.) It would also be possible to use `malloc()` to allocate the `answer` buffer, and to parameterize the buffer size (with something like

```
#define ANSWERSIZE 100).
```

7.2

Question: Why can't I get **strcat** to work? I tried

```
char *s1 = "Hello, ";
char *s2 = "world!";
char *s3 = strcat(s1, s2);
```

but I got strange results.

Answer: As in question 7.1, the main problem here is that space for the concatenated result is not properly allocated. C does not provide an automatically managed string type. C compilers allocate memory only for objects explicitly mentioned in the source code (in the case of "strings," this includes character arrays and string literals). The programmer must arrange for sufficient space for the results of run-time operations, such as string concatenation, typically by declaring arrays or by calling `malloc`.

The `strcat` function performs no allocation; the second string is appended to the first one, in place. The first (destination) string must be writable and have enough room for the concatenated result. Therefore, one fix would be to declare the first string as an array:

```
char s1[20] = "Hello, ";
```

In production code, of course, we wouldn't use magic numbers like "20"; we'd use more robust mechanisms to guarantee sufficient space.

Since `strcat` returns the value of its first argument (`s1`, in this case), the variable `s3` in the question above is superfluous.

The original call to `strcat` in the question actually has two problems: not only is the string literal pointed to by `s1` not being big enough for any concatenated text, it is not necessarily writable at all. See question 1.32.

References: CT&P §3.2 p. 32

7.3

Question: But the documentation for `strcat` says that it takes two `char *` pointers as arguments. How am I supposed to know to allocate things?

Answer: In general, you *always* have to consider memory allocation when using pointers, if only to make sure that the compiler is doing it for you. If a library function's documentation does not explicitly mention allocation, it is usually the caller's problem.

The Synopsis section at the top of a UNIX-style man page or in the ANSI C standard can be misleading. The code fragments presented there are closer to the function definitions used by an implementor than the invocations used by the caller. In particular, many functions that accept pointers (e.g., to structures or to strings) are usually called with the address of an object (a structure or an array—see questions 6.3 and 6.4). Other common examples are `time` (see question 13.12) and `stat`.

7.4

Question: I'm reading lines from a file into an array, with this code:

```
char linebuf[80];
char *lines[100];
int i;

for(i = 0; i < 100; i++) {
        char *p = fgets(linebuf, 80, fp);
        if(p == NULL) break;
        lines[i] = p;
}
```

Why do all the lines end up containing copies of the last line?

Answer: You have allocated memory for only one line: `linebuf`. Each time you call `fgets`, the previous line is overwritten. No memory is allocated by `fgets`: unless it reaches EOF or encounters an error, the pointer it returns is the same pointer you handed it as its first argument (in this case, a pointer to the single `linebuf` array).

To make code like this work, you'll need to allocate memory for each line. See question 20.2 for an example.

References: K&R1 §7.8 p. 155
K&R2 §7.7 pp. 164–5
ANSI §4.9.7.2
ISO §7.9.7.2
H&S §15.7 p. 356

7.5

Question: I have a function that is supposed to return a string, but when the function returns to its caller, the returned string is garbage. Why?

Answer: Whenever a function returns a pointer, make sure that the pointed-to memory is properly allocated. The returned pointer should be to a statically allocated buffer, to a buffer passed in by the caller, or to memory obtained with `malloc`, but *not* to a local (automatic) array. In other words, never do something like this:

```
#include <stdio.h>

char *itoa(int n)
{
        char retbuf[20];                /* WRONG */
        sprintf(retbuf, "%d", n);
        return retbuf;                  /* WRONG */
}
```

When a function returns, its automatic, local variables are discarded, so the returned pointer in this case is invalid (it points to an array that no longer exists).

One fix would be to declare the return buffer as

```
static char retbuf[20];
```

This fix is imperfect, since a function using static data is not reentrant. Furthermore, successive calls to this version of `itoa` keep overwriting the same return buffer: The caller won't be able to call it several times and keep all the return values around simultaneously.

Another fix is to have the caller pass space for the result:

```
char *itoa(int n, char *retbuf)
{
        sprintf(retbuf, "%d", n);
        return retbuf;
}

...

        char str[20];
        itoa(123, str);
```

A third alternative is to use `malloc`:

```
#include <stdlib.h>

char *itoa(int n)
{
        char *retbuf = malloc(20);
        if(retbuf != NULL)
                sprintf(retbuf, "%d", n);
        return retbuf;
}

...

        char *str = itoa(123);
```

In this case, the caller must remember to free the returned pointer when it is no longer needed.

See also questions 12.21 and 20.1.

References: ANSI §3.1.2.4
            ISO §6.1.2.4

Calling `malloc`

When you need more flexibly allocated data than you can achieve with static allocation, it's time to take the plunge and begin allocating memory dynamically, usually using `malloc`. The questions in this section cover the basics of calling `malloc`; the next section moves on to some of `malloc`'s failure modes.

7.6

Question: Why am I getting "warning: assignment of pointer from integer lacks a cast" for calls to **malloc**?

Answer: Have you included `<stdlib.h>` or otherwise arranged for `malloc` to be declared properly? If not, the compiler assumes that it returns an int (see question 1.25), which is not correct. (The same problem could arise for `calloc` or `realloc`.) See also question 7.15.

References: H&S §4.7 p. 101

7.7

Question: Why does some code carefully cast the values returned by **malloc** to the pointer type being allocated?

Answer: Before ANSI/ISO Standard C introduced the void * generic pointer type, these casts were typically required to silence warnings (and perhaps induce conversions) when assigning between incompatible pointer types.

Under ANSI/ISO Standard C, these casts are no longer necessary. Indeed, it can also be argued that they are now to be discouraged, since they can camouflage important warnings that would otherwise be generated if `malloc` happened not to be declared correctly; see question 7.6. Furthermore, well-defined, low-risk implicit conversions, such as those that C has always performed between integer and floating-point types, can be considered a feature.

On the other hand, some programmers prefer to make *every* conversion explicit, to record that they have considered each case and decided exactly what should happen (see also question 17.5). This book uses explicit casts mostly to make its code fragments more accessible to any readers with pre-ANSI compilers.

(By the way, the language in sections 6.5 and 7.8.5 of K&R2 suggesting that the casts are required is "overenthusiastic.")

Whether you use these casts or not is a matter of style; see Chapter 17.

References: H&S §16.1 pp. 386–7

7.8

Question: I see code like this:

```
char *p = malloc(strlen(s) + 1);
strcpy(p, s);
```

Shouldn't that be **malloc((strlen(s) + 1) * sizeof(char))**?

Answer: It's never necessary to multiply by `sizeof(char)`, which is, by definition, exactly 1. (On the other hand, multiplying by `sizeof(char)` doesn't hurt and may help by introducing a `size_t` into the expression; see question 7.15.) See also questions 8.9 and 8.10.

References: ANSI §3.3.3.4
ISO §6.3.3.4
H&S §7.5.2 p. 195

7.9

Question: I wrote this little wrapper around **malloc**. Why doesn't it work?

```
#include <stdio.h>
#include <stdlib.h>

mymalloc(void *retp, size_t size);
{
        retp = malloc(size);
        if(retp == NULL) {
                fprintf(stderr, "out of memory\n");
                exit(EXIT_FAILURE);
        }
}
```

Answer: See question 4.8. (In this case, you'll want to have `mymalloc` return the allocated pointer.)

7.10

Question: I'm trying to declare a pointer and allocate some space for it, but it's not working. What's wrong with this code?

```
char *p;
*p = malloc(10);
```

Answer: See question 4.2.

7.11

Question: How can I dynamically allocate arrays?

Answer: See questions 6.14 and 6.16.

7.12

Question: How can I find out how much memory is available?

Answer: See question 19.22.

7.13

Question: What should **malloc(0)** do: return a null pointer or a pointer to 0 bytes?

Answer: See question 11.26.

7.14

Question: I've heard that some operating systems don't allocate memory obtained via **malloc** until the program tries to use it. Is this legal?

Answer: It's hard to say. The standard doesn't say that systems can act this way, but it doesn't explicitly say that they can't, either. (Such a "deferred failure" implementation would not seem to conform to the implied requirements of the standard.)

The conspicuous problem is that by the time the program gets around to trying to use the memory, there might not be any. The program in this case must typically be killed by the operating system, since the semantics of C provide no recourse. (Obviously, **malloc** is supposed to return a null pointer if there's no memory, so that the program—as long as it checks **malloc**'s return value at all—never tries to use more memory than is available.)

Systems that do this "lazy allocation" usually provide extra signals indicating that memory is dangerously low, but portable or naïve programs won't catch them. Some systems that do lazy allocation also provide a way to turn it off (reverting to traditional `malloc` semantics) on a per process or per user basis, but the details vary from system to system.

References: ANSI §4.10.3
ISO §7.10.3

Problems with `malloc`

7.15

Question: Why is `malloc` returning crazy pointer values? I *did* read question 7.6, and I have included the declaration **extern void *malloc();** before I call it.

Answer: The argument to `malloc` is a value of type `size_t`, which may be defined as `unsigned long`. If you are passing `ints` (or even `unsigned ints`), `malloc` may be receiving garbage (or, similarly, if you are passing a `long` but `size_t` is `int`).

In general, it is much, much safer to declare standard library functions by including the appropriate header files rather than typing `extern` declarations yourself. See also question 7.16.

A related problem is that it is not safe to print `size_t` values, including the result of `sizeof`, using `printf`'s `%d` format. The portable approach is to use an explicit `(unsigned long)` cast and `%lu` format: `printf("%lu\n", (unsigned long)sizeof(int))`. See also question 15.3.

References: ANSI §4.1.5, §4.1.6
ISO §7.1.6, §7.1.7

7.16

Question: I'm allocating a large array for some numeric work, using the line

```
double *array = malloc(256 * 256 * sizeof(double));
```

Although **malloc** isn't returning null, the program is acting strangely, as if it's overwriting memory or **malloc** isn't allocating as much as I asked for. Why?

Answer: Notice that 256×256 is 65,536, which will not fit in a 16-bit int, even before you multiply it by sizeof(double). If you need to allocate this much memory, you'll have to be careful. If size_t (the type accepted by malloc) is a 32-bit type on your machine but int is 16 bits, you might be able to get away with writing 256 * (256 * sizeof(double)) (see question 3.14). Otherwise, you'll have to break up your data structure into smaller chunks, use a 32-bit machine, or use some nonstandard memory allocation routines. See also questions 7.15 and 19.23.

7.17

Question: I've got 8 MB of memory in my PC. Why does **malloc** seem to allocate only 640K or so?

Answer: Under the segmented architecture of PC compatibles, it can be difficult to use more than 640K with any degree of transparency. See also question 19.23.

7.18

Question: My application depends heavily on dynamic allocation of nodes for data structures, and **malloc/free** overhead is becoming a bottleneck. What can I do?

Answer: One improvement, particularly attractive if all nodes are the same size, is to place unused nodes on your own free list rather than actually calling free on them. (This approach works well when one kind of data structure dominates a program's memory use, but it can cause as many problems as it solves if so much memory is tied up in the list of unused nodes that it isn't available for other purposes.)

Question: My program is crashing, apparently somewhere down inside `malloc`, although I can't see anything wrong with it. What's wrong?

Answer: It is unfortunately very easy to corrupt `malloc`'s internal data structures, and the resulting problems can be stubborn. The most common source of problems is writing more to a `malloc` region than it was allocated to hold; a particularly common bug is to call `malloc(strlen(s))` instead of `strlen(s) + 1`.* Other problems may involve using pointers to freed storage (see question 7.20), allocating 0-sized objects (see question 11.26), reallocating null pointers (see question 7.30), and freeing pointers that were not obtained from `malloc`, that are null, or that have already been freed. (A few of these are sanctioned by the standard: on an ANSI-compatible system, you may safely allocate 0-sized objects and reallocate or free null pointers, although older implementations often have problems.) Consequences of any of these errors can show up long after the actual mistake and in unrelated sections of code, making diagnosis of the problem quite difficult.

Most implementations of `malloc` are particularly vulnerable to these problems because they store crucial pieces of internal information directly adjacent to the blocks of memory they return, making them easy prey for stray user pointers.

See also questions 7.15, 7.26, 16.8, and 18.2.

Freeing Memory

Memory allocated with `malloc` can persist as long as you need it. It is never deallocated automatically (except when your program exits; see question 7.24). When your program uses memory on a transient basis, it can—and should—recycle it by calling `free`.

---

*A more subtle bug is `malloc(strlen(s + 1))`; another common problem is `p = malloc (sizeof(p))`.

7.20

Question: Dynamically allocated memory can't be used after freeing it, can it?

Answer: No. Some early documentation for `malloc` stated that the contents of freed memory were "left undisturbed," but this ill-advised guarantee was never universal and is not required by the C standard.

Few programmers would use the contents of freed memory deliberately, but it is easy to do so accidentally. Consider the following (correct) code for freeing a singly linked list:

```
struct list *listp, *nextp;
for(listp = base; listp != NULL; listp = nextp) {
        nextp = listp->next;
        free((void *)listp);
}
```

Notice that if the code used the more obvious loop iteration expression `listp = listp->next` (without the temporary `nextp` pointer), it would be trying to fetch `listp->next` from freed memory.

References: K&R2 §7.8.5 p. 167
ANSI §4.10.3
ISO §7.10.3
Rationale §4.10.3.2
H&S §16.2 p. 387
CT&P §7.10 p. 95

7.21

Question: Why isn't a pointer null after calling **free**? How unsafe is it to use (assign, compare) a pointer value after it's been freed?

Answer: When you call `free`, the memory pointed to by the passed pointer is freed, but the value of the pointer in the caller remains unchanged, because C's pass-by-value semantics mean that called functions never permanently change the values of their arguments. (See also question 4.8.)

A pointer value that has been freed is, strictly speaking, invalid, and *any* use of it, even if is not dereferenced (i.e., even if the use of it is a seemingly innocuous assignment or comparison) can theoretically lead to trouble. (We can probably assume that as a quality of implementation issue, most implementations will not go out of their way to generate exceptions for innocuous uses of invalid pointers, but the standard is clear in saying that nothing is guaranteed, and such exceptions would be quite natural under some system architectures.)

When pointers are repeatedly allocated and freed within a program, it is often useful to set them to NULL immediately after freeing them, to explicitly record their state.

References: ANSI §4.10.3
ISO §7.10.3
Rationale §3.2.2.3

7.22

Question: When I call **malloc** to allocate memory for a local pointer, do I have to explicitly free it?

Answer: Yes. Remember that a pointer is different from what it points to. Local variables* are deallocated when the function returns, but in the case of a pointer variable, this means that the *pointer* is deallocated, not what it points to. Memory allocated with malloc always persists until you explicitly free it. (If the only pointer to a block of memory is a local pointer and if that pointer disappears, that block cannot be freed.) In general, for every call to malloc, there should be a corresponding call to free.

7.23

Question: I'm allocating structures containing pointers to other dynamically allocated objects. When I free a structure, do I have to free each subsidiary pointer first?

Answer: Yes. The malloc and free functions know nothing about structure declarations or about the contents of allocated memory; they especially do not know whether allocated memory contains pointers to other allocated memory. In general, you must arrange that each pointer returned from malloc be individually passed to free, exactly once (if it is freed at all).

---

*Strictly speaking, it is *automatic* variables that are deallocated when a function returns.

A good rule of thumb is that for each call to `malloc` in a program, you should be able to point at the call to `free` that frees the memory allocated by that `malloc` call.

See also question 7.24.

7.24

Question: Must I free allocated memory before the program exits?

Answer: You shouldn't have to. It's the operating system's job to reclaim all memory when a program exits; the system cannot afford to have memory integrity depend on the whims of random programs. (Strictly speaking, it is not even `free`'s job to return memory to the operating system; see question 7.25.) Nevertheless, some personal computers are said not to reliably recover memory unless it was freed before exiting, and all that can be inferred from the ANSI/ISO C Standard is that this issue is one of "quality of implementation."

In any case, it can be considered good practice to explicitly free all memory—for example, in case the program is ever rewritten to perform its main task more than once (perhaps under a graphical user interface).* On the other hand, some programs, such as interpreters, don't know what memory they're done with (i.e., what memory could be freed) until it's time to exit, and since all memory should be released at exit, it would be a needless, potentially expensive, and error-prone exercise for the program to explicitly free all of it.

References: ANSI §4.10.3.2
           ISO §7.10.3.2

7.25

Question: I have a program that allocates and later frees a lot of memory, but memory usage doesn't seem to go back down. Why?

Answer: Most implementations of `malloc`/`free` do not return freed memory to the operating system (if there is one) but merely make it available for future `malloc` calls within the same program.

---

*Also, unless a program frees all memory it knows about, it's much more difficult to see real memory leaks detected by a "leak checking" tool (see question 18.2).

Sizes of Allocated Blocks

Each block of memory allocated by `malloc` obviously has a known, fixed size, but once it's allocated, you can't ask the `malloc` package what that size is. (For one thing, if you could ask, should it tell you the size you asked for or the possibly larger size it gave you?)

7.26

Question: How does **free()** know how many bytes to free?

Answer: The `malloc`/`free` implementation remembers the size of each block allocated and returned, so it is not necessary to remind it of the size when freeing. (Typically, the size is stored adjacent to the allocated block, which is why things usually break badly if the bounds of the allocated block are even slightly overstepped; see also question 7.19.)

7.27

Question: So can I query the **malloc** package to find out how big an allocated block is?

Answer: Not portably. If you need to know, you'll have to keep track of it yourself.

7.28

Question: Why doesn't **sizeof** tell me the size of the block of memory pointed to by a pointer?

Answer: The `sizeof` operator does not know that `malloc` has been used to allocate a pointer; `sizeof` tells you the size of the pointer itself. There is no portable way to find out the size of a block allocated by `malloc`.

Other Allocation Functions

Most dynamic memory allocation involves `malloc` and `free`, but the complete set of standard functions includes `realloc` and `calloc`.

7.29

Question: Having dynamically allocated an array (as in question 6.14), can I change its size?

Answer: Yes. This is exactly what `realloc` is for. To change the size of a dynamically allocated array (e.g., `dynarray` from question 6.14), use code like this:

```
dynarray = (int *)realloc((void *)dynarray, 20 * sizeof(int));
```

Note that `realloc` may not always be able to enlarge* memory regions in place. When it is able to, it simply gives you back the same pointer you handed it, but if it must go to some other part of memory to find enough contiguous space, it will return a different pointer, and the previous pointer value will become unusable.

If `realloc` cannot find enough space at all, it returns a null pointer and leaves the previous region allocated.[†] Therefore, you usually don't want to immediately assign the new pointer to the old variable. Instead, use a temporary pointer:

```
    #include <stdio.h>
    #include <stdlib.h>

    int *newarray =
        (int *)realloc((void *)dynarray, 20 * sizeof(int));
    if(newarray != NULL)
        dynarray = newarray;
    else {
        fprintf(stderr, "Can't reallocate memory\n");
        /* dynarray remains allocated */
    }
```

---

*Nor, for that matter, is `realloc` always able to shrink regions in place.
[†]Beware, though, that some pre-ANSI implementations were not always able to preserve the prior region when `realloc` failed.

When reallocating memory, be careful if any other pointers point into ("alias") the same piece of memory: If `realloc` must locate the new region somewhere else, those other pointers must also be adjusted. Here is a contrived example (which is also careless of `malloc`'s return value):

```
#include <stdio.h>
#include <stdlib.h>
#include <string.h>

char *p, *p2, *newp;
int tmpoffset;

p = malloc(10);
strcpy(p, "Hello,");      /* p is a string */
p2 = strchr(p, ',');      /* p2 points into that string */

tmpoffset = p2 - p;
newp = realloc(p, 20);
if(newp != NULL) {
        p = newp;              /* p may have moved */
        p2 = p + tmpoffset; /* relocate p2 as well */
        strcpy(p2, ", world!");
}

printf("%s\n", p);
```

It is safest to recompute pointers based on offsets, as shown. The alternative—relocating pointers based on the difference, `newp - p`, between the base pointer's value before and after the `realloc`—is not guaranteed to work, because pointer subtraction is defined only when performed on pointers into the same object. See also questions 7.21 and 7.30.

References: K&R2 §B5 p. 252
          ANSI §4.10.3.4
          ISO §7.10.3.4
          H&S §16.3 pp. 387–8

7.30

Question: Is it legal to pass a null pointer as the first argument to `realloc()`? Why would you want to?

Answer: ANSI C sanctions this usage (and the related realloc(..., 0), which frees), although several earlier implementations do not support it, so it may not be fully portable. Passing an initially null pointer to realloc can make it easier to write a self-starting incremental allocation algorithm.

For example, here is a function that reads an arbitrarily long line into dynamically allocated memory, reallocating the input buffer as necessary. (The caller must free the returned pointer when it is no longer needed.)

```
#include <stdio.h>
#include <stdlib.h>


/* read a line from fp into malloc'ed memory */
/* returns NULL on EOF or error */
/* (use feof or ferror to distinguish) */

char *agetline(FILE *fp)
{
        char *retbuf = NULL;
        size_t nchmax = 0;
        register int c;
        size_t nchread = 0;
        char *newbuf;

        while((c = getc(fp)) != EOF) {
            if(nchread >= nchmax) {
                nchmax += 20;
                newbuf = realloc(retbuf, nchmax + 1);
                                 /* +1 for \0 */
                if(newbuf == NULL) {
                        free(retbuf);
                        return NULL;
                }

                retbuf = newbuf;
            }

            if(c == '\n')
                    break;

            retbuf[nchread++] = c;
        }
```

```
    if(retbuf != NULL) {
            retbuf[nchread] = '\0';

            newbuf = realloc(retbuf, nchread + 1);
            if(newbuf != NULL)
                    retbuf = newbuf;
    }

    return retbuf;
}
```

In production code, a line like `nchmax += 20` can prove troublesome, as the function may do lots of reallocating. Many programmers favor multiplicative reallocation, e.g., `nchmax *= 2`, although it obviously isn't quite as self-starting and can run into problems if it has to allocate a huge array but memory is limited.

References: ANSI §4.10.3.4
 ISO §7.10.3.4
 H&S §16.3 p. 388

7.31

Question: What's the difference between `calloc` and `malloc`? Which should I use? Is it safe to take advantage of `calloc`'s zero-filling? Does `free` work on memory allocated with `calloc`, or do you need a `cfree`?

Answer: A call to `calloc(m, n)` is essentially equivalent to

```
p = malloc(m * n);
memset(p, 0, m * n);
```

There is no important difference between the two other than the number of arguments and the zero fill.*

Use whichever function is convenient. Don't rely on `calloc`'s zero fill too much; usually, it's best to initialize data structures yourself, on a field-by-field basis, especially if there are pointer fields. Since `calloc`'s zero fill is all bits zero, it is guaranteed to yield the value 0 for all integral types (including `'\0'` for character types). But it does *not* guarantee useful null pointer values (see Chapter 5) or floating-point zero values.

---

*It is sometimes argued that `calloc`'s 0-fill guarantees early (nonlazy) allocation; see question 7.14.

Yes, `free` is properly used to free the memory allocated by `calloc`; there is no standard `cfree` function.

One imagined distinction that is *not* significant between `malloc` and `calloc` is whether a single element or an array of elements is being allocated. Although `calloc`'s two-argument calling convention suggests that it is supposed to be used to allocate an array of m items of size n, there is no such requirement; it is perfectly permissible to allocate one item with `calloc` (by passing one argument as 1) or to allocate an array with `malloc` (by doing the multiplication yourself; see, for example, the code fragment in question 6.14). (Nor does structure padding enter into the question; any padding necessary to make arrays of structures work correctly is always handled by the compiler and is reflected by `sizeof`. See question 2.13.)

References: ANSI §4.10.3 to 4.10.3.2
ISO §7.10.3 to 7.10.3.2
H&S §16.1 p. 386, §16.2 p. 386
PCS §11 pp. 141–2

7.32

Question: What is **alloca** and why is its use discouraged?

Answer: The nonstandard `alloca` function allocates memory that is automatically freed when the function that called `alloca` returns. That is, memory allocated with `alloca` is local to a particular function's "stack frame," or context.

Implementing `alloca` is difficult, especially on a machine without a conventional stack.* Its use is problematic (and the obvious implementation on a stack-based machine fails) when its return value is passed directly to another function, as in `fgets(alloca(100), 100, stdin)`.[†] Therefore, `alloca` is not standard and cannot be used in programs that must be widely portable.

See also question 7.22.

References: Rationale §4.10.3

---

*Although an "almost portable" implementation of `alloca` exists in the public domain, its author intended it as a stopgap measure and recommends against use of `alloca` in new code.

[†]If a call to `alloca` tries to allocate some memory on the stack in the middle of the preparation, on the same stack, of the argument list for another function call (`fgets`, in this case), the argument list may well be perturbed.

8 Characters and Strings

C has no built-in string type; by convention, a string is represented as an array of characters terminated with '\0'. Furthermore, C hardly has a character type; a character is represented by its integer value in the machine's character set. Because these representations are laid bare and are visible to C programs, programs have a tremendous amount of control over how characters and strings are manipulated. The downside is that to some extent, programs *have* to exert this control: The programmer must remember whether a small integer is being interpreted as a numeric value or as a character (see question 8.6) and must remember to maintain arrays (and allocated blocks of memory) containing strings correctly.

See also questions 13.1 through 13.7, which cover library functions for string handling.

8.1

Question: Why doesn't `strcat(string, '!');` work?

Answer: Characters and strings are very different, and `strcat` concatenates *strings*.

A character constant like `'!'` represents a single character. A string literal between double quotes usually represents multiple characters. Although string literal like `"!"` seems to represent a single character, it contains two: the ! you requested and the \0 that terminates all strings in C.

Characters in C are represented by small integers corresponding to their character set values (see also question 8.6). Strings are represented by arrays of characters; you usually manipulate a pointer to the first character of the array. It is never correct to use one when the other is expected. To append ! to a string, use

```
strcat(string, "!");
```

See also questions 1.32, 7.2, and 16.6.

References: CT&P §1.5 pp. 9–10

8.2

Question: I'm checking a string to see whether it matches a particular value. Why isn't this code working?

```
char *string;
...
if(string == "value") {
        /* string matches "value" */
    ...
}
```

Answer: Strings in C are represented as arrays of characters, and C never manipulates (assigns, compares, etc.) arrays as a whole. The == operator in the code fragment compares two pointers—the value of the pointer variable `string` and a pointer to the string literal `"value"`—to see whether they are equal, that is, if they point to the same place. They probably don't, so the comparison never succeeds.

To compare two strings, you generally use the library function `strcmp`:

```
if(strcmp(string, "value") == 0) {
        /* string matches "value" */
        ...
}
```

8.3

Question: If I can say

```
char a[] = "Hello, world!";
```

why can't I say

```
char a[14];
a = "Hello, world!";
```

Answer: Strings are arrays, and you can't assign arrays directly. Use `strcpy` instead:

```
strcpy(a, "Hello, world!");
```

See also questions 1.32, 4.2, 6.5, and 7.2.

8.4

Question: Why can't I get **strcat** to work? I tried

```
char *s1 = "Hello, ";
char *s2 = "world!";
char *s3 = strcat(s1, s2);
```

but I got strange results.

Answer: See question 7.2.

8.5

Question: What is the difference between these initializations?

```
char a[] = "string literal";
char *p  = "string literal";
```

My program crashes if I try to assign a new value to **p[i]**.

Answer: See question 1.32.

8.6

Question: How can I get the numeric value (i.e., ASCII or other character set code) corresponding to a character, or vice versa?

Answer: Characters are represented in C by small integers corresponding to their values (in the machine's character set), so you don't need a conversion routine: If you have the character, you have its value. The fragment

```
int c1 = 'A', c2 = 65;
printf("%c %d %c %d\n", c1, c1, c2, c2);
```

prints

```
A 65 A 65
```

on an ASCII machine. See also questions 8.9 and 20.10.

8.7

Question: Does C have anything like the "substr" (extract substring) routine present in other languages?

Answer: See question 13.3.

8.8

Question: I'm reading strings typed by the user into an array and then printing them out later. When the user types a sequence like **\n**, why isn't it being handled properly?

Answer: Character sequences like \n are interpreted at compile time. When a backslash and an adjacent n appear in a character constant or a string literal, they are translated immediately into a single newline character. (Analogous translations occur, of course, for the other character escape sequences.) When you're reading strings from the user or a file, however, no interpretation like this is performed: A backslash is read and printed just like any other character, with no particular interpretation. (Some interpretation of the newline character may be done during run-time I/O but for a completely different reason; see question 12.40.) See also question 12.6.

8.9

Question: I just noticed that **sizeof('a')** is 2, not 1 (i.e., not **sizeof(char)**). Is something wrong with my compiler?

Answer: Perhaps surprisingly, character constants in C are of type int, so sizeof('a') is sizeof(int) (though it's different in C++). See also question 7.8.

References: ANSI §3.1.3.4
ISO §6.1.3.4
H&S §2.7.3 p. 29

8.10

Question: I'm starting to think about multinational character sets. Should I worry about the implications of making **sizeof(char)** be 2 so that 16-bit character sets can be represented?

Answer: If type char were made 16 bits, sizeof(char) would still be 1, and CHAR_BIT in <limits.h> would be 16, and it would simply be impossible to declare (or allocate with malloc) a single 8-bit object.

Traditionally, a byte is not necessarily 8 bits but merely a smallish region of memory, usually suitable for storing one character. The C standard follows this usage, so the bytes used by `malloc` and `sizeof` can be more than 8 bits.* (The standard does not allow them to be less.)

To allow manipulation of multinational character sets without requiring an expansion of type `char`, ANSI/ISO C defines the "wide" character type `wchar_t`, and corresponding wide character constants and string literals, and functions for manipulating and converting strings of wide characters.

See also question 7.8.

References: ANSI §2.2.1.2, §3.1.3.4, §3.1.4, §4.1.5, §4.10.7, §4.10.8
   ISO §5.2.1.2, §6.1.3.4, §6.1.4, §7.1.6, §7.10.7, §7.10.8
   Rationale §2.2.1.2
   H&S §2.7.3 pp. 29–30, §2.7.4 p. 33, §11.1 p. 293, §§11.7, 11.8 pp. 303–10

---

*Formally, bytes of exactly 8 bits are referred to as "octets."

9 Boolean Expressions and Variables

C provides no formal, built-in Boolean type. Boolean values are just integers (though with greatly reduced range!), so they can be held in any integral type. C interprets a zero value as "false" and *any* nonzero value as "true." The relational and logical operators, such as ==, !=, <, >=, &&, and ||, return the value 1 for "true," so 1 is slightly more distinguished as a truth value than the other nonzero values (but see question 9.2).

9.1

Question: What is the right type to use for Boolean values in C? Why isn't it a standard type? Should I use #defines or enums for the true and false values?

Answer: C does not provide a standard Boolean type, in part because picking one involves a space/time tradeoff that can best be decided by the programmer. (Using an int may be faster, whereas using char may save data space.* Smaller types may make the generated code bigger or slower, though, if they require lots of conversions to and from int.)

---

*Bitfields may be even more compact; see also question 2.26. An unsigned bitfield would be required; a 1-bit signed bitfield cannot portably hold the value +1.

The choice between #defines and enumeration constants for the true/false values is arbitrary and not terribly interesting (see also questions 2.22 and 17.10). If you prefer not to use raw 1 and 0, use any of:

```
#define TRUE  1                    #define YES 1
#define FALSE 0                    #define NO  0


enum bool {false, true};          enum bool {no, yes};
```

(Do try to be consistent within one program or project, however.) An enumeration may be preferable if your debugger shows the names of enumeration constants when examining variables.

You may also want to use a typedef:

```
typedef int bool;
```

or

```
typedef char bool;
```

or

```
typedef enum {false, true} bool;
```

Some people prefer variants like

```
#define TRUE (1==1)
#define FALSE (!TRUE)
```

or define "helper" macros, such as

```
#define Istrue(e) ((e) != 0)
```

These don't buy anything (see question 9.2; see also questions 5.12 and 10.2).

9.2

Question: Isn't defining TRUE to be 1 dangerous, since any nonzero value is considered "true" in C? What if a built-in logical or a relational operator "returns" something other than 1?

Answer: Even though any nonzero value is considered true in C, this applies only "on input," i.e., where a Boolean value is expected. When a Boolean value is generated by a built-in operator, such as ==, !=, and <=, it is guaranteed to be 1 or 0. Therefore, a test like

```
if((a == b) == TRUE)
```

would work as expected (as long as TRUE is 1), but it is obviously silly. In general, explicit tests against TRUE and FALSE are inappropriate. In particular, and unlike the built-in operators, some library functions (notably isupper, isalpha, etc.) return, on success, a nonzero value that is *not* necessarily 1, so comparing their return values against a single value, such as TRUE, is quite risky and likely not to work.

(Besides, if you believe that

```
if((a == b) == TRUE)
```

is an improvement over

```
if(a == b)
```

why stop there? Why not use

```
if(((a == b) == TRUE) == TRUE)
```

or even

```
if((((a == b) == TRUE) == TRUE) == TRUE)
```

See also Lewis Carroll's essay "What the Tortoise Said to Achilles.")

Given that if(a == b) is a perfectly legitimate conditional, so is this:

```
#include <ctype.h>
...
if(isupper(c))
        { ... }
```

The reason is that isupper is known to return zero/nonzero for false/true. Similarly, there should not be any reluctance to use code like

```
int isvegetable;                 /* really a bool */
...
if(isvegetable)
        { ... }
```

or

```
extern int fileexists(char *);     /* returns true/false */
...
if(fileexists(outfile))
        { ... }
```

In these examples, `isvegetable` and `fileexists()` are of "conceptual Boolean type." Alternatives such as

```
if(isvegetable == TRUE)
```

or

```
if(fileexists(outfile) == YES)
```

are not really any improvement. (They can be thought of as "safer" or "better style," but they can also be thought of as risky or poor style. They certainly don't read as smoothly. See question 17.10.)

A good rule of thumb is to use `TRUE` and `FALSE` (or the like) only for assignment to a Boolean variable or function parameter or as the return value from a Boolean function, never in a comparison.

See also question 5.3.

References: K&R1 §2.6 p. 39, §2.7 p. 41
K&R2 §2.6 p. 42, §2.7 p. 44, §A7.4.7 p. 204, §A7.9 p. 206
ANSI §3.3.3.3, §3.3.8, §3.3.9, §3.3.13, §3.3.14, §3.3.15, §3.6.4.1, §3.6.5
ISO §6.3.3.3, §6.3.8, §6.3.9, §6.3.13, §6.3.14, §6.3.15, §6.6.4.1, §6.6.5
H&S §7.5.4 pp. 196–7, §7.6.4 pp. 207–8, §7.6.5 pp. 208–9, §7.7 pp. 217–8, §7.8 pp. 218–9, §8.5 pp. 238–9, §8.6 pp. 241–4
Carroll, "What the Tortoise Said to Achilles"

9.3

Question: Is `if(p)`, where `p` is a pointer, a valid conditional?

Answer: Yes. See question 5.3.

9.4

Question: Should I use symbolic names, such as `TRUE` and `FALSE`, for Boolean constants or use plain 1 and 0?

Answer: It's your choice. Preprocessor macros like these are used for code readability, not because the underlying values might ever change. It's a matter of style, not correctness, whether to use symbolic names or raw 1/0 values. (The same argument applies to the `NULL` macro. See also questions 5.10 and 17.10.)

On the one hand, using a symbolic name (e.g., TRUE or FALSE) reminds the reader that a Boolean value is involved. On the other hand, Boolean values and definitions can evidently be confusing, and some programmers feel that TRUE and FALSE macros only compound the confusion. (See also question 5.9.)

9.5

Question: A third-party header file I just started using is defining its own TRUE and FALSE values incompatibly with the code I've already developed. What can I do?

Answer: See question 10.10.

10 | The C Preprocessor

C's preprocessor provides reasonable solutions to a number of software engineering and configuration management problems, although its syntax is unlike the rest of C in several respects. As its name suggests, the preprocessor operates *before* formal parsing and compilation begin. Because it doesn't know about the structure of the code as seen by the rest of the compiler, it cannot do any processing that relates to declared types or function structure.

The first part of this chapter is arranged around the major preprocessor directives: #define (questions 10.1 through 10.5), #include (questions 10.6 through 10.11), and #if (questions 10.12 through 10.19). Questions 10.20 through 10.25 cover fancier macro replacement, and finally questions 10.26 and 10.27 cover a particular set of problems relating to the preprocessor's lack of support for variable-length macro argument lists.

Macro Definitions

Question: I'm trying to define a few simple little function-like macros, such as

```
#define square(x) x * x
```

but they're not always working. Why?

Answer: Macro expansion is purely textual. To avoid surprises, remember these three rules when defining function-like macros:

1. The macro expansion must always be parenthesized to protect any lower-precedence operators from the surrounding expression. Given the (incorrect) `square()` macro in the question, the invocation

   ```
   1 / square(n)
   ```

   would expand to

   ```
   1 / n * n
   ```

   which evaluates as `(1 / n) * n`. What you want, however, is

   ```
   1 / (n * n)
   ```

   In this case, the problem is one of associativity rather than precedence, but the effect is the same.

2. Within the macro definition, all occurrences of the parameters must be parenthesized to protect any low-precedence operators in the actual arguments from the rest of the macro expansion. Again given the `square()` macro, the invocation

   ```
   square(n + 1)
   ```

   would expand to

   ```
   n + 1 * n + 1
   ```

   But what you want is

   ```
   (n + 1) * (n + 1)
   ```

3. If a parameter appears several times in the expansion, the macro may not work properly if the actual argument is an expression with side effects. Yet again given the `square()` macro, the invocation

```
square(i++)
```

would expand to

```
i++ * i++
```

which is undefined (see question 3.2).

The proper definition of a `square` macro, to comply with rules 1 and 2, is

```
#define square(x)  ((x) * (x))
```

Complying with rule 3 is more difficult. Sometimes, careful exploitation of the short-circuiting behavior of the `&&`, `||`, or `?:` operators (see question 3.6) can arrange that a parameter appearing several times is guaranteed to be evaluated exactly once. Sometimes, the macro is just documented as being unsafe, and callers must remember not to use it on arguments with side effects. Other times, it may be advisable *not* to compose a function-like macro if it can't be made safe.

As a stylistic convention, macros are often defined with capitalized or all-uppercase names, to make it obvious that they are macros. It may be acceptable to define a function-like macro with an all-lowercase name if it truly simulates a function, but only if it complies with all three of these rules. Since the squaring macro we've been discussing does not, it should be defined as something like this if it is to be used at all:

```
#define Square(x)  ((x) * (x))              /* UNSAFE */
```

References: K&R1 §4.11 p. 87
K&R2 §4.11.2 p. 90
H&S §§3.3.6, 3.3.7 pp. 49–50
CT&P §6.2 pp. 78–80

10.2

Question: Here are some cute preprocessor macros:

```
#define begin      {
#define end        }
```

With these, I can write C code that looks more like Pascal.

Answer: Use of macros like these, though perhaps superficially attractive, is generally discouraged; in severe cases the practice is called "preprocessor abuse." Little can be gained by trying to redefine the syntax of a language to fit your own predilections, or to match some other language. Your predilections are unlikely to be shared by later readers or maintainers of the code, and any simulation of another language is most unlikely to be perfect (so any alleged convenience or utility will probably be outweighed by the nuisance of remembering the imperfections).

As a general rule, it's a good idea if the use of preprocessor macros follows the syntax of the C language. Macros without arguments should look like variables or other identifiers; macros with arguments should look like function calls. Ask yourself: "If I somehow presented this code to the compiler without running it through the preprocessor, how many syntax errors would I get?" (Of course, you'd get plenty of undefined symbols and non-constant array dimensions, but those aren't *syntax* errors.) This rule means that C code, plus macro invocations, still looks like C code. So-called nonsyntactic macros, such as `begin` and `end` or `CTRL(D)` (see question 10.21), can make C look like gobbledygook (see also question 20.36). This is of course largely a style issue; see also Chapter 17.

10.3

Question: How can I write a generic macro to swap two values?

Answer: This question has no good answer. If the values are integers, a well-known trick using exclusive-OR could perhaps be used, but it will not work for floating-point values or pointers or if the two values are the same variable.[*] If the macro is intended to be used on values of arbitrary type (the usual goal), any solution involving a temporary variable is problematic, because:

- It's difficult to give the temporary a name that won't clash with anything. Any name you pick might be the actual name of one of the variables being swapped. If you tried using `##` to concatenate the names of the two actual arguments, to ensure that it won't match either one, it might still not be unique if the concatenated name is longer than 31 characters,[†] and it wouldn't let you swap things (such as `a[i]`) that aren't simple identifiers.

---

[*] Also, the "obvious" supercompressed implementation for integral types `a^=b^=a^=b` is illegal, due to multiple side effects; see question 3.2.

[†] The C standard does not require compilers to look beyond the first 31 characters of an identifier.

You could probably get away with using a name like _tmp in the "no man's land" between the user and implementation namespaces; see question 1.29.

- Either the temporary can't be declared with the right type (because standard C does not provide a typeof operator), or (if it copies objects byte by byte, perhaps with memcpy, to a temporary array sized with sizeof) the macro can't be used on operands that are declared register.

The best all-around solution is probably to forget about using a macro, unless you're willing to pass in the type as a third argument. (Also, if you're trying to swap entire structures or arrays, you probably want to exchange pointers instead.)

If you're consumed by a passionate desire to solve this problem once and for all, please reconsider; there are better problems more worthy of your energies.

10.4

Question: What's the best way to write a multistatement macro?

Answer: The usual goal is to be able to invoke the macro as if it were an expression statement consisting of a function call:

```
MACRO(arg1, arg2);
```

This means that the "caller" will be supplying the final semicolon, so the macro body should not. The macro body cannot therefore be a simple brace-enclosed compound statement, because of the possibility that the macro could be used as the if branch of an if/else statement with an explicit else clause:

```
if(cond)
        MACRO(arg1, arg2);
else    /* some other code */
```

If the macro expanded to a simple compound statement, the final, caller-supplied semicolon would be a syntax error:

```
if(cond)
        {stmt1; stmt2;};
else    /* some other code */
```

The traditional solution, therefore, is to use

```
#define MACRO(arg1, arg2) do {        \
    /* declarations */                \
    stmt1;                            \
    stmt2;                            \
    /* ... */                         \
    } while(0)   /* (no trailing ;   ) */
```

When the caller appends a semicolon, this expansion becomes a single statement regardless of context. (An optimizing compiler will remove any "dead" tests or branches on the constant condition 0, although `lint` may complain.)

Another possibility might be

```
#define MACRO(arg1, arg2) if(1) {      \
    stmt1;                            \
    stmt2;                            \
    } else
```

This is inferior, however, since it quietly breaks the surrounding code if the caller happens to forget to append the semicolon on invocation.

If all of the statements in the intended macro are simple expressions, with no declarations or loops, another technique is to write a single, parenthesized expression using one or more comma operators:

```
#define FUNC(arg1, arg2) (expr1, expr2, expr3)
```

For an example, see the first `DEBUG()` macro in question 10.26. This technique also allows a value (in this case, `expr3`) to be "returned."

Some compilers, e.g., `gcc`, are also able to expand compact functions in line, either automatically or at the programmer's request, perhaps with a non-standard "`inline`" keyword or other extension.

References: H&S §3.3.2 p. 45
         CT&P §6.3 pp. 82–3

10.5

Question: What's the difference between using a typedef or a preprocessor macro for a user-defined type?

Answer: See question 1.13.

Header Files

10.6

Question: I'm splitting up a program into multiple source files for the first time. What should I put in .c files and what should I put in .h files? (What does ".h" mean, anyway?)

Answer: As a general rule, you should put these things in header (.h) files:

- Macro definitions (preprocessor #defines)
- Structure, union, and enumeration declarations
- Typedef declarations
- External function declarations (see also question 1.11)
- Global variable declarations

It's especially important to put a declaration or a definition in a header file when it will be shared among several other files. Don't repeat a declaration or macro definition at the top of two or more source files; do put it in a header file and use #include to bring the header wherever needed. The reason is not just to save typing: you want to set things up so that whenever a declaration or a definition changes, you have to change it in only one place, with the update propagated to all source files consistently. (In particular, never put external function prototypes in .c files. See also question 1.7.)

On the other hand, when a definition or a declaration should remain private to one source file, it's fine to leave it there. (Private file-scope functions and variables should also be declared static. See also question 2.4.)

Finally, you should not put actual code (i.e., function bodies) or global variable definitions (that is, defining or initializing instances) in header files. Also, when you are building a project out of multiple source files, you should compile each of them separately (using a compiler option to request compilation only) and use the linker to link the resultant object files together. (In an integrated development environment, all of this may be taken care of for you.) Don't try to "link" all of your source files together with #include; the #include directive should be used to pull in header files, not other .c files.

See also questions 1.7, 10.7, and 17.2.

References: K&R2 §4.5 pp. 81–2
H&S §9.2.3 p. 267
CT&P §4.6 pp. 66–7

10.7

Question: **Is it acceptable for one header file to include another?**

Answer: It's a question of style, and thus receives considerable debate.

Many people believe that "nested #include files" are to be avoided: the prestigious Indian Hill Style Guide (see question 17.9) disparages them; they can make it harder to find relevant definitions, they can lead to multiple-definition errors if a file is included twice, and they make manual Makefile maintenance very difficult.

On the other hand, nested #include files can be used in a modular way (a header file can include what it needs itself, rather than requiring each includer to do so). A tool like grep (or a tags file) makes it easy to find definitions no matter where they are. A popular trick can be used in each header file to make it "idempotent" so that it can safely be included multiple times:

```
#ifndef HFILENAME_USED
#define HFILENAME_USED
...header file contents...
#endif
```

(A different bracketing macro name is, of course, used for each header file.) Finally, automated Makefile maintenance tools (which are a virtual necessity in large projects anyway; see question 18.1) handle dependency generation in the face of nested #include files easily.

See also question 17.10.

References: Rationale §4.1.2

10.8

Question: **Where are header ("#include") files searched for?**

Answer: The exact behavior is implementation-defined (which means that it is supposed to be documented; see question 11.33). Typically, headers named with <> syntax are searched for in one or more standard places.* Header files named with " " syntax are searched for first in the "current directory" and

---

*Strictly speaking, <> headers do not have to exist as files at all. The <> syntax is usually reserved for system-defined headers.

then (if not found) in the same standard places. (This last rule, that " " files are additionally searched for as if they were <> files, is the only rule specified by the standard.)

Another distinction is the definition of "current directory" for " " files. Traditionally (especially under UNIX compilers), the current directory is taken to be the directory containing the file containing the #include directive. Under other compilers, however, the current directory is the directory in which the compiler was initially invoked. (Compilers running on systems without directories or without the notion of a current directory may, of course, use still different rules.)

It is also common for there to be a way (usually a command line option involving capital I or maybe an environment variable) to add additional directories to the list of standard places to search. Check your compiler documentation.

References: K&R2 §A12.4 p. 231
            ANSI §3.8.2
            ISO §6.8.2
            H&S §3.4 p. 55

10.9

Question: **Why am I getting strange syntax errors on the very first declaration in a file?**

Answer: Perhaps there's a missing semicolon at the end of the last declaration in the last header file you're including. See also questions 2.18, 11.29, and 16.1.

10.10

Question: I'm using header files that accompany two different third-party libraries, and they are "helpfully" defining common macros, such as TRUE, FALSE, Min(), and Max(), but the definitions clash with each other and with definitions I'd already established in my own header files. What can I do?

Answer: This is indeed an annoying situation. It's a classic namespace problem; see questions 1.9 and 1.29. Ideally, third-party vendors would be conscientious when defining symbols (both preprocessor macros and global variable and function names) to ensure that namespace collisions were unlikely. The best solution is to get the vendor(s) to fix their header files. As a workaround, you can sometimes undefine or redefine the offending macros between the conflicting #include directives.

10.11

Question: I seem to be missing the system header file <sgtty.h>. Where can I get a copy?

Answer: Standard headers exist in part so that definitions appropriate to your compiler, operating system, and processor can be supplied. You cannot pick up a copy of someone else's header file and expect it to work, unless that person is using exactly the same environment. Ask your compiler vendor why the file was not provided or to send a replacement copy.

In the case of nonstandard headers, the situation is a bit more complicated. Some headers (such as <dos.h>) are completely system or compiler specific. Others, such as those associated with popular add-on libraries, may be reasonably portable. If you have an add-on library but are missing its header file, look for the header where you got the library. If you have some source code that requires what appears to be an add-on header that you don't have, you probably don't have the library, either, and you'll need both (see question 13.25). Something like archie may help you find what you're looking for; see question 18.16.

Conditional Compilation

10.12

Question: How can I construct preprocessor `#if` expressions that compare strings?

Answer: You can't do it directly; preprocessor `#if` arithmetic uses only integers. You can define several manifest constants, however, and implement conditionals on those:

```
#define RED          1
#define BLUE         2
#define GREEN        3

#if COLOR == RED
/* red case */
#else
#if COLOR == BLUE
/* blue case */
#else
#if COLOR == GREEN
/* green case */
#else
/* default case */
#endif
#endif
#endif
```

(Standard C specifies a new `#elif` directive that makes if/else chains like these a bit cleaner.)

See also question 20.17.

References: K&R2 §4.11.3 p. 91
         ANSI §3.8.1
         ISO §6.8.1
         H&S §7.11.1 p. 225

10.13

Question: Does the `sizeof` operator work in preprocessor `#if` directives?

Answer: No. Preprocessing happens during an earlier phase of compilation, before type names have been parsed. Instead of using `sizeof`, consider using the predefined constants in ANSI's `<limits.h>`, if applicable, or perhaps a "configure" script. (Better yet, try to write code that is inherently insensitive to type sizes.)

References: ANSI §2.1.1.2, §3.8.1 footnote 83
          ISO §5.1.1.2, §6.8.1
          H&S §7.11.1 p. 225

10.14

Question: Can I use `#ifdef` in a `#define` line to define something in two different ways, like this?

```
#define a b \
#ifdef whatever
       c d
#else
       e f g
#endif
```

Answer: No. You can't "run the preprocessor on itself," so to speak. What you can do is use one of two completely separate `#define` lines, depending on the `#ifdef` setting:

```
#ifdef whatever
#define a b c d
#else
#define a b e f g
#endif
```

References: ANSI §3.8.3, §3.8.3.4
          ISO §6.8.3, §6.8.3.4
          H&S §3.2 pp. 40–1

10.15

Question: Is there anything like an #ifdef for typedefs?

Answer: Unfortunately, no. (There can't be, because types and typedefs haven't been parsed at preprocessing time.) See also questions 1.13 and 10.13.

References: ANSI §2.1.1.2, §3.8.1 footnote 83
       ISO §5.1.1.2, §6.8.1
       H&S §7.11.1 p. 225

10.16

Question: How can I use a preprocessor #if expression to tell whether a machine's byte order is big-endian or little-endian?

Answer: You probably can't. The usual techniques for detecting endianness involve pointers or arrays of char or maybe unions, but preprocessor arithmetic uses only long integers, and there is no concept of addressing. Furthermore, the integer formats used in preprocessor #if expressions are not necessarily the same as those that will be used at run time.

Are you sure you need to know the machine's endianness explicitly? Usually, it's better to write code that doesn't care (see, for example, the code fragments in question 12.42). See also question 20.9.

References: ANSI §3.8.1
       ISO §6.8.1
       H&S §7.11.1 p. 225

10.17

Question: Why am I getting strange syntax errors inside lines I've used #ifdef to disable?

Answer: See question 11.19.

10.18

Question: I inherited some code that contains far too many #ifdefs for my taste. How can I preprocess the code to leave only one conditional compilation set, without running it through the preprocessor and expanding all of the #includes and #defines as well?

Answer: Some programs floating around on the Internet, called unifdef, rmifdef, and scpp ("selective C preprocessor"), do exactly this. See question 18.16.

10.19

Question: How can I list all of the predefined macros?

Answer: There's no standard way, although it is a common need. If the compiler documentation is unhelpful, the most expedient way is probably to extract printable strings from the compiler or preprocessor executable with something like the UNIX strings utility. Beware that many traditional system-specific predefined identifiers (e.g., "unix") are nonstandard (because they clash with the user's namespace) and are being removed or renamed. (In any case, it's generally considered wise to keep conditional compilation to a minimum.)

Fancier Processing

Macro replacement can get fairly complicated—sometimes *too* complicated. For two somewhat popular tricks that used to work (if at all) by accident, namely, "token pasting" and replacement inside string literals, ANSI C introduces defined, supported mechanisms.

10.20

Question: I have some old code that tries to construct identifiers with a macro like

```
#define Paste(a, b) a/**/b
```

but it's not working any more. Why?

Answer: That macro worked only by accident. An undocumented feature of some early preprocessor implementations was that comments disappeared entirely and could therefore be used for token pasting. ANSI affirms (as did K&R1) that comments are replaced with white space, so they cannot portably be used in a `Paste()` macro. However, since the need for pasting tokens was demonstrated and real, ANSI introduced a well-defined token-pasting operator, `##`, which can be used like this:

```
#define Paste(a, b) a##b
```

Here is one other method you could try for pasting tokens under a pre-ANSI compiler:

```
#define   XPaste(s)    s
#define   Paste(a, b)  XPaste(a)b
```

See also question 11.17.

References: ANSI §3.8.3.3   Rationale §3.8.3.3
            ISO §6.8.3.3   H&S §3.3.9 p. 52

10.21

Question: I have an old macro

```
#define CTRL(c) ('c' & 037)
```

that doesn't seem to work any more. Why?

Answer: The intended use of this macro is in code like this:

```
tchars.t_eofc = CTRL(D);
```

This code is expected to expand to

```
tchars.t_eofc = ('D' & 037);
```

based on the assumption that the actual value of the parameter c will be substituted even inside the single quotes of a character constant. Preprocessing was never supposed to work this way, however; it was somewhat of an accident that a CTRL() macro like this ever worked. ANSI C defines a new "stringizing" operator (see question 11.17), but there is no corresponding "charizing" operator.

The best solution to this problem is probably to move the single quotes from the definition to the invocation, by rewriting the macro as

```
#define CTRL(c) (c & 037)
```

and invoking it as

```
CTRL('D')
```

Doing so also makes the macro "syntactic"; see question 10.2.

It may also be possible to use the stringizing operator and some indirection:

```
#define CTRL(c) (*#c & 037)
```

or

```
#define CTRL(c) (#c[0] & 037)
```

Neither of these would work as well as the original, however, since they wouldn't be valid in case labels or as global variable initializers. (Global variable initializers and case labels require various flavors of constant expressions in which string literals and indirection are not allowed.)

See also question 11.18.

References: ANSI §3.8.3 footnote 87
            ISO §6.8.3
            H&S §§7.11.2,7.11.3 pp. 226–7

10.22

Question: Why is the macro

```
#define TRACE(n) printf("TRACE: %d\n", n)
```

giving me the warning "macro replacement within a string literal"? It seems to be expanding TRACE(count); as

```
printf("TRACE: %d\count", count);
```

Answer: See question 11.18.

10.23

Question: How can I use a macro argument inside a string literal in the macro expansion?

Answer: See question 11.18.

10.24

Question: I'm trying to use the ANSI "stringizing" preprocessing operator '#' to insert the value of a symbolic constant into a message, but it keeps stringizing the macro's name rather than its value. Why?

Answer: See question 11.17.

10.25

Question: How can I do this really tricky preprocessing?

Answer: C's preprocessor is not intended as a general-purpose tool. (Note also that it is not guaranteed to be available as a separate program.) Rather than forcing the preprocessor to do something inappropriate, you might instead want to write your own little special-purpose preprocessing tool. You can easily get a utility like make to run it for you automatically.

If you are trying to preprocess something other than C, consider using a general-purpose preprocessor. (One older one available on most UNIX systems is m4.)

Macros with Variable-Length Argument Lists

There are sometimes good reasons for a function to accept a variable number of arguments (the canonical example is printf; see also Chapter 15). For the same sorts of reasons, it's sometimes wished that a function-like macro could accept a variable number of arguments; a particularly common wish is for a way to write a general-purpose `printf`-like `DEBUG()` macro.

10.26

Question: **How can I write a macro that takes a variable number of arguments or use the preprocessor to "turn off" a function call with a variable number of arguments?**

Answer: One popular trick is to define and invoke the macro with a single, parenthesized "argument," which in the macro expansion becomes the entire argument list, parentheses and all, for a function such as `printf`:

```
#define DEBUG(args) (printf("DEBUG: "), printf args)

if(n != 0) DEBUG(("n is %d\n", n));
```

The obvious disadvantage is that the caller must always remember to use the extra parentheses. Another problem is that the macro expansion cannot insert any additional arguments (that is, `DEBUG()` couldn't expand to something like `fprintf(debugfd, ...)`).

The GNU C compiler has an extension that allows a function-like macro to accept a variable number of arguments, but it's not standard. Other possible solutions are:

- Use different macros (`DEBUG1`, `DEBUG2`, etc.), depending on the number of arguments.
- Play games with commas:

```
#define DEBUG(args) (printf("DEBUG: "), printf(args))
#define _ ,

DEBUG("i = %d" _ i)
```

- Play horrendous games with mismatched parentheses:

```
#define DEBUG fprintf(stderr,

DEBUG "%d", x);
```

(These all require care on the part of the user, and all of them are rather ugly.)

It is often better to use a true function, which can take a variable number of arguments in a well-defined way. See questions 15.4 and 15.5.

When you want to turn the debugging printouts off, you can use a different version of your debug macro:

```
#define DEBUG(args) /* empty */
```

Or, if you're using real function calls, you can use still more preprocessor tricks to remove the function name but not the arguments, such as:

```
#define DEBUG (void)
```
or
```
#define DEBUG if(1) {} else printf
```
or
```
#define DEBUG 1 ? 0 : (void)
```

These tricks are predicated on the assumption that a good optimizer will remove any "dead" `printf` calls or degenerate cast-to-void parenthesized comma expressions. See also question 10.14.

10.27

Question: How can I include expansions of the `__FILE__` and `__LINE__` macros in a general-purpose debugging macro?

Answer: This question tends to reduce to question 10.26. One solution involves writing your debug macro in terms of a varargs function (see questions 15.4 and 15.5) and an auxiliary function that stashes the values of `__FILE__` and `__LINE__` away in static variables, as in:

```
#include <stdio.h>
#include <stdarg.h>

void debug(char *fmt, ...);
void dbginfo(int, char *);
#define DEBUG dbginfo(__LINE__, __FILE__), debug

static char *dbgfile;
static int dbgline;
```

```
void dbginfo(int line, char *file)
{
        dbgfile = file;
        dbgline = line;
}

void debug(char *fmt, ...)
{
        va_list argp;
        fprintf(stderr, "DEBUG: \"%s\", line %d: ",
                                        dbgfile, dbgline);

        va_start(argp, fmt);
        vfprintf(stderr, fmt, argp);
        va_end(argp);
        fprintf(stderr, "\n");
}
```

With this machinery in place, a call to

```
DEBUG("i is %d", i);
```

expands to

```
dbginfo(__LINE__, __FILE__), debug("i is %d", i);
```

and prints something like:

```
DEBUG: "x.c", line 10: i is 42
```

A cunning improvement is the idea of having the stashing function return a pointer to the varargs function:

```
void debug(char *fmt, ...);
void (*dbginfo(int, char *))(char *, ...);
#define DEBUG (*dbginfo(__LINE__, __FILE__))

void (*dbginfo(int line, char *file))(char *, ...)
{
        dbgfile = file;
        dbgline = line;
        return debug;
}
```

With these definitions, DEBUG("i is %d", i); gets expanded to:

```
(*dbginfo(__LINE__, __FILE__))("i is %d", i);
```

Another, perhaps easier way might simply be:

```
#define DEBUG printf("DEBUG: \"%s\", line %d: ", \
        __FILE__,__LINE__),printf
```

Now, `DEBUG("i is %d", i);` simply expands to:

```
printf("DEBUG: \"%s\", line %d: ",
    __FILE__,__LINE__),printf("i is %d", i);
```

11   ANSI/ISO Standard C

The release of the ANSI C Standard (X3.159-1989) in 1990 (now superseded by ISO 9899:1990 and its ongoing revisions) marked a major step in C's acceptance as a stable language. The standard clarified many existing ambiguities in the language, but it introduced a few new features and definitions that are occasionally troublesome. Misunderstandings also arise when an ambiguity was resolved contrary to someone's experience or when people with pre-ANSI compilers try to use code written since the standard became widely adopted.

Standard C can be referred to in several ways. It was originally written by a committee (X3J11) under the auspices of the American National Standards Institute, so it's often called "ANSI C." The ANSI C Standard was adopted internationally by the International Organization for Standardization, so it's sometimes called "ISO C." ANSI eventually adopted the ISO version (superseding the original), so it's now often called "ANSI/ISO C." Unless you're making a distinction about the wording of the original ANSI standard before ISO's modifications, there's no important difference among these terms, and it's correct to simply refer to "the C standard" or "standard C." (When the subject of C is implicit in the discussion, it's also common to use the word "standard" by itself, often capitalized.)

The Standard

Question: What is the "ANSI C Standard?"

Answer: In 1983, the American National Standards Institute (ANSI) commissioned a committee, X3J11, to standardize the C language. After a long, arduous process, including several widespread public reviews, the committee's work was finally ratified as ANS X3.159-1989 on December 14, 1989, and published in the spring of 1990. For the most part, ANSI C standardizes existing practice, with a few additions from C++ (most notably function prototypes) and support for multinational character sets (including the controversial trigraph sequences). The ANSI C Standard also formalizes the C runtime library support functions.

More recently, the standard has been adopted as an international standard, ISO/IEC 9899:1990, and this version replaces the earlier X3.159 even within the United States. Its sections are numbered differently (briefly, ISO sections 5 through 7 correspond roughly to the old ANSI sections 2 through 4). As an ISO standard, it is subject to ongoing revision through the release of Technical Corrigenda and Normative Addenda.

In 1994, Technical Corrigendum 1 amended the standard in about 40 places, most of them minor corrections or clarifications. More recently, Normative Addendum 1 added about 50 pages of new material, mostly specifying new library functions for internationalization. The production of Technical Corrigenda is an ongoing process, and a second one is expected in late 1995. In addition, both ANSI and ISO require periodic review of their standards. This process is beginning in 1995 and will likely result in a completely revised standard (nicknamed "C9X," on the assumption of completion by 1999).

The original ANSI standard included a "Rationale" explaining many of its decisions and discussing a number of subtle points, including several of those covered here. (The Rationale was "not part of ANSI Standard X3.159-1989, but … included for information only" and is not included with the ISO standard.)

11.2

Question: How can I get a copy of the standard?

Answer: Copies are available in the United States from

- American National Standards Institute
  11 W. 42nd St., 13th floor
  New York, NY 10036
  (212) 642-4900
- Global Engineering Documents
  15 Inverness Way E
  Englewood, CO 80112
  (303) 397-2715 or (800) 854-7179 (U.S. and Canada)

In other countries, contact the appropriate national standards body or ISO in Geneva at:

- ISO Sales
  Case Postale 56
  CH-1211 Geneve 20
  Switzerland

At the time of this writing, the cost is $130.00 from ANSI or $410.00 from Global. Copies of the original X3.159 (including the Rationale) may still be available at $205.00 from ANSI or $162.50 from Global. Note that ANSI derives revenues to support its operations from the sale of printed standards, so electronic copies are *not* available.

In the United States, it may be possible to get a copy of the original ANSI X3.159 (including the Rationale) as "FIPS PUB 160" from:

- National Technical Information Service (NTIS)
  U.S. Department of Commerce
  Springfield, VA 22161
  (703) 487-4650

The *Annotated ANSI C Standard*, with annotations by Herbert Schildt, contains most of the text of ISO 9899; it is published by Osborne/McGraw-Hill, ISBN 0-07-881952-0. Unfortunately, the book contains numerous errors and omissions, primarily in the annotations, and a few pages of the standard itself are missing. Many people on the Internet recommend ignoring the annotations entirely. A review of the annotations ("annotated annotations") by Clive Feather can be found on the World-Wide Web at http://www.lysator. liu.se/c/schildt.html.

The text of the Rationale (not the full standard) can be obtained by anonymous ftp from ftp.uu.net (see question 18.16) in directory doc/standards/ ansi/X3.159-1989 and is also available on the World-Wide Web at http://www.lysator.liu.se/c/rat/title.html. The Rationale has also been printed by Silicon Press, ISBN 0-929306-07-4.

Function Prototypes

The most significant introduction in ANSI C is the *function prototype* (borrowed from C++), which allows a function's argument types to be declared. To preserve backward compatibility, nonprototype declarations are still acceptable, which makes the rules for prototypes somewhat more complicated.

11.3

Question: **Why does my ANSI compiler complain about a mismatch when it sees**

```
extern int func(float);

int func(x)
float x;
{ ... }
```

Answer: You have mixed the new-style prototype function declaration "extern int func(float);" with the old-style, non-prototyped definition "int func(x) float x;". It is usually safe to mix the two styles (see question 11.4) but not in this case.

Old C (and ANSI C, in the absence of prototypes and in variable-length argument lists; see question 15.2) "widens" certain arguments when they are passed to functions: floats are promoted to double, and characters and short integers are promoted to `int`. (For old-style function definitions, the values are automatically converted back to the corresponding narrower types within the body of the called function, if they are declared that way there.) Therefore, the old-style definition in the question actually says that `func` takes a `double` (which will be converted to `float` inside the function).

This problem can be fixed in two ways. One is to use new-style syntax consistently in the definition:

```
int func(float x) { … }
```

Alternatively, you can change the new-style prototype declaration to match the old-style definition:

```
extern int func(double);
```

In this case, it would be clearest to change the old-style definition to use `double` as well.*

It may also be safer to avoid "narrow" (`char`, `short int`, and `float`) function arguments and return types altogether.

See also question 1.25.

References: K&R1 §A7.1 p. 186
K&R2 §A7.3.2 p. 202
ANSI §3.3.2.2, §3.5.4.3
ISO §6.3.2.2, §6.5.4.3
Rationale §3.3.2.2, §3.5.4.3
H&S §9.2 pp. 265–7, §9.4 pp. 272–3

11.4

Question: **Is it possible to mix old-style and new-style function syntax?**

Answer: Doing so is perfectly legal and can be useful for backward compatibility, as long as you're careful (see especially question 11.3). Note, however, that old-style syntax is marked as obsolescent, so official support for it may be removed some day.

References: ANSI §3.7.1, §3.9.5
ISO §6.7.1, §6.9.5
H&S §9.2.2 pp. 265–7, §9.2.5 pp. 269–70

---

*Changing a parameter's type may require additional changes if the address of that parameter is taken and must have a particular type.

11.5

Question: Why does the declaration

```
extern f(struct x *p);
```

give me an obscure warning message about "struct x introduced in prototype scope" or "struct x declared inside parameter list"?

Answer: In a quirk of C's normal block scoping rules, a structure declared (or even mentioned) for the first time within a function prototype cannot be compatible with other structures declared in the same source file. The problem is that the structure and the tag go out of scope at the end of the prototype; see question 1.29.

To resolve the problem, you should probably rearrange things so that the actual declaration of the structure precedes the function prototype(s) using it. (Usually, both the prototype and the structure declaration will end up in the same header file, so that the one can reference the other.) If you must mention a hitherto unseen structure in a prototype, precede the prototype with the line:

```
struct x;
```

This vacuous-looking declaration places an (incomplete) declaration of `struct x` at file scope, so that all following declarations involving `struct x` can at least be sure they're referring to the same `struct x`.

References: ANSI §3.1.2.1, §3.1.2.6, §3.5.2.3
          ISO §6.1.2.1, §6.1.2.6, §6.5.2.3

11.6

Question: I had a frustrating problem that turned out to be caused by the line

```
printf("%d", n);
```

where n was actually a `long int`. Aren't ANSI function prototypes supposed to guard against argument type mismatches like this?

Answer: See question 15.3.

11.7

Question: I heard that you have to include `<stdio.h>` before calling `printf`. Why?

Answer: See question 15.1.

The `const` Qualifier

Another introduction from C++ is an additional dimension to the type system: type qualifiers. Type qualifiers can modify pointer types in several ways (affecting either the pointer or the object pointed to), so qualified pointer declarations can be tricky. (The questions in this section refer to `const`, but most of the issues apply to the other qualifier, `volatile`, as well.)

11.8

Question: Why can't I use `const` values in initializers and array dimensions, as in:

```
const int n = 5;
int a[n];
```

Answer: The `const` qualifier really means "read-only"; an object so qualified is a run-time object that cannot (normally) be assigned to. The value of a `const`-qualified object is therefore *not* a constant expression in the full sense of the term and cannot be used for array dimensions, case labels, and the like. (C is unlike C++ in this regard.) When you need a true compile-time constant, use a preprocessor `#define`.

References: ANSI §3.4
          ISO §6.4
          H&S §§7.11.2,7.11.3 pp. 226–7

11.9

Question: What's the difference between `const char *p`, `char const *p`, and `char * const p`?

Answer: The first two are interchangeable; they declare a pointer to a constant character (which means that you can't change the character). On the other hand, `char * const p` declares a constant pointer to a (variable) character (i.e., you can't change the pointer). Read these declarations "inside out" to understand them; see question 1.21.

References: ANSI §3.5.4.1 examples
            ISO §6.5.4.1
            Rationale §3.5.4.1
            H&S §4.4.4 p. 81

11.10

Question: Why can't I pass a `char **` to a function that expects a `const char **`?

Answer: You can use a pointer to T (for any type T) where a pointer to const T is expected. However, the rule (an explicit exception) that permits slight mismatches in qualified pointer types is not applied recursively but only at the top level. (Since `const char **` is pointer to pointer to const char, the exception does not apply.)

The reason you cannot assign a `char **` value to a `const char **` pointer is somewhat obscure. Given that the `const` qualifier exists at all, the compiler would like to help you keep your promises not to modify `const` values. That's why you can assign a `char *` to a `const char *` but not the other way around: It's clearly safe to "add" `const`-ness to a simple pointer, but it would be dangerous to take it away. However, suppose that you performed the following, more complicated series of assignments:

```
const char c = 'x';         /* 1 */
char *p1;                    /* 2 */
const char **p2 = &p1;      /* 3 */
*p2 = &c;                    /* 4 */
*p1 = 'X';                   /* 5 */
```

In line 3, we assign a `char **` to a `const char **`. (The compiler should complain.) In line 4, we assign a `const char *` to a `const char *`; this is clearly legal. In line 5, we modify what a `char *` points to—this is supposed to be legal. However, p1 ends up pointing to c, which is `const`. This came about in line 4, because *p2 was really p1. This was set up in line 3, which is an assignment of a form that is disallowed, and this is exactly *why* line 3 is disallowed.*

Assigning a `char **` to a `const char **` (as in line 3 and in the question) is not immediately dangerous. But it sets up a situation in which p2's promise—that the ultimately pointed-to value won't be modified—cannot be kept. When you want to make such an assignment anyway, you must use an explicit cast (e.g., `(const char) **` in this case) when the pointers which have qualifier mismatches at other than the first level of indirection.

References: ANSI §3.1.2.6, §3.3.16.1, §3.5.3
            ISO §6.1.2.6, §6.3.16.1, §6.5.3
            H&S §7.9.1 pp. 221–2

11.11

Question: I've got the declarations

```
typedef char *charp;
const charp p;
```

Why is p turning out `const` instead of the characters pointed to?

Answer: Typedef substitutions are not purely textual. (This is one of the advantages of typedefs; see question 1.13.) In the declaration

```
const charp p;
```

p is `const` for the same reason that `const int i` declares i as `const`. The declaration of p does not "look inside" the typedef to see that a pointer is involved.

Reference: H&S §4.4.4 pp. 81–2

---

*C++ has more complicated rules for assigning `const`-qualified pointers, allowing you to make more kinds of assignments without incurring warnings but still protecting against inadvertent attempts to modify `const` values. C++ would still not allow assigning a `char **` to a `const char **`, but it would let you get away with assigning a `char **` to a `const char * const *`.

Using main()

Although every C program must by definition supply a function named main, the declaration of main is unique because it has two acceptable argument lists, and the rest of the declaration (in particular, the return type) is dictated by a factor outside of the program's control, namely, the startup code that will actually call main.

11.12

Question: **Can I declare main as void to shut off these warnings about main not returning a value?**

Answer: No; main must be declared as returning an int and as taking either zero or two arguments, of the appropriate types. In other words, there are just two valid declarations:

```
int main(void)
int main(int argc, char **argv)
```

However, these declarations can be written in a variety of ways. The second parameter may be declared char *argv[] (see question 6.4), you can use any names for the two parameters, and you can use old-style syntax:

```
int main()

int main(argc, argv)
int argc; char **argv;
```

Finally, the int return value can be omitted, since int is the default (see question 1.25).

If you're calling exit but still getting warnings, you may have to insert a redundant return statement (or use some kind of "not reached" directive, if available).

Declaring a function as void does not merely shut off or rearrange warnings; it may also result in a different function call/return sequence, incompatible with what the caller (in main's case, the C run-time startup code) expects. That is, if the calling sequences for void- and int-valued functions differ, the startup code is going to be calling main using specifically the int-valued conventions. If `main` has been improperly declared as `void`, it may not work. (See also question 2.18.)

(Note that this discussion of `main` pertains only to "hosted" implementations, not to "freestanding" implementations, which may not even have `main`. However, freestanding implementations are comparatively rare, and if you're using one, you probably know it. If you've never heard of the distinction, you're probably using a hosted implementation, and these rules apply.)

References: ANSI §2.1.2.2.1, §F.5.1
          ISO §5.1.2.2.1, §G.5.1
          H&S §20.1 p. 416
          CT&P §3.10 pp. 50–1

11.13

Question: What about `main`'s third argument, `envp`?

Answer: It's a nonstandard (though common) extension. If you really need to access the environment in ways beyond what the standard `getenv` function provides, though, the global variable `environ` is probably a better avenue (though it's equally nonstandard).

References: ANSI §F.5.1
          ISO §G.5.1
          H&S §20.1 pp. 416–7

11.14

Question: I believe that declaring `void main()` can't fail, since I'm calling `exit` instead of returning. Anyway, my operating system ignores a program's exit/return status.

Answer: It doesn't matter whether `main` returns or not, or whether anyone looks at the status; the problem is that when `main` is misdeclared, its caller (the runtime startup code) may not even be able to *call* it correctly (due to the potential clash of calling conventions; see question 11.12).

It's true that declaring `void main()` does appear to work on many systems. If you find it convenient and don't mind so much about portability, no one's stopping you from using it.

11.15

Question: But why do all my books declare `main` as `void`?

Answer: They're wrong, or they're assuming that everyone writes code for systems on which it happens to work.

11.16

Question: Is `exit(status)` truly equivalent to returning the same `status` from `main`?

Answer: Yes and no. The standard says that a return from the initial call to `main` is equivalent to calling `exit`. However, a few older, nonconforming systems may have problems with one or the other form. Also, a `return` from `main` cannot be expected to work if data local to `main` might be needed during cleanup; see also question 16.4. (Finally, the two forms are obviously not equivalent in a recursive call to `main`.)

References: K&R2 §7.6 pp. 163–4
ANSI §2.1.2.2.3
ISO §5.1.2.2.3

Preprocessor Features

ANSI C introduced a few new features into the C preprocessor, including the "stringizing" and "token pasting" operators and the `#pragma` directive.

11.17

Question: I'm trying to use the ANSI "stringizing" preprocessing operator '#' to insert the value of a symbolic constant into a message, but it keeps stringizing the macro's name rather than its value. Why?

Answer: The definition of # says that it's supposed to stringize a macro argument immediately, without further expanding it (if the argument happens to be the name of another macro). You can use something like the following two-step procedure to force a macro to be both expanded and stringized:

```
#define Str(x) #x
#define Xstr(x) Str(x)
#define OP plus
char *opname = Xstr(OP);
```

This code sets `opname` to `"plus"` rather than to `"OP"`. (It works because the `Xstr()` macro expands its argument, and then `Str()` stringizes it.)

An equivalent circumlocution is necessary with the token-pasting operator ## when the values (rather than the names) of two macros are to be concatenated.

Note that both # and ## operate only during preprocessor macro expansion. You cannot use them in normal source code, only in macro definitions.

References: ANSI §3.8.3.2, §3.8.3.5 example
           ISO §6.8.3.2, §6.8.3.5

11.18

Question: **What does the message "warning: macro replacement within a string literal" mean?**

Answer: Some pre-ANSI compilers/preprocessors interpreted macro definitions like

```
#define TRACE(var, fmt) printf("TRACE: var = fmt\n", var)
```

such that invocations like `TRACE(i, %d);` were expanded as

```
printf("TRACE: i = %d\n", i);
```

In other words, macro parameters were expanded even inside string literals and character constants. (This interpretation may even have been an accident of early implementations, but it can prove useful for macros like this.)

Macro expansion is *not* defined in this way by K&R or by the C standard. (It can be dangerous and confusing; see question 10.22.) When you do want to turn macro arguments into strings, you can use the new # preprocessing operator, along with string literal concatenation (another new ANSI feature):

```
#define TRACE(var, fmt) \
        printf("TRACE: " #var " = " #fmt "\n", var)
```

See also question 11.17.

Reference: H&S §3.3.8 p. 51

11.19

Question: **Why am I getting strange syntax errors inside lines I've used `#ifdef` to disable?**

Answer: Under ANSI C, the text inside a "turned off" #if, #ifdef, or #ifndef must still consist of "valid preprocessing tokens." This means that there must be no newlines inside quotes and no unterminated comments or quotes. (Note particularly that an apostrophe within a contracted word looks like the beginning of a character constant.) Therefore, natural-language comments and pseudocode should always be written between the "official" comment delimiters /* and */. (But see questions 20.20 and also 10.25.)

References: ANSI §2.1.1.2, §3.1
         ISO §5.1.1.2, §6.1
         H&S §3.2 p. 40

11.20

Question: **What is the `#pragma` directive and what is it good for?**

Answer: The #pragma directive provides a single, well-defined "escape hatch" that can be used for all sorts of implementation-specific controls and extensions: source listing control, structure packing, warning suppression (like lint's old /* NOTREACHED */ comments), etc.

References: ANSI §3.8.6
         ISO §6.8.6
         H&S §3.7 p. 61

11.21

Question: What does "#pragma once" mean? I found it in some header files.

Answer: It is an extension implemented by some preprocessors to help make header files idempotent, that is, to make sure that their contents are processed exactly once even if they are included multiple times. It is essentially equivalent to the #ifndef trick mentioned in question 10.7. Some people claim that #pragma once can be implemented "more efficiently" (of course, only compilation efficiency is a factor here), but in fact a preprocessor that is serious about compilation efficiency can arrange for the portable #ifndef trick to be handled just as efficiently.

Other ANSI C Issues

11.22

Question: Is char a[3] = "abc"; legal? What does it mean?

Answer: It is legal in ANSI C (and perhaps in a few pre-ANSI systems) but is useful only in rare circumstances. It declares an array of size 3, initialized with the three characters 'a', 'b', and 'c', *without* the usual terminating '\0' character. The array is therefore not a true C string and cannot be used with strcpy, printf's %s format, etc.

Most of the time, you should let the compiler count the initializers when initializing arrays (in the case of the initializer "abc", of course, the computed size will be 4).

References: ANSI §3.5.7   H&S §4.6.4 p. 98
        ISO §6.5.7

11.23

Question: Since array references decay into pointers, if array is an array, what's the difference between array and &array?

Answer: See question 6.12.

11.24

Question: Why can't I perform arithmetic on a `void *` pointer?

Answer: The compiler doesn't know the size of the pointed-to objects. (Remember that pointer arithmetic is always in terms of the pointed-to size; see also question 4.4.) Therefore, arithmetic on a `void *` is disallowed (although some compilers allow it as an extension). Before performing arithmetic, convert the pointer either to `char *` or to the pointer type you're trying to manipulate (but see also questions 4.5 and 16.7).

References: ANSI §3.1.2.5, §3.3.6
ISO §6.1.2.5, §6.3.6
H&S §7.6.2 p. 204

11.25

Question: What's the difference between `memcpy` and `memmove`?

Answer: The function offers guaranteed behavior if the memory regions pointed to by the source and destination arguments overlap; `memcpy` makes no such guarantee and may therefore be more efficiently implementable. When in doubt, it's safer to use `memmove`.

It seems simple enough to implement `memmove`; the overlap guarantee apparently requires only an additional test:

```
void *memmove(void *dest, void const *src, size_t n)
{
        register char *dp = dest;
        register char const *sp = src;
        if(dp < sp) {
                while(n-- > 0)
                        *dp++ = *sp++;
        } else {
                dp += n; sp += n;
                while(n-- > 0)
                        *--dp = *--sp;
        }

        return dest;
}
```

The problem with this code is in that additional test; the pointer comparison (dp < sp) is not quite portable (it compares two pointers that do not necessarily point within the same object) and may not be as cheap as it looks. On some machines, particularly segmented architectures, it may be tricky and significantly less efficient* to implement.

References: K&R2 §B3 p. 250
ANSI §4.11.2.1, §4.11.2.2
ISO §7.11.2.1, §7.11.2.2
Rationale §4.11.2
H&S §14.3 pp. 341–2
PCS §11 pp. 165–6

11.26

Question: What should `malloc(0)` do: return a null pointer or a pointer to 0 bytes?

Answer: The ANSI/ISO C Standard says that it may do either; the behavior is implementation-defined (see question 11.33). Portable code must either take care not to call `malloc(0)` or be prepared for the possibility of a null return.

References: ANSI §4.10.3
ISO §7.10.3
PCS §16.1 p. 386

11.27

Question: Why does the ANSI standard not guarantee more than six case-insensitive characters of external identifier significance?

Answer: The problem is older linkers, which are under the control of neither the ANSI/ISO C Standard nor the C compiler developers on the systems that have them. The limitation is only that identifiers be *significant* in the first

---

*For example, a correct test under a segmented architecture might require pointer normalization.

six characters, not that they be restricted to six characters in length. This limitation is annoying, but certainly not unbearable, and is marked in the standard as "obsolescent," i.e., a future revision will likely relax it.

This concession to current, restrictive linkers really had to be made (the Rationale notes that its retention was "most painful"). Several tricks have been proposed by which a compiler burdened with a restrictive linker could present the C programmer with the appearance of more significance in external identifiers; the excellently worded §3.1.2 in the X3.159 Rationale (see question 11.1) discusses some of these schemes and explains why they could not be mandated. You can rely on uniqueness of longer or mixed-case identifiers if your environment supports them, but be prepared for extra work if you ever have to port such code to a more restrictive environment.

References: ANSI §3.1.2, §3.9.1
             ISO §6.1.2, §6.9.1
             Rationale §3.1.2
             H&S §2.5 pp. 22–3

11.28

Question: What was `noalias` and what ever happened to it?

Answer: The type qualifier `noalias` (in the same syntactic class as `const` and `volatile`), was intended to assert that an object was not pointed to ("aliased") by other pointers. The primary application would have been for the formal parameters of functions designed to perform computations on large arrays. A compiler cannot usually take advantage of vectorization or other parallelization hardware (on supercomputers that have it) unless it can ensure that the source and destination arrays do not overlap.

The `noalias` keyword was not backed up by any "prior art," and it was introduced late in the review and approval process. It was surprisingly difficult to define precisely and explain coherently, and sparked widespread, acrimonious debate. It had far-ranging implications, particularly for several standard library interfaces, for which easy fixes were not readily apparent.

Because of the criticism and the difficulty of defining `noalias` well, the committee declined to adopt it, in spite of its superficial attractions. (When writing a standard, features cannot be introduced halfway; their full integration, and all implications, must be understood.) The need for an explicit mechanism to support parallel implementation of nonoverlapping operations remains unfilled, although some work is being done on the problem.

References: ANSI §3.9.6
         ISO §6.9.6

Old or Nonstandard Compilers

Although ANSI C largely standardized existing practice, it introduced sufficient new functionality that ANSI code is not necessarily acceptable to older compilers. Furthermore, any compiler may provide nonstandard extensions or may accept (and therefore seem to condone) code that the standard says is suspect.

11.29

Question: Why is my compiler rejecting the simplest possible test programs, with all kinds of syntax errors? It's complaining about the first line of

```
main(int argc, char **argv)
{
        return 0;
}
```

Answer: Perhaps it is a pre-ANSI compiler, unable to accept function prototypes and the like. See also questions 1.31, 10.9, and 11.30.

If you don't have access to an ANSI compiler and you need to convert some newer code (such as that in this book) so that you can compile it, perform these steps:

1. Remove the argument type information from function prototype declarations and convert prototype-style function definitions to old style. The new-style declarations

   ```
   extern int f1(void);
   extern int f2(int);
   int main(int argc, char **argv) { … }
   int f3(void) { … }
   ```

   would be rewritten as

   ```
   extern int f1();
   extern int f2();
   int main(argc, argv) int argc; char **argv; { … }
   int f3() { … }
   ```

   (Beware of parameters with "narrow" types; see question 11.3.)

2. Replace `void *` with `char *`.

3. Perhaps insert explicit casts where converting between "generic" pointers (`void *`, which you've just replaced with `char *`) and other pointer types (for instance, in calls to `malloc` and `free` and in `qsort` comparison functions; see questions 7.7 and 13.9).

4. Insert casts when passing the "wrong" numeric types as function arguments, e.g., `sqrt((double)i)`.

5. Remove `const` and `volatile` qualifiers.

6. Modify any initialized automatic aggregates (see question 1.31).

7. Use older library functions (see question 13.24).

8. Rework any preprocessor macros involving `#` or `##` (see questions 10.20, 10.21, and 11.18).

9. Convert from the facilities of `<stdarg.h>` to `<varargs.h>` (see question 15.7).

10. Cross your fingers. (In other words, the steps listed here are not always sufficient; more complicated changes, not covered by any cookbook conversions, may be required.)

    See also question 11.31.

11.30

Question: Why are some ANSI/ISO C Standard library functions showing up as undefined, even though I've got an ANSI compiler?

Answer: It's possible to have a compiler available that accepts ANSI syntax but not to have ANSI-compatible header files or run-time libraries installed. (In fact, this situation is rather common when using a non-vendor-supplied compiler, such as gcc.) See also questions 11.29, 13.25, and 13.26.

11.31

Question: Does anyone have a tool for converting old-style C programs to ANSI C, or vice versa, or for automatically generating prototypes?

Answer: Two programs, protoize and unprotoize, convert back and forth between prototyped and old-style function definitions and declarations. (These programs do *not* handle full-blown translation between "classic" C and ANSI C.) These programs are part of the FSF's GNU C compiler distribution; see question 18.3.

The unproto program (pub/unix/unproto5.shar.Z on ftp.win.tue.nl) is a filter that sits between the preprocessor and the next compiler pass, converting most of ANSI C to traditional C on the fly.

The GNU GhostScript package comes with a little program called ansi2knr.

Before converting ANSI C back to old style, beware that such a conversion cannot always be made both safely and automatically. ANSI C introduces new features and complexities not found in K&R C. You'll especially need to be careful of prototyped function calls; you'll probably need to insert explicit casts. See also questions 11.3 and 11.29.

Several prototype generators exist, many as modifications to lint. A program called CPROTO was posted to comp.sources.misc in March 1992. There is another program, called "cextract." Many vendors supply simple utilities like these with their compilers. See also question 18.16. (But be careful when generating prototypes for old functions with "narrow" parameters; see question 11.3.)

Finally, are you sure you really need to convert lots of old code to ANSI C? The old-style function syntax is still acceptable, and a hasty conversion can easily introduce bugs. (See question 11.3.)

11.32

Question: Why won't my C compiler, which claims to be ANSI compliant, accept this code? I know that the code is ANSI, because gcc accepts it.

Answer: Many compilers support a few nonstandard extensions, gcc more so than most. Are you sure that the code being rejected doesn't rely on such an extension? The compiler may have an option to disable extensions; it may be wise to use such an option if you're not certain your code is ANSI compatible. (To its credit, gcc includes a -pedantic option, which turns off extensions and attempts to enforce strict ANSI compliance.)

It is usually a bad idea to perform experiments with a particular compiler to determine properties of a language; the applicable standard may permit variations, or the compiler may be wrong. See also question 11.35.

Compliance

Obviously, the whole point of having a standard is so that programs and compilers can be compatible with it (and therefore with each other). Compatibility is not a simple black-or-white issue, however: There are degrees of compliance, and the scope of the standard's definitions is not always as comprehensive as might be expected. In keeping with the "spirit of C," several issues are not precisely specified; portable programs must simply avoid depending on these issues.

11.33

Question: People seem to make a point of distinguishing among implementation-defined, unspecified, and undefined behavior. What do these terms mean?

Answer: First of all, all three of these represent areas in which the C standard does *not* specify exactly what a particular construct, or a program that uses it, must do. This looseness in C's definition is traditional and deliberate:

It permits compiler writers to (1) make choices that allow efficient code to be generated by arranging that various constructs are implemented as "however the hardware does them" (see also question 14.4), and (2) ignore (that is, avoid worrying about generating correct code for) certain marginal constructs that are too difficult to define precisely and that probably aren't useful to well-written programs, anyway (see, for example, the code fragments in questions 3.1, 3.2, and 3.3).

The three variations on "not precisely defined by the standard" are defined as:

- Implementation-defined: The implementation must pick some behavior; it may not fail to compile the program. (The program using the construct is not incorrect.) The choice must be documented. The standard may specify a set of allowable behaviors from which to choose, or it may impose no particular requirements.

- Unspecified: Like implementation-defined, except that the choice need not be documented.

- Undefined: Anything at all can happen; the standard imposes no requirements. The program may fail to compile, execute incorrectly (either crashing or silently generating incorrect results), or fortuitously do exactly what the programmer intended.

Note that since the standard imposes absolutely no requirements on the behavior of a compiler faced with an instance of undefined behavior, the compiler (more important, any generated code) can do absolutely anything. In particular, there is no guarantee that at most the undefined bit of the program will behave badly and that the rest of the program will perform normally. It's perilous to think that you can tolerate undefined behavior in a program, imagining that its undefinedness can't hurt; the undefined behavior can be more undefined than you think it can. (See question 3.2 for a relatively simple example.)

If you're interested in writing portable code, you can ignore the distinctions, as you'll want to avoid code that depends on any of the three behaviors. See also questions 3.9 and 11.34.

References: ANSI §1.6
              ISO §3.10, §3.16, §3.17
              Rationale §1.6

11.34

Question: I'm appalled that the ANSI standard leaves so many issues undefined. Isn't a standard's whole job to standardize these things?

Answer: It has always been a characteristic of C that certain constructs behaved in whatever way a particular compiler or a particular piece of hardware chose to implement them. This deliberate imprecision often allows compilers to generate more efficient code for common cases, without having to burden all programs with extra code to ensure well-defined behavior of cases deemed to be less reasonable. Therefore, the standard is simply codifying existing practice.

A programming language standard can be thought of as a treaty between the language user and the compiler implementor. Parts of that treaty consist of features that the compiler implementor agrees to provide and that the user may assume will be available. Other parts, however, consist of rules that the user agrees to follow and that the implementor may assume will be followed. As long as both sides uphold their guarantees, programs have a fighting chance of working correctly. If *either* side reneges on any of its commitments, nothing is guaranteed to work.

See also questions 11.35 and 19.42.

References: Rationale §1.1

11.35

Question: People keep saying that the behavior of `i = i++` is undefined, but I just tried it on an ANSI-conforming compiler and got the results I expected. Is it really undefined?

Answer: A compiler may do anything it likes when faced with undefined behavior (and, within limits, with implementation-defined and unspecified behavior), including doing what you expect. It's unwise to depend on it, though.

Here is another way of looking at it, thanks to Roger Miller:

> Somebody told me that in basketball you can't hold the ball and run. I got a basketball and tried it and it worked just fine. He obviously didn't understand basketball.

See also questions 11.32, 11.33, and 11.34.

12 The Standard I/O Library

A program isn't very useful unless you can tell it what to do and it can tell you what it has done. Almost any program must therefore do some I/O. C's I/O is through library functions—those in the standard I/O, or "stdio" library*—and these functions are therefore some of the most used in C's libraries.

In keeping with C's minimalist philosophy, the stdio functions assume a fairly bare-bones, least-common-denominator I/O model. You can open, read from, and write to files. Files are treated as sequential character streams, although seeking is possible. You can make a distinction between text and binary files if it's meaningful. You name a file by a string that represents an arbitrary file name or pathname; its interpretation is specific to the underlying operating system. There is no notion of directories except as embedded in pathnames, and there is no standard way to create or list directories (see Chapter 19). Three predefined I/O streams are opened for your program implicitly: You can read from `stdin`, which is often an interactive keyboard, and you can write to `stdout` or `stderr`, both of which are often the user's

---

*When we refer to "the stdio library," we really mean "the stdio functions within the standard C run-time library," or "the functions described by `<stdio.h>`."

screen. There is, however, very little defined functionality concerning the details of keyboards and screens (again, see Chapter 19).

Much of this chapter concerns `printf` (questions 12.6 through 12.11) and `scanf` (questions 12.12 through 12.20). Questions 12.21 through 12.26 cover other stdio functions. When you need access to a specific file, you can either open it with `fopen` (questions 12.27 through 12.32) or redirect a standard stream to it (questions 12.33 through 12.36). If you're not content to do text I/O, you can resort to "binary" streams (questions 12.37 through 12.42). Before delving into all those particulars, however, here are a few simple, introductory I/O questions.

Basic I/O

12.1

Question: **What's wrong with this code?**

```
char c;
while((c = getchar()) != EOF) …
```

Answer: For one thing, the variable to hold `getchar`'s return value must be an `int`. EOF is an "out of band" return value from `getchar`, distinct from all possible `char` values that `getchar` can return. (On modern systems, it does not reflect any actual end-of-file character stored in a file; it is a signal that no more characters are available.) The values returned by `getchar` must be stored in a variable larger than `char` so that it can hold all possible `char` values *and* EOF.

Two failure modes are possible if, as in the preceding fragment, `getchar`'s return value is assigned to a `char`.

1. If type `char` is signed and if EOF is defined (as is usual) as −1, the character with the decimal value 255 (`'\377'` or `'\xff'` in C) will be sign extended and will compare equal to EOF, prematurely terminating the input.*

---

*The value 255 assumes that type `char` is 8 bits. On some systems chars are larger, but the possibility of analogous failure modes remains.

2. If type `char` is unsigned, an `EOF` value will be truncated (by having its higher-order bits discarded, probably resulting in 255 or `0xff`) and will *not* be recognized as `EOF`, resulting in effectively infinite input.*

The bug can go undetected for a long time, however, if `chars` are signed and if the input is all 7-bit characters. (Whether plain `char` is signed or unsigned is implementation-defined.)

References: K&R1 §1.5 p. 14
  K&R2 §1.5.1 p. 16
  ANSI §3.1.2.5, §4.9.1, §4.9.7.5
  ISO §6.1.2.5, §7.9.1, §7.9.7.5
  H&S §5.1.3 p. 116, §15.1 pp. 345–6, §15.6 pp. 354–5
  CT&P §5.1 p. 70
  PCS §11 p. 157

12.2

Question: **Why does the simple line-copying loop**

```
while(!feof(infp)) {
        fgets(buf, MAXLINE, infp);
        fputs(buf, outfp);
}
```

copy the last line twice?

Answer: In C, EOF is indicated only *after* an input routine has tried to read and has reached end of file. (In other words, C's I/O is not like Pascal's.) Usually, you should just check the return value of the input routine:

```
while(fgets(buf, MAXLINE, infp) != NULL)
        fputs(buf, outfp);
```

Generally, you don't need to use `feof` at all. (Occasionally, `feof` or its companion `ferror` is useful *after* a stdio call has returned `EOF` or `NULL`, to distinguish between an end-of-file condition and a read error.)

References: K&R2 §7.6 p. 164
  ANSI §4.9.3, §4.9.7.1, §4.9.10.2
  ISO §7.9.3, §7.9.7.1, §7.9.10.2
  H&S §15.14 p. 382

---

*As in the previous paragraph, the value 255 assumes that type `char` is 8 bits. On some systems `chars` are larger, but the possibility of analogous failure modes remains.

12.3

Question: I'm using **fgets** to read lines from a file into an array of pointers. Why do all the lines end up containing copies of the last line?

Answer: See question 7.4.

12.4

Question: My program's prompts and intermediate output don't always show up on the screen, especially when I pipe the output through another program. Why not?

Answer: It's best to use an explicit `fflush(stdout)` whenever output should definitely be visible.* Several mechanisms attempt to perform the `fflush` for you, at the "right time," but they tend to apply only when `stdout` is an interactive terminal. (See also question 12.24.)

References: ANSI §4.9.5.2
ISO §7.9.5.2

12.5

Question: How can I read one character at a time without waiting for the Return key?

Answer: See question 19.1.

---

*Another possibility might be to use `setbuf` or `setvbuf` to turn off buffering of the output stream, but buffering is a Good Thing, and completely disabling it can lead to crippling inefficiencies.

`printf` **Formats**

Question: How can I print a `'%'` character in a **printf** format string? I tried `\%`, but it didn't work.

Answer: Simply double the percent sign: `%%` .

The reason it's tricky to print `%` signs with `printf` is that `%` is essentially `printf`'s escape character. Whenever `printf` sees a `%`, it expects it to be followed by a character telling it what to do next. The two-character sequence `%%` is defined to print a single `%`.

To understand why `\%` can't work, remember that the backslash `\` is the *compiler's* escape character and controls how the compiler interprets source code characters at compile time. In this case, however, we want to control how `printf` interprets its format string at run time. As far as the compiler is concerned, the escape sequence `\%` is undefined and probably results in a single `%` character. It would be unlikely for both the `\` and the `%` to make it through to `printf`, even if `printf` were prepared to treat the `\` specially.

See also questions 8.8 and 19.17.

References: K&R1 §7.3 p. 147
           K&R2 §7.2 p. 154
           ANSI §4.9.6.1
           ISO §7.9.6.1

Question: Why doesn't this code work?

```
long int n = 123456;
printf("%d\n", n);
```

Answer: Whenever you print long ints, you must use the 1 (lowercase letter "ell") modifier in the printf format (e.g., %ld). Since printf can't know the types of the arguments you've passed to it, you must let it know by using the correct format specifiers.

12.8

Question: Aren't ANSI function prototypes supposed to guard against argument type mismatches?

Answer: See question 15.3.

12.9

Question: Someone told me that it is wrong to use %lf with **printf**. How can **printf** use %f for type **double** if **scanf** requires %lf?

Answer: It's true that printf's %f specifier works with both float and double arguments.* Due to the "default argument promotions" (which apply in variable-length argument lists,† such as printf's, whether or not prototypes are in scope), values of type float are promoted to double, and printf therefore sees only doubles. See also question 15.2.

This situation is completely different for scanf, which accepts pointers for which no such promotions apply. Storing into a float (via a pointer) is very different from storing into a double, so scanf distinguishes between %f and %lf.

The following table lists the argument types expected by printf and scanf for the various format specifiers.

---

*Everything said here is equally true of %e and %g and the corresponding scanf formats %le and %lg.
†In fact, the default argument promotions apply only in the variable-length part of variable-length argument lists; see Chapter 15.

Format	`printf`	`scanf`
`%c`	int	char *
`%d, %i`	int	int *
`%o, %u, %x`	unsigned int	unsigned int *
`%ld, %li`	long int	long int *
`%lo, %lu, %lx`	unsigned long int	unsigned long int *
`%hd, %hi`	int	short int *
`%ho, %hu, %hx`	unsigned int	unsigned short int *
`%e, %f, %g`	double	float *
`%le, %lf, %lg`	n/a	double *
`%s`	char *	char *
`%[...]`	n/a	char *
`%p`	void *	void **
`%n`	int *	int *
`%%`	none	none

(Strictly speaking, `%lf` is undefined under `printf`, although many systems probably accept it. To ensure portability, always use `%f`.)

See also question 12.13.

References: K&R1 §7.3 pp. 145–7, §7.4 pp. 147–50
K&R2 §7.2 pp. 153–4, §7.4 pp. 157–9
ANSI §4.9.6.1, §4.9.6.2
ISO §7.9.6.1, §7.9.6.2
H&S §15.8 pp. 357-64, §15.11 pp. 366–78
CT&P §A.1 pp. 121–33

12.10

Question: How can I implement a variable field width with `printf`? That is, instead of something like `%8d`, I want the width to be specified at run time.

Answer: Use `printf("%*d", width, n)`. The asterisk in the format specifier indicates that an `int` value from the argument list will be used for the field width. (Note that in the argument list, the width precedes the value to be printed.) See also question 12.15.

References: K&R2 §7.2 p. 154
ANSI §4.9.6.1
ISO §7.9.6.1
H&S §15.11.4 p. 370
CT&P §A.1 pp. 132–3

12.11

Question: How can I print numbers with commas separating the thousands? What about currency-formatted numbers?

Answer: The functions in <locale.h> begin to provide some support for these operations, but there is no standard function for doing either task. (The only thing printf does in response to a custom locale setting is to change its decimal-point character.)

Here is a little function for formatting comma-separated numbers, using the locale's thousands separator, if available:

```
#include <locale.h>

char *commaprint(unsigned long n)
{
        static int comma = '\0';
        static char retbuf[30];
        char *p = &retbuf[sizeof(retbuf)-1];
        int i = 0

        if(comma == '\0') {
                struct lconv *lcp = localeconv();
                if(lcp != NULL) {
                        if(lcp->thousands_sep != NULL &&
                                *lcp->thousands_sep != '\0')
                                comma = *lcp->thousands_sep;
                        else    comma = ',';
                }
        }

        *p = '\0';

        do {
                if(i%3 == 0 && i != 0)
                        *--p = comma;
                *--p = '0' + n % 10;
                n /= 10;
                i++;
        } while(n != 0);

        return p;
}
```

A better implementation would use the `grouping` field of the `lconv` structure rather than assuming groups of three digits. A safer size for `retbuf` might be `4*(sizeof(long)*CHAR_BIT+2)/3/3+1`. See question 12.21.

References: ANSI §4.4
ISO §7.4
H&S §11.6 pp. 301–4

scanf Formats

12.12

Question: Why doesn't the call `scanf("%d", i)` work?

Answer: The arguments you pass to `scanf` must always be pointers: For each value converted, `scanf` "returns" it by filling in one of the locations you've passed pointers to. (See also question 20.1.) To fix the preceding fragment, change it to `scanf("%d", &i)`.

12.13

Question: Why doesn't this code work?

```
double d;
scanf("%f", &d);
```

Answer: Unlike `printf`, `scanf` uses `%lf` for values of type `double` and `%f` for `float`.* The `%f` format tells `scanf` to expect a pointer to `float`, not the pointer to `double` you gave it. Either use `%lf` or declare the receiving variable as a `float`. See also question 12.9.

---

*Everything said here is equally true of `%e` and `%g` and their companion formats `%le` and `%lg`.

12.14

Question: Why doesn't this code work?

```
short int s;
scanf("%d", &s);
```

Answer: When converting %d, scanf expects a pointer to an int. To convert to a short int, use %hd . (See also the table in question 12.9.)

12.15

Question: How can I specify a variable width in a **scanf** format string?

Answer: You can't; an asterisk in a scanf format string means to suppress assignment. You may be able to use ANSI stringizing and string concatenation to construct a constant format specifier based on a preprocessor macro containing the desired width:

```
#define WIDTH 3

#define Str(x) #x
#define Xstr(x) Str(x)    /* see question 11.17 */

scanf("%" Xstr(WIDTH) "d", &n);
```

If the width is a run-time variable, though, you'll have to build the format specifier at run time, too:

```
char fmt[10];
sprintf(fmt, "%%%dd", width);
scanf(fmt, &n);
```

(Such scanf formats are unlikely when reading from standard input but might find some usefulness with fscanf or sscanf.)

See also questions 11.17 and 12.10.

Question: How can I read data from data files with particular formats? How can I read 10 **floats** without having to use a jawbreaker **scanf** format mentioning **%f** 10 times? How can I read an arbitrary number of fields from a line into an array?

Answer: In general, there are three main ways of parsing data lines:

1. Use **fscanf** or **sscanf**, with an appropriate format string. Despite the limitations mentioned in this chapter (see question 12.20), the **scanf** family is quite powerful. Although whitespace-separated fields are always the easiest to deal with, **scanf** format strings can also be used with more compact, column-oriented, FORTRAN-style data. For instance, the line

   ```
   1234ABC5.678
   ```

   could be read with **"%d%3s%f"**. (See also the last example in question 12.19.)

2. Break the line into fields separated by whitespace (or some other delimiter), using **strtok** or the equivalent (see question 13.6); then deal with each field individually, perhaps with functions such as **atoi** and **atof**. (Once the line is broken up, the code for handling the fields is much like the traditional code in **main()** for handling the **argv** array; see question 20.3.) This method is particularly useful for reading an arbitrary (i.e., not known in advance) number of fields from a line into an array.

   Here is a simple example that copies a line of up to 10 floating-point numbers (separated by whitespace) into an array:

   ```c
   #include <stdlib.h>
   #define MAXARGS 10

   char *av[MAXARGS];
   int ac, i;
   double array[MAXARGS];

   ac = makeargv(line, av, MAXARGS);
   for(i = 0; i < ac; i++)
       array[i] = atof(av[i]);
   ```

(See question 13.6 for the definition of **makeargv**.)

3. Use whatever pointer manipulations and library functions are handy to parse the line in an ad hoc way. (The ANSI `strtol` and `strtod` functions are particularly useful for this style of parsing because they can return a pointer indicating where they stopped reading.) This is obviously the most general way, but it's also the most difficult and error prone: The thorniest parts of many C programs are those that use lots of tricky little pointers to pick apart strings.

When possible, design data files and input formats so that they don't require arcane manipulations, but can instead be parsed with easier techniques, such as 1 and 2. Dealing with the files will then be much more pleasant all around.

scanf Problems

Though it seems to be an obvious complement to `printf`, `scanf` has a number of fundamental limitations that lead some programmers to recommend avoiding it entirely.

12.17

Question: When I read numbers from the keyboard with **scanf** and a **"%d\n"** format, like this:

```
int n;
scanf("%d\n", &n);
printf("you typed %d\n", n);
```

it seems to hang until I type one extra line of input. Why?

Answer: Perhaps surprisingly, \n in a `scanf` format string does *not* mean to expect a newline but rather to read and discard characters as long as each is a whitespace character. (In fact, any whitespace character in a `scanf` format string means to read and discard whitespace characters. Furthermore, formats such as %d also discard leading whitespace, so you usually don't need explicit whitespace in `scanf` format strings at all.)

The \n in "%d\n" therefore causes scanf to read characters until it finds a nonwhitespace character, and it may need to read another line before it can find that nonwhitespace character. In this case, the fix is just to use "%d" without the \n (although your program may then need to skip over the unread newline; see question 12.18).

The scanf functions were designed for free-format input, which is seldom what you want when reading from the keyboard. By "free format" we mean that scanf does not treat newlines differently from other whitespace. The format "%d %d %d" would just as readily read the input

```
1 2 3
```

or

```
1
2
3
```

(By way of comparison, source code in such languages as C, Pascal, and LISP is free-format, whereas traditional BASIC and FORTRAN are not.)

If you're insistent, scanf *can* be told to match a newline, using the "scanset" directive:

```
scanf("%d%*[\n]", &n);
```

Scansets, though powerful, won't solve all scanf problems, however. See also question 12.20.

References: K&R2 §B1.3 pp. 245–6   ISO §7.9.6.2
           ANSI §4.9.6.2   H&S §15.8 pp. 357–64

12.18

Question: I'm reading a number with **scanf** and **%d** and then a string with **gets()**:

```
int n;
char str[80];

printf("enter a number: ");
scanf("%d", &n);
printf("enter a string: ");
gets(str);
printf("you typed %d and \"%s\"\n", n, str);
```

but the compiler seems to be skipping the call to **gets()**! Why?

Answer: If, in response to the program in the question, you type the two lines

```
42
a string
```

scanf will read the 42 but *not* the newline following it. That newline will remain on the input stream, where it will immediately satisfy gets(), which will therefore seem to read a blank line. The second line, "a string", will not be read at all.

If you had typed both the number and the string on the same line:

```
42 a string
```

the code would have worked more or less as you expected.

As a general rule, you shouldn't try to interlace calls to scanf with calls to gets() or any other input routines; scanf's peculiar treatment of newlines almost always leads to trouble. Use scanf to read either everything or nothing.

See also questions 12.20 and 12.23.

References: ANSI §4.9.6.2
           ISO §7.9.6.2
           H&S §15.8 pp. 357–64

12.19

Question: I figured I could use **scanf** more safely if I checked its return value to make sure that the user typed the numeric values I expect:

```
int n;

while(1) {
        printf("enter a number: ");
        if(scanf("%d", &n) == 1)
                break;
        printf("try again: ");
}

printf("you typed %d\n", n);
```

but sometimes it seems to go into an infinite loop.* Why?

---

*Don't try the code fragment in the question unless you have a working control-C key or are willing to reboot.

Answer: When `scanf` is attempting to convert numbers, any nonnumeric characters it encounters terminate the conversion *and are left on the input stream.* Therefore, unless some other steps are taken, unexpected nonnumeric input "jams" `scanf` again and again; `scanf` never gets past the bad character(s) to encounter later, valid data. If the user types a character such as 'x' in response to the preceding code, the code will loop printing "try again" forever, but it won't give the user a chance to try.

You may wonder why `scanf` leaves unmatchable characters on the input stream. Suppose that you had a compact data file containing lines consisting of a number and an alphabetic code string without intervening whitespace":

```
123CODE
```

You might want to parse this data file with `scanf`, using the format string `"%d%s"`. But if the `%d` conversion did not leave the unmatched character on the input stream, `%s` would incorrectly read `"ODE"` instead of `"CODE"`. (The problem is a standard one in lexical analysis: When scanning an arbitrary-length numeric constant or alphanumeric identifier, you never know where it ends until you've read "too far." This is one reason that `ungetc` exists.)

See also question 12.20.

References: ANSI §4.9.6.2
        ISO §7.9.6.2
        H&S §15.8 pp. 357–64

12.20

Question: Why does everyone say not to use **scanf**? What should I use instead?

Answer: As noted in questions 12.17, 12.18, and 12.19, `scanf` has a number of problems. Also, its `%s` format has the same problem that `gets()` has (see question 12.23)—it's difficult to guarantee that the receiving buffer won't overflow.*

---

*An explicit field width, as in `%20s`, may help; see also question 12.15.

More generally, scanf is designed for relatively structured, formatted input (its name is, in fact, derived from "scan formatted"). If you pay attention, it will tell you whether it succeeded or failed, but it can tell you only approximately where it failed and not at all how or why. You have very little opportunity to do any error recovery.

Yet interactive user input is the least structured input there is. A well-designed user interface will allow for the possibility of the user typing just about anything—not just letters or punctuation when digits were expected, but also more or fewer characters than were expected, no characters at all (i.e., just the Return key), premature EOF, or anything. It's nearly impossible to deal gracefully with all of these potential problems when using scanf; it's far easier to read entire lines (with fgets or the like), then interpret them, using either sscanf or other techniques. (Functions such as strtol, strtok, and atoi are often useful; see also questions 12.16 and 13.6.) If you do use sscanf, don't forget to check the return value to make sure that the expected number of items was found.

Note, by the way, that criticisms of scanf are not necessarily indictments of fscanf and sscanf. The standard input implicitly read by scanf is usually an interactive keyboard and is therefore the least constrained, leading to the most problems. When a data file has a known format, on the other hand, it may be appropriate to read it with fscanf. It's perfectly appropriate to parse strings with sscanf (as long as the return value is checked), because it's so easy to regain control, restart the scan, discard the input if it didn't match, etc.

Reference: K&R2 §7.4 p. 159

Other stdio Functions

12.21

Question: How can I tell how much destination buffer space I'll need for an arbitrary **sprintf** call? How can I avoid overflowing the destination buffer with **sprintf**?

Answer: No good answers exist (yet) to either of these excellent questions, and this represents perhaps the biggest deficiency in the traditional stdio library.

When the format string being used with sprintf is known and relatively simple, you can usually predict a buffer size in an ad hoc way. If the format consists of one or two %s's, you can count the fixed characters in the format string yourself (or let `sizeof` count them for you) and add in the result of calling `strlen` on the string(s) to be inserted. For example, to compute the buffer size that the call

```
sprintf(buf, "You typed \"%s\"", answer);
```

would need, you could write:

```
int bufsize = 13 + strlen(answer);
```

or

```
int bufsize = sizeof("You typed \"%s\"") + strlen(answer);
```

followed by

```
char *buf = malloc(bufsize);
if(buf != NULL)
        sprintf(buf, "You typed \"%s\"", answer);
```

You can conservatively estimate the size that %d will expand to with code such as:

```
#include <limits.h>
char buf[(sizeof(int) * CHAR_BIT + 2) / 3 + 1 + 1];
sprintf(buf, "%d", n);
```

This code computes the number of characters required for a base-8 representation of a number; a base-10 expansion is guaranteed to take as much room or less. (The +2 takes care of truncation if the size is not a multiple of 3, and the +1+1 leaves room for a leading - and a trailing \0.) An analogous technique could, of course, be used for `long int`, and the same buffer can obviously be used with %u, %o, and %x formats as well.

When the format string is more complicated or is not even known until run time, predicting the buffer size becomes as difficult as reimplementing `sprintf` and correspondingly error prone (and inadvisable). A last-ditch technique sometimes suggested is to use `fprintf` to print the same text to a temporary file and then to look at `fprintf`'s return value or the size of the file (but see question 19.12). (Using a temporary file for this application is admittedly clumsy and inelegant, but it's the only portable solution besides writing an entire `sprintf` format interpreter. If your system provides one, you can use a null or "bit bucket" device, such as /dev/null or NUL, instead of a temporary file.)

If there's any chance that the buffer might not be big enough, you won't want to call sprintf without some guarantee that the buffer will not overflow and overwrite some other part of memory. Several versions of the stdio library (including those in GNU and 4.4bsd) provide the obvious snprintf function, which can be used like this:

```
snprintf(buf, bufsize, "You typed \"%s\"", answer);
```

and we can hope that a future revision of the ANSI/ISO C Standard will include this function. (It's tremendously needed and no more difficult to implement than sprintf itself.) For computing the buffer size in the first place, it's possible that sprintf could be extended to accept a null pointer buffer argument, safely returning the correct size without storing anything.

12.22

Question: What's the deal on **sprintf**'s return value? Is it an **int** or a **char ***?

Answer: The standard says that it returns an int (the number of characters written, just like printf and fprintf). Once upon a time, in some C libraries, sprintf returned the char * value of its first argument, pointing to the completed result (i.e., analogous to strcpy's return value).

References: ANSI §4.9.6.5
ISO §7.9.6.5
PCS §11 p. 175

12.23

Question: Why does everyone say not to use **gets()**?

Answer: Unlike fgets(), gets() cannot be told the size of the buffer it's to read into, so it cannot be prevented from overflowing that buffer if an input line is longer than expected—and Murphy's Law says that sooner or later, a larger than expected input line *will* occur.* As a general rule, always use `fgets()`. (It's possible to convince yourself that for one reason or another, input lines longer than a particular maximum are impossible, but it's also possible to be mistaken,† and in any case, it's just as easy to use `fgets`.)

One other difference between `fgets()` and `gets()` is that `fgets()` retains the `'\n'`, but it is straightforward to strip it out. See question 7.1 for a code fragment illustrating the replacement of `gets()` with `fgets()`.

References: Rationale §4.9.7.2
        H&S §15.7 p. 356

12.24

Question: I thought I'd check **errno** after a long string of **printf** calls to see whether any of them had failed:

```
errno = 0;
printf("This\n");
printf("is\n");
printf("a\n");
printf("test.\n");
if(errno != 0)
    fprintf(stderr, "printf failed: %s\n", strerror(errno));
```

Why is it printing something strange like "printf failed: Not a typewriter" when I redirect the output to a file?

Answer: Many implementations of the stdio library adjust their behavior slightly if `stdout` is a terminal. To make the determination, these implementations perform some operation that happens to fail if `stdout` is not a terminal. Although the output operation goes on to complete successfully, `errno` still contains the failure code. This behavior can be mildly confusing, but it is not strictly incorrect, because it is meaningful for a program to inspect the contents of `errno` only after an error has been reported. (More

---

*When discussing the drawbacks of `gets()`, it is customary to point out that the 1988 "Internet worm" exploited a call to `gets()` in the UNIX finger daemon as one of its methods of attack. It overflowed `gets`'s buffer with carefully contrived binary data that overwrote a return address on the stack such that control flow transferred into the binary data.

†You may think that your operating system imposes a maximum length on keyboard input lines, but what if input is redirected from a file?

precisely, `errno` is meaningful only after a library function that sets `errno` on error has returned an error code.)

In general, it's best to detect errors by checking a function's return value. To check for any accumulated error after a long string of stdio calls, you can use `ferror`. See also questions 12.2 and 20.4.

References: ANSI §4.1.3, §4.9.10.3
ISO §7.1.4, §7.9.10.3
CT&P §5.4 p. 73
PCS §14 p. 254

12.25

Question: What's the difference between **fgetpos/fsetpos** and **ftell/fseek**? What are **fgetpos** and **fsetpos** good for?

Answer: The newer `fgetpos` and `fsetpos` functions use a special typedef, `fpos_t`, for representing offsets (positions) in a file. The type behind this typedef, if chosen appropriately, can represent arbitrarily large offsets, allowing `fgetpos` and `fsetpos` to be used with arbitrarily huge files. In contrast, `ftell` and `fseek` use `long int` and are therefore limited to offsets that can be represented in a `long int`. (Type `long int` is not guaranteed to hold values larger than $2^{31}-1$, limiting the maximum offset to 2 gigabytes.) See also question 1.4.

References: K&R2 §B1.6 p. 248
ANSI §4.9.1, §4.9.9.1, §4.9.9.3
ISO §7.9.1, §7.9.9.1, §7.9.9.3
H&S §15.5 p. 252

12.26

Question: How can I flush pending input so that a user's typeahead isn't read at the next prompt? Will **fflush(stdin)** work?

Answer: In standard C, `fflush` is defined only for output streams. Since its definition of "flush" is to complete the writing of buffered characters (not to discard them), discarding unread input would not be an analogous meaning for `fflush` on input streams.

There is no standard way to discard unread characters from a stdio input stream. Some vendors do implement `fflush` so that `fflush(stdin)` discards unread characters, although portable programs cannot depend on this. (Some versions of the stdio library implement `fpurge` or `fabort` calls that do the same thing, but these aren't standard, either.) Note, too, that flushing stdio input buffers is not necessarily sufficient; unread characters can also accumulate in other, OS-level input buffers.

If you need to flush input, you'll have to use a system-specific technique, such as `fflush(stdin)` if it happens to work, or some other operating system–dependent routines as in questions 19.1 and 19.2. Keep in mind that users can become frustrated if you discard input that happened to be typed too quickly.

References: ANSI §4.9.5.2
ISO §7.9.5.2
H&S §15.2 p. 347

Opening and Manipulating Files

12.27

Question: I wrote this function, which opens a file:

```
myfopen(char *filename, FILE *fp)
{
        fp = fopen(filename, "r");
}
```

But when I call it like this:

```
        FILE *infp;
        myfopen("filename.dat", infp);
```

the `infp` variable in the caller doesn't get set properly. Why not?

Answer: Functions in C always receive copies of their arguments, so a function can never "return" a value to the caller by assigning to an argument. See question 4.8.

For this example, one fix is to change `myfopen` to return a FILE *:

```
FILE *myfopen(char *filename)
{
        FILE *fp = fopen(filename, "r");
        return fp;
}
```

and to call it like this:

```
        FILE *infp;
        infp = myfopen("filename.dat");
```

Alternatively, have `myfopen` accept a *pointer* to a FILE * (a pointer to pointer to FILE):

```
myfopen(char *filename, FILE **fpp)
{
        FILE *fp = fopen(filename, "r");
        *fpp = fp;
}
```

and call it like this:

```
        FILE *infp;
        myfopen("filename.dat", &infp);
```

12.28

Question: I can't even get a simple **fopen** call to work! What's wrong with this call?

```
FILE *fp = fopen(filename, 'r');
```

The problem is that **fopen**'s mode argument must be a string, such as **"r"**, not a character (**'r'**). See also question 8.1.

12.29

Question: Why can't I open a file by its explicit path? This call is failing:

```
fopen("c:\newdir\file.dat", "r")
```

Answer: You probably need to double those backslashes. See question 19.17.

12.30

Question: I'm trying to update a file in place by using **fopen** mode **"r+"**, reading a certain string, and writing back a modified string, but it's not working. Why not?

Answer: Be sure to call **fseek** before you write, both to seek back to the beginning of the string you're trying to overwrite and because an **fseek** or **fflush** is always required between reading and writing in the read/write **"+"** modes. Also, remember that you can overwrite characters only with the same number of replacement characters; there is no way to insert or delete characters in place (see also question 19.14).

References: ANSI §4.9.5.3
          ISO §7.9.5.3

12.31

Question: How can I insert or delete a line (or record) in the middle of a file?

Answer: See question 19.14.

12.32

Question: How can I recover the file name given an open stream?

Answer: See question 19.15.

Redirecting stdin and stdout

12.33

Question: How can I redirect **stdin** or **stdout** to a file from within a program?

Answer: Use freopen. If you'd like a function f() that normally writes to stdout to send its output to a file instead, and you don't have the option of rewriting f, you can use a sequence like this:

```
freopen(file, "w", stdout);
f();
```

See, however, question 12.34.

References: ANSI §4.9.5.4
           ISO §7.9.5.4
           H&S §15.2 pp. 347–8

12.34

Question: Once I've used **freopen**, how can I get the original **stdout** (or **stdin**) back?

Answer: There isn't a good way. If you need to switch back, the best solution is not to have used freopen in the first place. Try using your own explicit output (or input) stream variable, which you can reassign at will, while leaving the original stdout (or stdin) undisturbed. For example, declare a global

```
FILE *ofp;
```

and replace all calls to printf(...) with fprintf(ofp, ...). (Obviously, you'll have to check for calls to putchar and puts, too.) Then you can set ofp to stdout or to anything else.

You might wonder whether you could skip `freopen` entirely and do something like

```
FILE *savestdout = stdout;
stdout = fopen(file, "w");        /* WRONG */
```

leaving yourself able to restore `stdout` later by doing

```
stdout = savestdout;              /* WRONG */
```

Code like this is *not* likely to work, because `stdout` (and `stdin` and `stderr`) are typically constants, which cannot be reassigned (which is why `freopen` exists in the first place).

It is barely possible to save away information about a stream before calling `freopen` to open another file in its place, such that the original stream can later be restored, but the methods involve system-specific calls, such as `dup`, or copying or inspecting the contents of a `FILE` structure, which is exceedingly nonportable and unreliable.

Under some systems, you can explicitly open the controlling terminal (see question 12.36), but this isn't necessarily what you want, since the original input or output (i.e., what `stdin` or `stdout` had been before you called `freopen`) could have been redirected from the command line.

If you're trying to capture the result of a subprogram execution, `freopen` probably won't work anyway; see question 19.30 instead.

12.35

Question: How can I tell whether standard input or output is redirected, i.e., whether "<" or ">" was used on the invocation command line?

Answer: You can't tell directly, but you can usually look at a few other things to make whatever decision you need to. If you want your program to take input from `stdin` when not given any input files, you can do so if `argv` doesn't mention any input files (see question 20.3) or perhaps if you're given a placeholder, such as "-", instead of a file name. If you want to suppress prompts if input is not coming from an interactive terminal, on some systems (e.g., UNIX, and usually MS-DOS), you can use `isatty(0)` or `isatty(fileno(stdin))` to make the determination.

12.36

Question: I'm trying to write a program like "more." How can I get back to the interactive keyboard if `stdin` is redirected?

Answer: There is no portable way of doing this. Under UNIX, you can open the special file `/dev/tty`. Under MS-DOS, you can try opening the "file" CON or use routines or BIOS calls, such as `getch`, that may go to the keyboard whether or not input is redirected.

"Binary" I/O

A normal stream is assumed to consist of printable text and may undergo certain translations to match the conventions of the underlying operating system. When you want to read and write arbitrary bytes exactly, without any translations, you want "binary" I/O.

12.37

Question: I want to read and write numbers directly between files and memory a byte at a time, not as formatted characters the way `fprintf` and `fscanf` do. How can I do this?

Answer: What you're trying to do is usually called "binary" I/O. First, make sure that you are calling `fopen` with the `"b"` modifier (`"rb"`, `"wb"`, etc.; see question 12.38). Then use the `&` and `sizeof` operators to get a handle on the sequences of bytes you are trying to transfer. Usually, the `fread` and `fwrite` functions are what you want to use; see question 2.11 for an example.

Note, though, that `fread` and `fwrite` do not necessarily imply binary I/O. If you've opened a file in binary mode, you can use any I/O calls on it (see, for example, the examples in question 12.42); if you've opened it in text mode, you can use `fread` or `fwrite` if they're convenient.

Finally, note that binary data files are not very portable; see question 20.5. See also question 12.40.

12.38

Question: How can I read a binary data file properly? I'm occasionally seeing 0x0a and 0x0d values getting garbled, and it seems to hit EOF prematurely if the data contains the value 0x1a.

Answer: When you're reading a binary data file, you should specify "rb" mode when calling fopen, to make sure that text file translations do not occur. Similarly, when writing binary data files, use "wb". (Under operating systems such as UNIX that don't distinguish between text and binary files, "b" may not be required but is harmless.)

Note that the text/binary distinction is made when you open the file. Once a file is open, it doesn't matter which I/O calls you use on it. See also questions 12.40, 12.42, and 20.5.

References: ANSI §4.9.5.3
ISO §7.9.5.3
H&S §15.2.1 p. 348

12.39

Question: I'm writing a "filter" for binary files, but stdin and stdout are preopened as text streams. How can I change their mode to binary?

Answer: There is no standard way to do this. UNIX-like systems have no text/binary distinction, so there is no need to change the mode. Some MS-DOS compilers supply a setmode call. Otherwise, you're on your own.

12.40

Question: What's the difference between text and binary I/O?

Answer: In text mode, a file is assumed to consist of lines of printable characters (perhaps including tabs). The routines in the stdio library (getc, putc, and all the rest) translate between the underlying system's end-of-line representation and the single \n used in C programs. C programs that simply read and write text therefore don't have to worry about the underlying system's newline conventions: When a C program writes a ' \n ', the stdio library writes the appropriate end-of-line indication, and when the stdio library detects an end of line while reading, it returns a single ' \n ' to the calling program.*

In binary mode, on the other hand, bytes are read and written between the program and the file without any interpretation. (On MS-DOS systems, binary mode also turns off testing for control-Z as an in-band end-of-file character.)

Text-mode translations also affect the apparent size of a file as it's read. Because the characters read from and written to a file in text mode do not necessarily match exactly the characters stored in the file, the size of the file on disk may not always match the number of characters that can be read from it. Furthermore, for analogous reasons, the fseek and ftell functions do not necessarily deal in pure byte offsets from the beginning of the file. (Strictly speaking, in text mode, the offset values used by fseek and ftell should not be interpreted at all; a value returned by ftell should be used only as a later argument to fseek, and *only* values returned by ftell should be used as arguments to fseek.)

In binary mode, fseek and ftell do use pure byte offsets. However, some systems may have to append a number of null bytes at the end of a binary file to pad it out to a full record.

See also questions 12.37 and 19.12.

References: ANSI §4.9.2
ISO §7.9.2
Rationale §4.9.2
H&S §15 p. 344, §15.2.1 p. 348

12.41

Question: How can I read/write structures from/to data files?

Answer: See question 2.11.

---

*Some systems may represent lines in text files as space-padded records. On these systems, trailing spaces are necessarily trimmed when lines are read in text mode, so any trailing spaces that were explicitly written are lost.

12.42

Question: How can I write code to conform to these old, binary data file formats?

Answer: It's difficult, because of word size and byte-order differences, floating-point formats, and structure padding. To get the control you need over these particulars, you may have to read and write things a byte at a time, shuffling and rearranging as you go. (This isn't always as bad as it sounds and gives you both code portability and complete control.)

For example, suppose that you want to read a data structure, consisting of a character, a 32-bit integer, and a 16-bit integer, from the stream fp into the C structure

```
struct mystruct {
        char c;
        long int i32;
        int i16;
};
```

You might use code like this:

```
s.c = getc(fp);

s.i32 = (long)getc(fp) << 24;
s.i32 |= (long)getc(fp) << 16;
s.i32 |= (unsigned)(getc(fp) << 8);
s.i32 |= getc(fp);

s.i16 = getc(fp) << 8;
s.i16 |= getc(fp);
```

This code assumes that getc reads 8-bit characters and that the data is stored most significant byte first ("big endian"). The casts to (long) ensure that the 16- and 24-bit shifts operate on long values (see question 3.14), and the cast to (unsigned) guards against sign extension. (In general, it's safer to use all unsigned types when writing code like this, but see question 3.19.)

The corresponding code to write the structure might look like:

```
putc(s.c, fp);

putc((unsigned)((s.i32 >> 24) & 0xff), fp);
putc((unsigned)((s.i32 >> 16) & 0xff), fp);
putc((unsigned)((s.i32 >> 8) & 0xff), fp);
putc((unsigned)(s.i32 & 0xff), fp);

putc((s.i16 >> 8) & 0xff, fp);
putc(s.i16 & 0xff, fp);
```

See also questions 2.12, 12.38, 16.7, and 20.5.

13 Library Functions

Once upon a time, a specific run-time library was not a formal part of the C language. With the advent of ANSI/ISO Standard C, much of the traditional run-time library (including the stdio functions of Chapter 12) also became standard.

Some particularly important library functions have their own chapters; see Chapter 7 for information on functions dealing with memory allocation (`malloc`, `free`, etc.) and Chapter 12 for information on the "standard I/O" functions described in `<stdio.h>`. This chapter is divided as follows:

String Functions	13.1–13.7
Sorting	13.8–13.11
Date and Time	13.12–13.14
Random Numbers	13.15–13.21
Other Library Functions	13.22–13.28

The last few questions (13.25 through 13.28) concern problems (e.g., "undefined external" errors) that crop up during linking.

String Functions

13.1

Question: How can I convert numbers to strings (the opposite of `atoi`)? Is there an `itoa` function?

Answer: Just use `sprintf`:

```
sprintf(string, "%d", number);
```

(Don't worry that `sprintf` may be overkill, potentially wasting run time or code space; it works well in practice.) See also the examples in the answer to question 7.5 and also question 12.21.

You can obviously use `sprintf` to convert `long` or floating-point numbers to strings as well (using `%ld` or `%f`); in other words, `sprintf` can also be thought of as the opposite of `atol` and `atof`. In addition, you have quite a bit of control over the formatting. (It's for these reasons that C supplies `sprintf` as a general solution, and not `itoa`.)

If you simply must write an `itoa` function, here are some things to consider:

- K&R provides a sample implementation.
- You'll have to worry about return buffer allocation; see question 7.5.
- A naïve implementation usually doesn't handle the most negative integer (INT_MIN, usually −32,768 or −2,147,483,648) properly.

See also questions 12.21 and 20.10.

References: K&R1 §3.6 p. 60
K&R2 §3.6 p. 64

13.2

Question: Why does `strncpy` not always place a `'\0'` terminator in the destination string?

Answer: Since it was first designed to handle a now obsolete data structure, the fixed-length, not necessarily \0-terminated "string,"* strncpy is admittedly a bit cumbersome to use in other contexts; you must often append a '\0' to the destination string by hand. You can get around the problem by using strncat instead of strncpy. If the destination string starts out empty, strncat does what you probably wanted strncpy to do:

```
*dest = '\0';
strncat(dest, source, n);
```

This code copies up to n characters and always appends a \0.

Another possibility is

```
sprintf(dest, "%.*s", n, source)
```

Strictly speaking, however, this is guaranteed to work only for n ≤ 509.

When arbitrary bytes (as opposed to strings) are being copied, memcpy is usually a more appropriate function to use than strncpy.

13.3

Question: Does C have anything like the "substr" (extract substring) routine present in other languages?

Answer: Not as such. (One reason it doesn't is that, as mentioned in question 7.2 and Chapter 8, C has no managed string type.)

To extract a substring of length LEN starting at index POS in a source string, use something like

```
char dest[LEN+1];
strncpy(dest, &source[POS], LEN);
dest[LEN] = '\0';                /* ensure \0 termination */
```

Alternatively, use a variation on the trick from question 13.2:

```
char dest[LEN+1] = "";
strncat(dest, &source[POS], LEN);
```

---

*For example, early C compilers and linkers used 8-character fixed-length strings in their symbol tables, and many versions of UNIX still use 14-character file names. A related quirk of strncpy's is that it pads short strings with multiple \0's, out to the specified length; this can allow more efficient string comparisons, since they can blindly compare n bytes without also looking for '\0'.

You can also use pointer instead of array notation:

```
strncat(dest, source + POS, LEN);
```

(The expression source + POS is, by definition, identical to &source[POS]; see also Chapter 6.)

13.4

Question: How do I convert a string to all uppercase or all lowercase?

Answer: Some libraries have functions strupr and strlwr or strupper and strlower, but these are not standard or portable. It's a straightforward exercise to write upper-/lowercase functions in terms of the toupper and tolower macros in <ctype.h>; see also question 13.5. (The only tricky part is that the function will either have to modify the string in place or deal with the problem of returning a new string; see question 7.5.)

(Note also that converting characters and strings to upper- or lowercase is vastly more complicated when multinational character sets are being used.)

References: K&R1 §2.7 p. 40
           K&R2 §2.7 p. 43
           PCS §11 p. 178

13.5

Question: Why do some versions of **toupper** act strangely if given an uppercase letter? Why does some code call **islower** before **toupper**?

Answer: In earlier times, toupper was a function-like preprocessor macro and was defined to work only on lowercase letters; it misbehaved if applied to digits, punctuation, or letters that were already uppercase. Similarly, tolower worked only on uppercase letters. Therefore, old code (or code written for wide portability) tends to call islower before toupper and isupper before tolower.

The C standard, however, says that `toupper` and `tolower` must work correctly on all characters, i.e., characters that don't need changing are left alone.

References: ANSI §4.3.2
ISO §7.3.2
H&S §12.9 pp. 320–1
PCS §11 p. 182

13.6

Question: How can I split up a string into whitespace-separated fields? How can I duplicate the process by which `main()` is handed `argc` and `argv`?

Answer: The only standard function available for this kind of "tokenizing" is `strtok`, although it can be tricky to use* and may not do everything you want it to. (For instance, it does not handle quoting.) Here is a usage example that simply prints each field as it's extracted:

```
#include <string.h>
char string[] = "this is a test"; /* not char *; see Q16.6 */
char *p;
for(p = strtok(string, " \t\n"); p != NULL;
                p = strtok(NULL, " \t\n"))
        printf("\"%s\"\n", p);
```

As an alternative, here is a function I use for building an `argv` all at once:

```
#include <ctype.h>

int makeargv(char *string, char *argv[], int argvsize)
{
        char *p = string;
        int i;
        int argc = 0;

        for(i = 0; i < argvsize; i++) {
                /* skip leading whitespace */
                while(isspace(*p))
                        p++;
```

---

*Also, `strtok` relies on some internal state during a series of calls and is therefore not reentrant.

```
                if(*p != '\0')
                        argv[argc++] = p;
                else {
                        argv[argc] = 0;
                        break;
                }

                /* scan over arg */
                while(*p != '\0' && !isspace(*p))
                        p++;
                /* terminate arg: */
                if(*p != '\0' && i < argvsize-1)
                        *p++ = '\0';
        }

        return argc;
}
```

Calling makeargv is straightforward:

```
char *av[10];
int i, ac = makeargv(string, av, 10);
for(i = 0; i < ac; i++)
        printf("\"%s\"\n", av[i]);
```

If you want each separator character to be significant—for instance, if you want two tabs in a row to indicate an omitted field—it's probably more straightforward to use strchr:

```
#include <string.h>

char *p = string;

while(1) {            /* break in middle */
        char *p2 = strchr(p, '\t');
        if(p2 != NULL)
                *p2 = '\0';
        printf("\"%s\"\n", p);
        if(p2 == NULL)
                break;
        p = p2 + 1;
}
```

All the code fragments presented here modify the input string by inserting \0's to terminate each field. If you'll need the original string later, make a copy before breaking it up.

References: K&R2 §B3 p. 250
ANSI §4.11.5.8
ISO §7.11.5.8
H&S §13.7 pp. 333–4
PCS §11 p. 178

13.7

Question: **Where can I get some code to do regular expression and wildcard matching?**

Answer: Make sure that you recognize the difference between:

- Classic regular expressions, variants of which are used in such UNIX utilities as ed and grep. In regular expressions, a dot (.) usually matches any single character, and the sequence .* usually matches any string of characters. (Of course, full-blown regular expressions have several more features as well.)

- Filename wildcards, variants of which are used by most operating systems. There is considerably more variation here, but it is often the case that ? matches any single character and that * matches any string of characters.

A number of packages are available for matching regular expressions. Most packages use a pair of functions: one for "compiling" the regular expression and one for "executing" it (i.e., matching strings against it). Look for header files named <regex.h> or <regexp.h> and functions called regcmp/regex, regcomp/regexec, or re_comp/re_exec. (These functions may exist in a separate regexp library.) A popular, freely redistributable regexp package by Henry Spencer is available from ftp.cs.toronto.edu in pub/regexp.shar.Z or in several other archives. The GNU project has a package called rx. See also question 18.16.

Filename wildcard matching (sometimes called "globbing") is done in a variety of ways on different systems. On UNIX, the shell automatically expands wildcards before a process is invoked, so programs rarely have to worry about them explicitly. Under MS-DOS compilers, there is often a special object file that can be linked in to a program to expand wildcards while argv is being built. Several systems (including MS-DOS and VMS) provide system services for listing or opening files specified by wildcards. Check your compiler/library documentation.

Here is a quick little wildcard matcher by Arjan Kenter:

```
int match(char *pat, char *str)
{
        switch(*pat) {
        case '\0':  return !*str;
        case '*':   return match(pat+1, str) ||
                            *str && match(pat, str+1);
        case '?':   return *str && match(pat+1, str+1);
        default:    return *pat == *str &&
                            match(pat+1,str+1);
        }
}
```

With this definition, the call match("a*b.c", "aplomb.c") would return 1.

Reference: Schumacher, ed., *Software Solutions in C* §3 pp. 35–71

Sorting

13.8

Question: I'm trying to sort an array of strings with qsort, using strcmp as the comparison function, but it's not working. Why not?

Answer: By "array of strings," you probably mean "array of pointers to char." The arguments to qsort's comparison function are pointers to the objects being sorted—in this case, pointers to pointers to char. Because strcmp accepts simple pointers to char, however, it can't be used directly. Write an intermediate comparison function like this:

```
/* compare strings via pointers */
int pstrcmp(const void *p1, const void *p2)
{
        return strcmp(*(char * const *)p1, *(char * const *)p2);
}
```

The comparison function's arguments are expressed as "generic pointers," `const void *`. They are converted back to what they "really are" (`char **`) and dereferenced, yielding `char *`'s, which can be passed to `strcmp`. (Under a pre-ANSI compiler, declare the pointer parameters as `char *` instead of `void *` and drop the `const`s.)

The call to `qsort` might look like this:

```
#include <stdlib.h>
char *strings[NSTRINGS];
int nstrings;
/* nstrings cells of strings[] are to be sorted */
qsort(strings, nstrings, sizeof(char *), pstrcmp);
```

(Don't be misled by the discussion in K&R2 §5.11 pp. 119–20, which is not discussing the standard library's `qsort` and makes a quiet, unnecessary assumption about the equivalence of `char *` and `void *`.)

For more information on `qsort` comparison functions—how they are called and how they must be declared—see question 13.9.

References: ANSI §4.10.5.2
      ISO §7.10.5.2
      H&S §20.5 p. 419

13.9

Question: Now I'm trying to sort an array of structures with `qsort`. My comparison function takes pointers to structures, but the compiler complains that the function is of the wrong type for `qsort`. How can I cast the function pointer to shut off the warning?

Answer: The conversions must be in the comparison function, which must be declared as accepting "generic pointers" (`const void *`) as discussed in question 13.8. Suppose that you have this hypothetical little date structure:

```
struct mystruct {
        int year, month, day;
};
```

The comparison function might look like* this:

```
int mystructcmp(const void *p1, const void *p2)
{
        const struct mystruct *sp1 = p1;
        const struct mystruct *sp2 = p2;
        if(sp1->year < sp2->year) return -1;
        else if(sp1->year > sp2->year) return 1;
        else if(sp1->month < sp2->month) return -1;
        else if(sp1->month > sp2->month) return 1;
        else if(sp1->day < sp2->day) return -1;
        else if(sp1->day > sp2->day) return 1;
        else return 0;
}
```

(The conversions from generic pointers to struct mystruct pointers happen in the initializations sp1 = p1 and sp2 = p2; the compiler performs the conversions implicitly, since p1 and p2 are void pointers. Explicit casts and char * pointers would be required under a pre-ANSI compiler. See also question 7.7.)

For this version of mystructcmp, the call to qsort might look like this:

```
#include <stdlib.h>
struct mystruct dates[NDATES];
int ndates;
/* ndates cells of dates[] are to be sorted */
qsort(dates, ndates, sizeof(struct mystruct), mystructcmp);
```

If, on the other hand, you're sorting pointers to structures, you'll need indirection, as in question 13.8. The comparison function would begin with

```
int myptrstructcmp(const void *p1, const void *p2)
{
    struct mystruct *sp1 = *(struct mystruct * const *)p1;
    struct mystruct *sp2 = *(struct mystruct * const *)p2;
```

---

*This version of mystructcmp uses explicit comparisons rather than the more obvious subtractions to decide whether to return a negative, zero, or positive value. In general, it's safer to write comparison functions this way: Subtraction can easily overflow (and cause either an abort or a quiet wrong answer) when a very large positive number is compared with a very large negative number. (In this example, of course, overflow would be unlikely in any case.)

and the call would look like this:

```
struct mystruct *dateptrs[NDATES];
qsort(dateptrs, ndates, sizeof(struct mystruct *),
                                    myptrstructcmp);
```

To understand why the curious pointer conversions in a qsort comparison function are necessary (and why a cast of the function pointer when calling qsort can't help), it's useful to think about how qsort works: It doesn't know anything about the type or representation of the data being sorted; it just shuffles around little chunks of memory. (All it knows about the chunks is their size, which you specify in qsort's third argument.) To determine whether two chunks need swapping, qsort calls your comparison function. (To swap them, it uses the equivalent of memcpy.)

Since qsort deals in a generic way with chunks of memory of unknown type, it uses generic pointers (void *) to refer to them. When qsort calls your comparison function, it passes as arguments two generic pointers to the chunks to be compared. Since it passes generic pointers, your comparison function must *accept* generic pointers, and it must convert the pointers back to their appropriate type before manipulating them (i.e., before performing the comparison). A void pointer is not the same type as a structure pointer; on some machines, it may have a different size or representation (which is why these casts are required for correctness).

Suppose that you were sorting an array of structures and had a comparison function accepting structure pointers:

```
int mywrongstructcmp(struct mystruct *, struct mystruct *);
```

If you called qsort as

```
qsort(dates, ndates, sizeof(struct mystruct),
     (int (*)(const void *, const void *))mywrongstructcmp);
                            /* WRONG */
```

the cast (int (*)(const void *, const void *)) would do nothing except, perhaps, silence the message from the compiler telling you that this comparison function may *not* work with qsort. The implications of any cast you use when calling qsort will have been forgotten by the time qsort gets around to calling your comparison function: It will call them with const void * arguments, so that is what your function must accept. No prototype mechanism exists that could operate down inside qsort to convert the void pointers to struct mystruct pointers just before calling mywrongstructcmp.

In general, it is a bad idea to insert casts just to "shut the compiler up." Compiler warnings are usually trying to tell you something, and unless you really know what you're doing, you ignore or muzzle them at your peril. See also question 4.9.

References: ANSI §4.10.5.2
ISO §7.10.5.2
H&S §20.5 p. 419

13.10

Question: How can I sort a linked list?

Answer: Sometimes, it's easier to keep the list in order as you build it (or perhaps to use a tree instead). Algorithms such as insertion sort and merge sort lend themselves ideally to use with linked lists. If you want to use a standard library function, you can allocate a temporary array of pointers, fill it in with pointers to all your list nodes, call qsort, and finally rebuild the list pointers based on the sorted array.

References: Knuth Vol. 3 §5.2.1 pp. 80–102, §5.2.4 pp. 159–68
Sedgewick §8 pp. 98–100, §12 pp. 163–75

13.11

Question: How can I sort more data than will fit in memory?

Answer: You want an "external sort," which you can read about in Knuth, Volume 3. The basic idea is to sort the data in chunks (as much as will fit in memory at one time), write each sorted chunk to a temporary file, and then merge the files. If your operating system provides a general-purpose sort utility, you can try invoking it from within your program; see questions 19.27 and 19.30 and the example in question 19.28.

References: Knuth Vol. 3 §5.4 pp. 247–378
Sedgewick §13 pp. 177–87

Date and Time

13.12

Question: **How can I get the current date or time of day in a C program?**

Answer: Just use the time, ctime, and/or localtime functions. (These functions have been around for years and are in the ANSI standard.) Here is a simple example:*

```
#include <stdio.h>
#include <time.h>

main()
{
        time_t now;
        time(&now);
        printf("It's %.24s.\n", ctime(&now));
        return 0;
}
```

Calls to localtime and strftime look like this:

```
struct tm *tmp = localtime(&now);
char fmtbuf[30];
printf("It's %d:%02d:%02d\n",
        tmp->tm_hour, tmp->tm_min, tmp->tm_sec);
strftime(fmtbuf, sizeof fmtbuf, "%A, %B %d, %Y", tmp);
printf("on %s\n", fmtbuf);
```

(Note that these functions take a *pointer* to the time_t variable, even when they will not be modifying it.†)

References: K&R2 §B10 pp. 255–7
ANSI §4.12
ISO §7.12
H&S §18.2 p. 399, §18.3 p. 400, §18.4 p. 401, §18.6 p. 403–4

---

*Note, though, that according to ANSI, time can fail, returning (time_t)(-1).

†These pointers are basically a holdover from the earliest days of C, before type long was invented; back then, an array of two ints was used to hold time values.

13.13

Question: I know that the library function `localtime` will convert a `time_t` into a broken-down `struct tm` and that `ctime` will convert a `time_t` to a printable string. How can I perform the inverse operations of converting a `struct tm` or a string into a `time_t`?

Answer: ANSI C specifies a library function, `mktime`, that converts a `struct tm` to a `time_t`.

Converting a string to a `time_t` is more difficult, because of the wide variety of date and time formats that might be encountered. Some systems provide a `strptime` function, which is basically the inverse of `strftime`. Other popular functions are `partime` (widely distributed with the RCS package) and `getdate` (and a few others, from the C news distribution). See question 18.16.

References: K&R2 §B10 p. 256
 ANSI §4.12.2.3
 ISO §7.12.2.3
 H&S §18.4 pp. 401–2

13.14

Question: How can I add *n* days to a date? How can I find the difference between two dates?

Answer: The ANSI/ISO Standard C `mktime` and `difftime` functions provide some support for both problems. Nonnormalized dates are acceptable to `mktime`, so it is straightforward to take a filled-in `struct tm`, add or subtract from the `tm_mday` field, and call `mktime` to normalize the year, month, and day fields (and, incidentally, convert to a `time_t` value). The `difftime` function computes the difference, in seconds, between two `time_t` values; `mktime` can be used to compute `time_t` values for two dates to be subtracted.

These solutions are guaranteed to work correctly only for dates in the range that can be represented as `time_t`s. The `tm_mday` field is an `int`, so day offsets of more than 32,736 or so may cause overflow. Note also that at daylight saving time changeovers, local days are not 24 hours long, so be careful if you try to divide by 86,400 seconds/day.

Here is a code fragment to compute the date 90 days past October 24, 1994:

```
#include <stdio.h>
#include <time.h>

tm1.tm_mon = 10 - 1;
tm1.tm_mday = 24;
tm1.tm_year = 1994 - 1900;
tm1.tm_hour = tm1.tm_min = tm1.tm_sec = 0;
tm1.tm_isdst = -1;

tm1.tm_mday += 90;

if(mktime(&tm1) == -1)
        fprintf(stderr, "mktime failed\n");
else  printf("%d/%d/%d\n",
            tm1.tm_mon+1, tm1.tm_mday, tm1.tm_year+1900);
```

(Setting tm_isdst to −1 helps to guard against daylight saving time anomalies; setting tm_hour to 12 would, too.)

Here is a piece of code to compute the difference in days between February 28 and March 1 in the year 2000:

```
struct tm tm1, tm2;
time_t t1, t2;

tm1.tm_mon = 2 - 1;
tm1.tm_mday = 28;
tm1.tm_year = 2000 - 1900;
tm1.tm_hour = tm1.tm_min = tm1.tm_sec = 0;
tm1.tm_isdst = -1;

tm2.tm_mon = 3 - 1;
tm2.tm_mday = 1;
tm2.tm_year = 2000 - 1900;
tm2.tm_hour = tm2.tm_min = tm2.tm_sec = 0;
tm2.tm_isdst = -1;

t1 = mktime(&tm1);
t2 = mktime(&tm2);
```

```
if(t1 == -1 || t2 == -1)
        fprintf(stderr, "mktime failed\n");
else {
        long d = (difftime(t2, t1) + 86400L/2) / 86400L;
        printf("%ld\n", d);
}
```

(The addition of `86400L/2` rounds the difference to the nearest day; see also question 14.6.)

Another approach to both problems is to use "Julian day" numbers, or the number of days since January 1, 4013 BC.* It's convenient to declare a pair of Julian day conversion functions:

```
/* returns Julian for month, day, year */
long ToJul(int month, int day, int year);


/* returns month, day, year for jul */
void FromJul(long jul, int *monthp, int *dayp, int *yearp);
```

Then, adding n days to a date can be implemented as

```
int n = 90;
int month, day, year;
FromJul(ToJul(10, 24, 1994) + n, &month, &day, &year);
```

and the number of days between two dates is

```
ToJul(3, 1, 2000) - ToJul(2, 28, 2000)
```

Implementations of Julian day conversion functions can be found in the file JULCAL10.ZIP from the Simtel/Oakland archives (see question 18.16) and Burki's "Date Conversions" article.

See also questions 13.13, 20.31, and 20.32.

References: K&R2 §B10 p. 256
           ANSI §4.12.2.2, §4.12.2.3
           ISO §7.12.2.2, §7.12.2.3
           H&S §18.4, §18.5 pp. 401–2
           Burki, "Date Conversions"

---

*Specifically, since noon GMT on that date. Note that the Julian day number is different from the "Julian dates" sometimes used in data processing and that neither one has anything to do with dates in the Julian calendar.

Random Numbers

13.15

Question: How can I generate random numbers?

Answer: The standard C library has a random number generator: `rand`. The implementation on your system may not be perfect, but writing a better one isn't necessarily easy, either.

If you do find yourself needing to implement your own random number generator, there is plenty of literature out there; see the references. Also, any number of packages are available on the Internet; look for r250, RANLIB, and FSULTRA (see question 18.16).

Here is a portable C implementation of the "minimal standard" generator proposed by Park and Miller:

```
#define a 16807
#define m 2147483647
#define q (m / a)
#define r (m % a)

static long int seed = 1;

long int PMrand()
{
        long int hi = seed / q;
        long int lo = seed % q;
        long int test = a * lo - r * hi;
        if(test > 0)
                seed = test;
        else  seed = test + m;
        return seed;
}
```

(The "minimal standard" is adequately good; it is something "against which all others should be judged" and is recommended for use "unless one has access to a random number generator *known* to be better.")

This code implements the generator

$$X \leftarrow (aX + c) \bmod m$$

for $a = 16807$, $m = 2147483647$ (which is $2^{31}-1$), and $c = 0$. (Since the modulus is prime, this generator does not have the problem described in question 13.18.) The multiplication is carried out using a technique described by Schrage, ensuring that the intermediate result aX does not overflow. The preceding implementation returns `long int` values in the range [1,2147483646]; that is, it corresponds to C's `rand` with a `RAND_MAX` of 2147483646, *except* that it never returns 0. To alter it to return floating-point numbers in the range (0, 1) (as in the Park and Miller paper), change the declaration to

```
double PMrand()
```

and the last line to

```
return (double)seed / m;
```

For slightly better statistical properties, Park and Miller now recommend using $a = 48271$.

References: K&R2 §2.7 p. 46, §7.8.7 p. 168
ANSI §4.10.2.1
ISO §7.10.2.1
H&S §17.7 p. 393
PCS §11 p. 172
Knuth Vol. 2 Chap. 3 pp. 1–177
Park and Miller, "Random Number Generators: Good Ones Are Hard to Find"

13.16

Question: How can I get random integers in a certain range?

Answer: The obvious way:

```
rand() % N        /* POOR */
```

(which tries to return numbers from 0 to N-1) is poor, because the low-order bits of many random number generators are distressingly *non*random. (See question 13.18.) A better method is something like

```
(int)((double)rand() / ((double)RAND_MAX + 1) * N)
```

If you're worried about using floating point, you could use

```
rand() / (RAND_MAX / N + 1)
```

Both methods obviously require knowing RAND_MAX (which ANSI defines in <stdlib.h>) and assume that N is much less than RAND_MAX.

When N is close to RAND_MAX, and if the range of the random number generator is not a multiple of N (i.e., if (RAND_MAX+1) % N != 0), all of these methods break down: Some outputs occur more often than others. (Using floating point does *not* help; the problem is that rand returns RAND_MAX+1 distinct values, which cannot always be evenly divvied up into N buckets.) If this is a problem, about the only thing you can do is to call rand multiple times, discarding certain values:

```
unsigned int x = (RAND_MAX + 1u) / N;
unsigned int y = x * N;
unsigned int r;
do {
    r = rand();
} while(r >= y);
return r / x;
```

For any of these techniques, it's straightforward to shift the range, if necessary; numbers in the range [M, N] could be generated with something like

```
M + rand() / (RAND_MAX / (N - M + 1) + 1)
```

(Note, by the way, that RAND_MAX is a *constant* telling you what the fixed range of the C library rand function is. You cannot set RAND_MAX to some other value, and there is no way of requesting that rand return numbers in some other range.)

If you're starting with a random number generator that returns floating-point values between 0 and 1 (such as the last version of PMrand alluded to in question 13.15 or drand48 in question 13.21), all you have to do to get integers from 0 to N-1 is multiply the output of that generator by N:

```
(int)(drand48() * N)
```

References: K&R2 §7.8.7 p. 168
          PCS §11 p. 172

13.17

Question: Each time I run my program, I get the same sequence of numbers back from **rand**. Why?

Answer: It's a characteristic of most pseudo-random number generators (and a defined property of the C library **rand**) that they always start with the same number and go through the same sequence. (Among other things, a bit of predictability can make debugging much easier.) When you don't want this predictability, you can call **srand** to seed the pseudo-random number generator with a truly random initial value. Popular seed values are the time of day or the elapsed time before the user presses a key (although keypress times are difficult to determine portably; see question 19.37). Here's an example, using the time of day as a seed:

```
#include <stdlib.h>
#include <time.h>

srand((unsigned int)time((time_t *)NULL));
```

(Note also that it's rarely useful to call **srand** more than once during a run of a program; in particular, don't try calling **srand** before each call to **rand**, in an attempt to get "really random" numbers.)

References: K&R2 §7.8.7 p. 168
            ANSI §4.10.2.2
            ISO §7.10.2.2
            H&S §17.7 p. 393

13.18

Question: I need a random true/false value, so I'm just taking **rand() % 2**, but it's alternating 0, 1, 0, 1, 0.... Why?

Answer: Poor pseudo-random number generators (such as the ones unfortunately supplied with some systems) are not very random in the low-order bits. (In fact, for a pure linear congruential random number generator with period 2^e, and this tends to be how random number generators for e-bit machines are written, the low-order n bits repeat with period 2^n.) For this reason, it's preferable to use the higher-order bits: see question 13.16.

Reference: Knuth §3.2.1.1 pp. 12–4

13.19

Question: **How can I return a sequence of random numbers that don't repeat at all?**

Answer: What you're looking for is often called a "random permutation" or "shuffle." One way is to initialize an array with the values to be shuffled, then randomly interchange each of the cells with another one later in the array:

```
int a[10], i, nvalues = 10;

for(i = 0; i < nvalues; i++)
        a[i] = i + 1;

for(i = 0; i < nvalues-1; i++) {
        int c = randrange(nvalues-i);
        int t = a[i]; a[i] = a[i+c]; a[i+c] = t;  /* swap */
}
```

Here, `randrange(N)` is `rand() / (RAND_MAX/(N) + 1)` or one of the other expressions from question 13.16.

Reference: Knuth §3.4.2 pp. 137–8

13.20

Question: **How can I generate random numbers with a normal, or Gaussian, distribution?**

Answer: You can do this in at least three ways:

1. Exploit the Central Limit Theorem ("law of large numbers") and add up several uniformly distributed random numbers:

```
#include <stdlib.h>
#include <math.h>

#define NSUM 25

double gaussrand()
{
        double x = 0;
        int i;
        for(i = 0; i < NSUM; i++)
                x += (double)rand() / RAND_MAX;

        x -= NSUM / 2.0;
        x /= sqrt(NSUM / 12.0);

        return x;
}
```

(Don't overlook the sqrt(NSUM / 12.) correction, although it's easy to do so accidentally, especially when NSUM is 12.)

2. Use a method described by Abramowitz and Stegun:

```
#include <stdlib.h>
#include <math.h>

#define PI 3.141592654

double gaussrand()
{
        static double U, V;
        static int phase = 0;
        double Z;

        if(phase == 0) {
                U = (rand() + 1.) / (RAND_MAX + 2.);
                V = rand() / (RAND_MAX + 1.);
                Z = sqrt(-2 * log(U)) * sin(2 * PI * V);
        } else
                Z = sqrt(-2 * log(U)) * cos(2 * PI * V);

        phase = 1 - phase;

        return Z;
}
```

3. Use a method described by Box and Muller and discussed in Knuth:

```c
#include <stdlib.h>
#include <math.h>

double gaussrand()
{
        static double V1, V2, S;
        static int phase = 0;
        double X;

        if(phase == 0) {
                do {
                        double U1 = (double)rand() / RAND_MAX;
                        double U2 = (double)rand() / RAND_MAX;

                        V1 = 2 * U1 - 1;
                        V2 = 2 * U2 - 1;
                        S = V1 * V1 + V2 * V2;
                        } while(S >= 1 || S == 0);

                X = V1 * sqrt(-2 * log(S) / S);
        } else
                X = V2 * sqrt(-2 * log(S) / S);

        phase = 1 - phase;

        return X;
}
```

These methods all generate numbers with mean 0 and standard deviation 1. (To adjust to another distribution, multiply by the standard deviation and add the mean.) Method 1 is poor "in the tails" (especially if NSUM is small), but methods 2 and 3 perform quite well. See the references for more information.

References: Knuth Vol. 2 §3.4.1 p. 117
        Box and Muller, "A Note on the Generation of Random Normal Deviates"
        Marsaglia and Bray, "A Convenient Method for Generating Normal Variables"
        Abramowitz and Stegun, *Handbook of Mathematical Functions*
        Press *et al.*, *Numerical Recipes in C* §7.2 pp. 288–90

13.21

Question: I'm porting a program, and it calls a function **drand48**, which my library doesn't have. What is it?

Answer: The UNIX System V function drand48 returns floating-point random numbers (presumably with 48 bits of precision) in the half-open interval [0, 1). (Its companion seed function is srand48; neither is in the C standard.) It's easy to write a low-precision replacement:

```
#include <stdlib.h>

double drand48()
{
        return rand() / (RAND_MAX + 1.);
}
```

To more accurately simulate drand48's semantics, you can try to give it closer to 48 bits worth of precision:

```
#define PRECISION 2.82e14     /* 2**48, rounded up */

double drand48()
{
        double x = 0;
        double denom = RAND_MAX + 1.;
        double need;

        for(need = PRECISION; need > 1;
                    need /= (RAND_MAX + 1.)) {
            x += rand() / denom;
            denom *= RAND_MAX + 1.;
        }

        return x;
}
```

Before using code like this, though, beware that it is numerically suspect, particularly if (as is usually the case) the period of rand is on the order of RAND_MAX. (If you have a longer-period random number generator available, such as BSD random, definitely use it when simulating drand48.)

Reference: PCS §11 p. 149

Other Library Functions

13.22

Question: Is exit(status) truly equivalent to returning the same status from main?

Answer: See question 11.16.

13.23

Question: What's the difference between memcpy and memmove?

Answer: See question 11.25.

13.24

Question: I'm trying to port this old program. Why do I get "undefined external" errors for:

index?

rindex?

bcopy?

bcmp?

bzero?

Answer: Those functions are variously obsolete; you should instead use:

strchr.

strrchr.

memmove, after interchanging the first and second arguments (see also question 11.25).

memcmp.

memset, with a second argument of 0.

If, on the other hand, you're using an older system that is missing the functions in the second column, you may be able to implement them in terms of, or substitute, the functions in the first. See also questions 12.22 and 13.21.

Reference: PCS §11

13.25

Question: I keep getting errors due to library functions being undefined, even though I'm including all the right header files.

Answer: In general, a header file gives you only the declarations of library functions, not the library functions themselves. Header files happen at compile time; libraries happen at link time.

In some cases (especially if the functions are nonstandard), you may have to explicitly ask for the correct libraries to be searched when you link the program. (Some systems may be able to arrange that whenever you include a header, its associated library, if nonstandard, is automatically requested at link time, but such a facility is not widespread.) See also questions 11.30, 13.26, and 14.3.

13.26

Question: I'm still getting errors due to library functions being undefined, even though I'm explicitly requesting the right libraries while linking.

Answer: Many linkers make one pass over the list of object files and libraries you specify and extract from libraries only those modules that satisfy references that have so far come up as undefined. Therefore, the order in which libraries are listed with respect to object files (and one another) is significant; usually, you want to search the libraries last.

For example, under UNIX, a command line such as

```
cc -lm myprog.c          # WRONG
```

usually won't work. Instead, put any -l options at the end of the command line:

```
cc myprog.c -lm
```

If you list a library first, the linker doesn't know that it needs anything out of it yet and passes it by. See also question 13.28.

13.27

Question: Why is my simple program, which hardly does more than print "Hello, world!" in a window, compiling to such a huge executable (several hundred K)? Should I include fewer header files?

Answer: What you're seeing is the current (poor) state of the "art" in library design. Run-time libraries tend to accumulate more and more features (especially having to do with graphical user interfaces). When one library function calls another library function to do part of its job (which ought to be a Good Thing; that's what library functions are for), it can happen that calling anything in the library (particularly something relatively powerful such as `printf`) eventually pulls in practically everything else, leading to horribly bloated executables.

Including fewer header files probably won't help, because declaring a few functions that you don't call (which is mostly all that happens when you include a header you don't need) shouldn't result in those functions being placed in your executable, unless they do in fact get called. See also question 13.25.

You may be able to track down and derail a chain of unnecessarily coupled functions that are bloating your executable or perhaps complain to your vendor to clean up the libraries.

References: H&S §4.8.6 pp. 103–4

13.28

Question: What does it mean when the linker says that _end is undefined?

Answer: That message is a quirk of the old UNIX linkers. You get an error about _end being undefined only when other things are undefined, too. Fix the others, and the error about _end will disappear. (See also questions 13.25 and 13.26.)

14 Floating Point

Floating-point calculations often seem somewhat troubling and mysterious, and the problems are a bit worse in C because it has not traditionally been targeted at programs that use floating point extensively.

14.1

Question: When I set a `float` variable to, say, 3.1, why is `printf` printing it as 3.0999999?

Answer: Most computers use base 2 for floating-point numbers as well as for integers, and just as for base 10, not all fractions are representable exactly in base 2. It's well-known that in base 10, a fraction like 1/3 = 0.333333 ... repeats infinitely. It turns out that in base 2, 1/1010 (that is, 1/10 decimal) is also an infinitely repeating fraction: its binary representation is 0.0001100110011.... Depending on how carefully your compiler's binary/decimal conversion routines (such as those used by `printf`) have been written, you may see discrepancies when numbers (especially low-precision `floats`) not exactly representable in base 2 are assigned or read in and then printed (i.e., are converted from base 10 to base 2 and back again).* See also questions 14.4 and 14.6.

---

*Converting binary floating-point numbers to and from base 10 without discrepancies is an interesting problem; two excellent papers on the subject by Clinger, Steele, and White are mentioned in the bibliography.

14.2

Question: I'm trying to take some square roots, and I've simplified the code down to

```
main()
{
        printf("%f\n", sqrt(144.));
}
```

but I'm still getting crazy numbers. Why?

Answer: Make sure that you have included `<math.h>` and correctly declared other functions returning `double`. (Another library function to be careful with is `atof`, which is declared in `<stdlib.h>`.) See also questions 1.25, 14.3, and 14.4.

Reference: CT&P §4.5 pp. 65–6

14.3

Question: I'm trying to do some simple trig, and I am including `<math.h>`, but the linker keeps complaining that functions such as `sin` and `cos` are undefined. Why?

Answer: Make sure that you're actually linking with the math library. For instance, under UNIX, you usually need to use the `-lm` option, at the *end* of the command line, when compiling/linking. See also questions 13.25 and 13.26.

14.4

Question: My floating-point calculations are acting strangely and giving me different answers on different machines. Why?

Answer: First, see question 14.2.
   If the problem isn't that simple, recall that digital computers usually use floating-point formats that provide a close, but by no means exact, simulation of real number arithmetic. Among other things, the associative and distributive

laws do not hold completely; that is, order of operation may be important, and repeated addition is not necessarily equivalent to multiplication. Underflow, cumulative precision loss, and other anomalies are often troublesome.

Don't assume that floating-point results will be exact, and especially don't assume that floating-point values can be compared for equality. (Don't throw haphazard "fuzz factors" in, either; see question 14.5.) Beware that some machines have more precision available in floating-point computation registers than in `double` values stored in memory, which can lead to floating-point inequalities when it would seem that two values just *have* to be equal.

These problems are no worse for C than for any other computer language. Certain aspects of floating point are usually defined as "however the processor does them" (see also questions 11.33 and 11.34); otherwise, a compiler for a machine without the "right" model would have to do prohibitively expensive emulations.

This book cannot begin to list the pitfalls associated with, and workarounds appropriate for, floating-point work. A good numerical programming text should cover the basics; see also the references. (Beware, though, that subtle problems can occupy numerical analysts for years.)

References: Kernighan and Plauger, *The Elements of Programming Style* §6 pp. 115–8
             Knuth, Volume 2 chapter 4
             Goldberg, "What Every Computer Scientist Should Know about Floating-Point Arithmetic"

14.5

Question: What's a good way to check for "close enough" floating-point equality?

Answer: Since the absolute accuracy of floating-point values varies, by definition, with their magnitude, the best way of comparing two floating-point values is to use an accuracy threshold that is relative to the magnitude of the numbers being compared. Rather than

```
double a, b;
...
if(a == b)     /* WRONG */
```

use something like

```
#include <math.h>

if(fabs(a - b) <= epsilon * a)
```

for a suitably chosen `epsilon`. The value of `epsilon` may still have to be chosen with care: Its appropriate value may be quite small and related only to the machine's floating-point precision, or it may be larger if the numbers being compared are inherently less accurate or are the result of a chain of calculations that compounds accuracy losses over several steps. (Also, you may have to make the threshold a function of b or of both a and b.)

A decidedly inferior approach, not generally recommended, would be to use an absolute threshold:

```
if(fabs(a - b) < 0.001)              /* POOR */
```

Absolute "fuzz factors," such as 0.001, never seem to work for very long, however. As the numbers being compared change, it's likely that two small numbers that should be taken as different happen to be within 0.001 of each other or that two large numbers, which should have been treated as equal, differ by more than 0.001 . (And, of course, the problems merely shift around and do not go away when the fuzz factor is tweaked to 0.005 or 0.0001 or any other absolute number.)

Doug Gwyn suggests using the following "relative difference" function. It returns the relative difference of two real numbers: 0.0 if they are exactly the same; otherwise, the ratio of the difference to the larger of the two:

```
#define Abs(x)      ((x) < 0 ? -(x) : (x))
#define Max(a, b) ((a) > (b) ? (a) : (b))

double RelDif(double a, double b)
{
        double c = Abs(a);
        double d = Abs(b);

        d = Max(c, d);

        return d == 0.0 ? 0.0 : Abs(a - b) / d;
}
```

Typical usage is

```
if(RelDif(a, b) <= TOLERANCE) ...
```

Reference: Knuth Volume 2 §4.2.2 pp. 217–8

14.6

Question: How do I round numbers?

Answer: The simplest and most straightforward way is with code such as

```
(int)(x + 0.5)
```

C's floating-to-integer conversion truncates (discards) the fractional part, so adding 0.5 before truncating arranges that fractions ≥ 0.5 will be rounded up. (This technique won't work properly for negative numbers, though.)

You can round to a certain precision by scaling:

```
(int)(x / precision + 0.5) * precision
```

Handling negative numbers or implementing even/odd rounding is slightly trickier.

Note that because truncation is otherwise the default, it's usually a good idea to use an explicit rounding step when converting floating-point numbers to integers. Unless you're careful, it's quite possible for a number you thought was 8.0 to be represented internally as 7.999999 and to be truncated to 7.

14.7

Question: Why doesn't C have an exponentiation operator?

Answer: One reason is probably that few processors have a built-in exponentiation instruction. C has a pow function (declared in <math.h>) for performing exponentiation, although explicit multiplication is often better for small positive integral exponents.* In other words, pow(x, 2.) is probably inferior to x * x. (If you're tempted to make a Square() macro, though, check question 10.1 first.)

References: ANSI §4.5.5.1
            ISO §7.5.5.1
            H&S §17.6 p. 393

---

*In particular, not all implementations of pow yield the expected results when both arguments are integral. For example, on some systems, (int)pow(2., 3.) gives 7 due to truncation; see also question 14.6.

14.8

Question: The predefined constant `M_PI` seems to be missing from my machine's copy of `<math.h>`. Shouldn't it be there?

Answer: That constant (which is apparently supposed to be the value of π, accurate to the machine's precision) is not standard; in fact a standard-conforming copy of `<math.h>` should *not* define a symbol `M_PI`.* If you need π, you'll have to define it yourself. (You could use a construction like

```
#ifndef M_PI
#define M_PI 3.1415926535897932385
#endif
```

to provide your own definition only if a system header file has not.)

Reference: PCS §13 p. 237

14.9

Question: How do I set variables to or test for IEEE NaN ("Not a Number") and other special values?

Answer: Many systems with high-quality IEEE floating-point implementations provide facilities (e.g. predefined constants and functions such as `isnan()`, either as nonstandard extensions in `<math.h>` or perhaps in `<ieee.h>` or `<nan.h>`) to deal with these values cleanly, and work is being done to formally standardize such facilities. A crude but usually effective test for NaN can be written based on the fact that an IEEE NaN never compares equal to anything, even another NaN; therefore, a number that doesn't compare equal to itself must be a NaN:

```
#define isnan(x) ((x) != (x))
```

Beware, though, that non-IEEE-aware compilers may optimize the test away. (Note also that even if you do have a predefined constant like `NAN`, you *cannot* use it in comparisons, such as `if(x == NAN)`, again because one NaN does not compare equal to another.)

---

*The concern here is one of "namespace pollution"; see also question 1.29.

Another possibility is to format the value in question by using `sprintf`: On many systems, it generates `"NaN"` and `"Inf"` strings, which you could compare for in a pinch.

To initialize variables with these values (and if your system does not provide cleaner solutions), you may be able to get away with some compile-time "arithmetic":

```
double nan = 0./0.;
double inf = 1./0.;
```

Don't be too surprised, though, if these don't work or if they abort the compiler with a floating-point exception.

(The most reliable way of setting up these special values would use a hex representation of their internal bit patterns, but initializing a floating-point value with a bit pattern would require using a union or some other type punning mechanism and would obviously be machine dependent.)

See also question 19.39.

14.10

Question: How can I handle floating-point exceptions gracefully?

Answer: See question 19.39.

14.11

Question: What's a good way to implement complex numbers in C?

Answer: It is straightforward to define a simple structure and some arithmetic functions to manipulate them.* Here is a tiny example, to give you a feel for it:

```
typedef struct {
        double real;
        double imag;
        } complex;
```

---

*Obviously, the manipulation would be even more straightforward in C++.

```
#define Real(c) (c).real
#define Imag(c) (c).imag

complex cpx_make(double real, double imag)
{
        complex ret;
        ret.real = real;
        ret.imag = imag;
        return ret;
}

complex cpx_add(complex a, complex b)
{
        return cpx_make(Real(a) + Real(b), Imag(a) + Imag(b));
}
```

You can use these functions with code like

```
complex a = cpx_make(1, 2);
complex b = cpx_make(3, 4);
complex c = cpx_add(a, b);
```

or, even more simply,

```
complex c = cpx_add(cpx_make(1, 2), cpx_make(3, 4));
```

See also questions 2.7, 2.10, and 14.12.

14.12

Question: Where can I find some code to do Fast Fourier Transforms (FFTs), matrix arithmetic (multiplication, inversion, etc.), and complex arithmetic?

Answer: Ajay Shah maintains an index of free numerical software; it is posted periodically and available where the on-line versions of this book are archived (see question 20.40). See also question 18.16.

14.13

Question: I'm having trouble with a Turbo C program that crashes and says something like "floating point formats not linked." What am I missing?

Answer: Some compilers for small machines, including Borland's (and Ritchie's original PDP–11 compiler), leave out certain floating-point support if it looks as though it will not be needed. In particular, the non-floating-point versions of `printf` and `scanf` save space by not including code to handle `%e`, `%f`, and `%g`. It happens that Borland's heuristics for determining whether the program uses floating point are insufficient, and the programmer must sometimes insert an extra, explicit call to a floating-point library function to force loading of floating-point support. (Any such required workarounds should be documented in the manuals; if not, complain! Borland tech note #645 supposedly addresses the problem.)

A partially related problem, resulting in a similar error message (perhaps "floating point not loaded") can apparently occur under some MS-DOS compilers when an incorrect variant of the floating-point library is linked. Check your compiler manual's description of the various floating-point libraries.

15 Variable-Length Argument Lists

C provides a mechanism, not widely understood, that allows a function to accept a variable number of arguments. Variable-length argument lists are relatively rare but are vital in the context of C's `printf` function and in related situations. (Variable-length argument lists are particularly troublesome because formal support for them arose only under the ANSI C Standard—prior to that standard, they were, strictly speaking, undefined.)

The terminology associated with variable-length argument lists can get a bit baroque. Formally, a variable-length argument list consists of two parts: a fixed part and a variable-length part. Thus, we find ourselves using bombastic expressions such as "the variable-length part of a variable-length argument list." (You will also see the terms "variadic" and "varargs" used: Both are adjectives meaning "having a variable number of arguments." Thus, we might speak of "a varargs function" or "a varargs argument.")

Manipulating a variable-length argument list involves three steps. First, a special "pointer" variable of type `va_list` is declared and initialized to point to the beginning of the argument list by calling `va_start`. Next, arguments are retrieved from the variable argument list by calling `va_arg`, which requires as parameters the `va_list` pointer and an indication of the type of the argument being retrieved. Finally, when processing is completed, `va_end` is called to perform any cleanup. (The `va_list` type is here referred to as a "pointer" in quotes because it is not necessarily a true pointer; `va_list` is a typedef that hides the details of the actual data structure used.)

Varargs functions may use special calling mechanisms, different from the ones used for conventional, fixed-argument functions. Therefore, a prototype must always be in scope before a varargs call (see question 15.1). However, a prototype obviously cannot specify the number and type(s) of the variable arguments. Therefore, the variable arguments receive the "default argument promotions" (see question 15.2), and no type checking can be performed (see question 15.3).

Calling Varargs Functions

15.1

Question: I heard that you have to include `<stdio.h>` before calling `printf`. Why?

Answer: So that a proper prototype for `printf` will be in scope.

A compiler may use a different calling sequence for functions that accept variable-length argument lists. (It might do so if calls using variable-length argument lists were less efficient than those using fixed length.) Therefore, a prototype (using the ellipsis notation " . . . " to indicate that the argument list is of variable length) must be in scope whenever a varargs function is called, so that the compiler knows to use the varargs calling mechanism.

References: ANSI §3.3.2.2, §4.1.6
         ISO §6.3.2.2, §7.1.7
         Rationale §3.3.2.2, §4.1.6
         H&S §9.2.4 pp. 268–9, §9.6 pp. 275–6

15.2

Question: How can %f be used for both float and double arguments in printf? Aren't they different types?

Answer: In the variable-length part of a variable-length argument list, the "default argument promotions" apply: Types char and short int are promoted to int, and float is promoted to double. (These are the same promotions that apply to function calls without a prototype in scope, also known as "old style" function calls; see question 11.3.) Therefore, printf's %f format always sees a double. (Similarly, %c always sees an int, as does %hd.) See also questions 12.9 and 12.13.

References: ANSI §3.3.2.2
ISO §6.3.2.2
H&S §6.3.5 p. 177, §9.4 pp. 272–3

15.3

Question: I had a frustrating problem that turned out to be caused by the line

```
printf("%d", n);
```

where n was actually a long int. Aren't ANSI function prototypes supposed to guard against argument type mismatches like this?

Answer: When a function accepts a variable number of arguments, its prototype does not (and cannot) provide any information about the number and types of those variable arguments. Therefore, the usual protections do *not* apply in the variable-length part of variable-length argument lists: The compiler cannot perform implicit conversions or (in general) warn about mismatches. The programmer must make sure that arguments match or must manually insert explicit casts.

In the case of printf-like functions, some compilers (including gcc) and some versions of lint are able to check the actual arguments against the format string, as long as the format string is an immediate string literal.

See also questions 5.2, 11.3, 12.9, and 15.2.

Implementing Varargs Functions

15.4

Question: How can I write a function that takes a variable number of arguments?

Answer: Use the facilities of the `<stdarg.h>` header.

Here is a function that concatenates an arbitrary number of strings into dynamically allocated memory:

```
#include <stdlib.h>          /* for malloc, NULL, size_t */
#include <stdarg.h>          /* for va_ stuff */
#include <string.h>          /* for strcat et al. */

char *vstrcat(char *first, ...)
{
        size_t len;
        char *retbuf;
        va_list argp;
        char *p;

        if(first == NULL)
               return NULL;

        len = strlen(first);

        va_start(argp, first);

        while((p = va_arg(argp, char *)) != NULL)
               len += strlen(p);

        va_end(argp);

        retbuf = malloc(len + 1);    /* +1 for trailing \0 */

        if(retbuf == NULL)
               return NULL;                 /* error */
```

```
        (void)strcpy(retbuf, first);

        va_start(argp, first);        /* restart for second scan */

        while((p = va_arg(argp, char *)) != NULL)
                (void)strcat(retbuf, p);

        va_end(argp);

        return retbuf;
}
```

(Note that a second call to `va_start` is needed to restart the scan when the argument list is processed a second time. Note the calls to `va_end`: They're important for portability, even if they don't seem to do anything.)

A call to `vstrcat` looks something like this:

```
char *str = vstrcat("Hello, ", "world!", (char *)NULL);
```

Note the cast on the last argument; see questions 5.2 and 15.3. (Also note that the caller is responsible for freeing the allocated memory.)

The preceding example was of a function that accepts a variable number of arguments, all of type `char *`. Here is an example that accepts a variable number of arguments of different types; it is a stripped-down version of the familiar `printf` function. Note that each invocation of `va_arg()` specifies the type of the argument being retrieved from the argument list.

(The `miniprintf` function here uses `baseconv` from question 20.10 to format numbers. It is significantly imperfect in that it will not usually be able to print the smallest integer, `INT_MIN`, properly.)

```
#include <stdio.h>
#include <stdarg.h>

extern char *baseconv(unsigned int, int);

void
miniprintf(char *fmt, ...)
{
        char *p;
        int i;
        unsigned u;
        char *s;
        va_list argp;
```

```
va_start(argp, fmt);

for(p = fmt; *p != '\0'; p++) {
        if(*p != '%') {
                putchar(*p);
                continue;
        }

        switch(*++p) {
        case 'c':
                i = va_arg(argp, int);
                /* not va_arg(argp, char); see Q 15.10 */
                putchar(i);
                break;

        case 'd':
                i = va_arg(argp, int);
                if(i < 0) {
                        /* XXX won't handle INT_MIN */
                        i = -i;
                        putchar('-');
                }
                fputs(baseconv(i, 10), stdout);
                break;

        case 'o':
                u = va_arg(argp, unsigned int);
                fputs(baseconv(u, 8), stdout);
                break;

        case 's':
                s = va_arg(argp, char *);
                fputs(s, stdout);
                break;

        case 'u':
                u = va_arg(argp, unsigned int);
                fputs(baseconv(u, 10), stdout);
                break;
```

```
        case 'x':
                u = va_arg(argp, unsigned int);
                fputs(baseconv(u, 16), stdout);
                break;

        case '%':
                putchar('%');
                break;
        }
    }

        va_end(argp);
    }
```

See also question 15.7.

References: K&R2 §7.3 p. 155, §B7 p. 254
            ANSI §4.8
            ISO §7.8
            Rationale §4.8
            H&S §11.4 pp. 296–9
            CT&P §A.3 pp. 139–41
            PCS §11 pp. 184–5, §13 p. 242

15.5

Question: How can I write a function that, like `printf`, takes a format string and a variable number of arguments, and passes them to `printf` to do most of the work?

Answer: Use `vprintf`, `vfprintf`, or `vsprintf`. These functions are like their counterparts `printf`, `fprintf`, and `sprintf`, except that instead of a variable-length argument list, they accept a single `va_list` pointer.

For example, here is an `error` function that prints an error message, preceded by the string "error: " and terminated with a newline:

```
#include <stdio.h>
#include <stdarg.h>

void error(char *fmt, ...)
{
        va_list argp;
        fprintf(stderr, "error: ");
        va_start(argp, fmt);
        vfprintf(stderr, fmt, argp);
        va_end(argp);
        fprintf(stderr, "\n");

}
```

See also question 15.7.

References: K&R2 §8.3 p. 174, §B1.2 p. 245   H&S §15.12 pp. 379–80
           ANSI §4.9.6.7, 4.9.6.8, 4.9.6.9   PCS §11 pp. 186–7
           ISO §7.9.6.7, §7.9.6.8, §7.9.6.9

15.6

Question: How can I write a function analogous to `scanf`, i.e., that accepts similar arguments, and calls `scanf` to do most of the work?

Answer: Unfortunately, `vscanf` and the like are not standard. You're on your own.

15.7

Question: I have a pre-ANSI compiler, without `<stdarg.h>`. What can I do?

Answer: An older header, `<varargs.h>`, offers about the same functionality. Here is the `vstrcat` function from question 15.4, rewritten to use `<varargs.h>`:

```
#include <stdio.h>
#include <varargs.h>
#include <string.h>

extern char *malloc();

char *vstrcat(va_alist)
va_dcl                              /* no semicolon */
{
        int len = 0;
        char *retbuf;
        va_list argp;
        char *p;

        va_start(argp);

        while((p = va_arg(argp, char *)) != NULL)
              len += strlen(p);

        va_end(argp);

        retbuf = malloc(len + 1);    /* +1 for trailing \0 */

        if(retbuf == NULL)
              return NULL;           /* error */

        retbuf[0] = '\0';

        va_start(argp);              /* restart for second scan */

        while((p = va_arg(argp, char *)) != NULL)
              strcat(retbuf, p);

        va_end(argp);

        return retbuf;
}
```

(Note that there is no semicolon after va_dcl, and that in this case, no special treatment for the first argument is necessary.) You may also have to declare the string functions by hand rather than using <string.h>.

If you can manage to find a system with vfprintf but without <stdarg.h>, the following is a version of the error function (from question 15.5) using <varargs.h>.

```
#include <stdio.h>
#include <varargs.h>

void error(va_alist)
va_dcl              /* no semicolon */
      {
      char *fmt;
      va_list argp;
      fprintf(stderr, "error: ");
      va_start(argp);
      fmt = va_arg(argp, char *);
      vfprintf(stderr, fmt, argp);
      va_end(argp);
      fprintf(stderr, "\n");
}
```

(Note that in contrast to <stdarg.h>, under <varargs.h> *all* arguments are variable, so the fmt argument must also be picked up via va_arg.)

References: H&S §11.4 pp. 296–9
          CT&P §A.2 pp. 134–9
          PCS §11 pp. 184–5, §13 p. 250

Extracting Variable-Length Arguments

15.8

Question: How can I discover how many arguments were used to call a function?

Answer: This information is not available to a portable program. Some old systems provided a nonstandard nargs function, but its use was always questionable, since it typically returned the number of words passed, not the number of arguments. (Structures, long ints, and floating-point values are usually passed as several words.)

Any function that takes a variable number of arguments must be able to determine *from the arguments themselves* how many of them there are. The printf functions, for example, do this by looking for formatting specifiers (%d and the like) in the format string (which is why these functions fail badly if the format string does not match the argument list). Another common technique, applicable when the arguments are all of the same type, is to use a sentinel value (often 0, −1, or an appropriately cast null pointer) at the end of the list (see the `execl` and `vstrcat` examples in questions 5.2 and 15.4). Finally, if their types are predictable, you can pass an explicit count of the number of variable arguments (although it's usually a nuisance for the caller to generate).

Reference: PCS §11 pp. 167–8

15.9

Question: My compiler isn't letting me declare a function

```
int f(...)
{
}
```

i.e., accepting a variable number of arguments but with no fixed arguments at all. Why not?

Answer: Standard C requires at least one fixed argument, in part so that you can hand it to `va_start`. (In any case, you often need a fixed argument to determine the number, and perhaps the types, of the variable arguments.)

References: ANSI §3.5.4, §3.5.4.3, §4.8.1.1
          ISO §6.5.4, §6.5.4.3, §7.8.1.1
          H&S §9.2 p. 263

15.10

Question: I have a varargs function that accepts a `float` parameter. Why isn't the call `va_arg(argp, float)` extracting it correctly?

Answer: In the variable-length part of variable-length argument lists, the old "default argument promotions" apply: Arguments of type `float` are always promoted (widened) to type `double`, and types `char` and `short int` are promoted to `int`. Therefore, it is never correct to invoke `va_arg(argp, float)`; instead, you should always use `va_arg(argp, double)`. Similarly, use `va_arg(argp, int)` to retrieve arguments that were originally `char`, `short`, or `int`. See also questions 11.3 and 15.2.

References: ANSI §3.3.2.2   Rationale §4.8.1.2
          ISO §6.3.2.2   H&S §11.4 p. 297

15.11

Question: I can't get `va_arg` to pull in an argument of type pointer to function. Why not?

Answer: Try using a `typedef` for the function pointer type.

The type-rewriting games the `va_arg` macro typically plays are stymied by overly complicated types, such as pointer to function. To illustrate, a simplified implementation of `va_arg` is:

```
#define va_arg(argp, type) \
       (*(type *)(((argp) += sizeof(type)) - sizeof(type)))
```

where `argp`'s type (`va_list`) is `char *`. When you attempt to invoke

```
va_arg(argp, int (*)())
```

the expansion is:

```
(*(int (*)() *)(((argp) += sizeof(int (*)())) -
       sizeof(int (*)())))
```

That expansion, however, is a syntax error (the first cast `(int (*)() *)` is meaningless).*

If you use a `typedef` for the function pointer type, however, all will be well. Given

```
typedef int (*funcptr)();
```

the expansion of

```
va_arg(argp, funcptr)
```

is

```
(*(funcptr *)(((argp) += sizeof(funcptr)) - sizeof(funcptr)))
```

This expansion works correctly.

See also questions 1.13, 1.17, and 1.21.

References: ANSI §4.8.1.2
          ISO §7.8.1.2
          Rationale §4.8.1.2

---

*The "right" expansion would have been
```
(*(int (**)())(((argp) += sizeof(int (*)())) - sizeof(int (*)())))
```

Harder Problems

You can pick apart variable-length argument lists at run time, as we've seen. But you can *create* them only at compile time. (We might say that strictly speaking, there are no truly variable-length argument lists; every actual argument list has some fixed number of arguments. A varargs function merely has the capability of accepting a different length of argument list with each call.) If you want to call a function with a list of arguments created on the fly at run time, you can't do so portably.

15.12

Question: How can I write a function that takes a variable number of arguments and passes them to another function (which takes a variable number of arguments)?

Answer: In general, you cannot. Ideally, you should provide a version of that other function that accepts a `va_list` pointer.

Suppose that you want to write a `faterror` function that will print a fatal error message, then exit. You might like to write it in terms of the `error` function of question 15.5:

```
void faterror(char *fmt, ...)
{
    error(fmt, what goes here? );
    exit(EXIT_FAILURE);
}
```

but it's not obvious how to hand `faterror`'s arguments off to `error`.

Proceed as follows. First, split up the existing `error` function to create a new `verror` that accepts not a variable argument list but a single `va_list` pointer. (Note that doing so is little extra work, because `verror` contains much of the code that used to be in `error`, and the new `error` becomes a simple wrapper around `verror`.)

```
#include <stdio.h>
#include <stdarg.h>

void verror(char *fmt, va_list argp)
{
        fprintf(stderr, "error: ");
        vfprintf(stderr, fmt, argp);
        fprintf(stderr, "\n");
}

void error(char *fmt, ...)
{
        va_list argp;
        va_start(argp, fmt);
        verror(fmt, argp);
        va_end(argp);
}
```

Now you can write `faterror` and have it call `verror`, too:

```
#include <stdlib.h>

void faterror(char *fmt, ...)
{
        va_list argp;
        va_start(argp, fmt);
        verror(fmt, argp);
        va_end(argp);
        exit(EXIT_FAILURE);
}
```

Note that the relation between `error` and `verror` is exactly that which holds between, for example, `printf` and `vprintf`. In fact, as Chris Torek has observed, whenever you find yourself writing a varargs function, it's a good idea to write two versions of it: one (like `verror`) that accepts a `va_list` and does the work, the other (like the revised `error`) that is a simple wrapper. The only real restriction on this technique is that a function like `verror` can scan the arguments just once; it has no way to reinvoke `va_start`.

If you do not have the option of rewriting the lower-level function (`error`, in this example) to accept a `va_list`, such that you find yourself needing to pass the variable arguments that one function (e.g., `faterror`) receives on to another as actual arguments, no portable solution is possible. (The problem

could perhaps be solved by resorting to machine-specific assembly language.)
One approach that would *not* work would be something like

```
void faterror(char *fmt, ...)
{
        va_list argp;
        va_start(argp, fmt);
        error(fmt, argp);        /* WRONG */
        va_end(argp);
        exit (EXIT_FAILURE);
}
```

A va_list is *not* itself a variable-length argument list; it's really sort of a pointer to one. That is, a function that accepts a va_list is not itself varargs, or vice versa.

Another kludge that is sometimes used and that sometimes works even though it is grossly nonportable is to use a lot of int arguments, hoping that there are enough of them and that they can somehow pass through pointer, floating-point, and other arguments as well:

```
void faterror(fmt, a1, a2, a3, a4, a5, a6)
char *fmt;
int a1, a2, a3, a4, a5, a6;
{
        error(fmt, a1, a2, a3, a4, a5, a6); /* VERY WRONG */
        exit (EXIT_FAILURE);
}
```

This example is presented only for the purpose of urging you *not* to use it; please don't try it just because you saw it here.

15.13

Question: How can I call a function with an argument list built up at run time?

Answer: There is no guaranteed or portable way to do this.

Instead of a conventional argument list, you might consider passing an array of generic (void *) pointers. The called function can then step through the array, much like main() might step through argv. (Obviously, this works only if you have control over all the called functions.)

See also question 19.36.

16 Strange Problems

It's not even worth asking the rhetorical question, Have you ever had a baffling bug that you just couldn't track down? Of course you have; everyone has. C has a number of splendid "gotcha!s" lurking in wait for the unwary; this chapter discusses a few of them. (In fact, any language powerful enough to be popular probably has its share of surprises like these.)

16.1

Question: Why is this loop always executing once?

```
for(i = start; i < end; i++);
        {
        printf("%d\n", i);
        }
```

Answer: The accidental extra semicolon hiding at the end of the line containing the `for` constitutes a null statement—which is, as far as the compiler is concerned, the loop body. The following brace-enclosed block, which you thought (and the indentation suggests) was a loop body, is actually the next statement, and it is traversed exactly once, regardless of the number of loop iterations.

See also question 2.18.

Reference: CT&P §2.3 pp. 20–1

16.2

Question: I'm getting strange syntax errors on the very first declaration in a file, but it looks fine.

Answer: See question 10.9.

16.3

Question: This program crashes before it even runs! (When single stepping with a debugger, it dies before the first statement in `main`.) Why?

Answer: You probably have one or more very large (kilobyte or more) local arrays. Many systems have fixed-size stacks, and those that perform dynamic stack allocation automatically (e.g., UNIX) can be confused when the stack tries to grow by a huge chunk all at once. It is often better to declare large arrays with `static` duration (unless, of course, you need a fresh set with each recursive call, in which case you could dynamically allocate them with `malloc`; see also question 1.31).

Other possibilities are that your program has been linked incorrectly (combining object modules compiled with different compilation options or using improper dynamic libraries), that run-time dynamic library linking is failing for some reason or that you have somehow misdeclared `main`.

See also questions 11.12, 16.4, 16.5, and 18.4.

16.4

Question: I have a program that seems to run correctly, but it crashes as it's exiting, *after* the last statement in `main()`. What could be causing this?

Answer: There are at least three things to look for:

1. If a semicolon in a previous declaration is missing, `main` might be inadvertently declared as returning a structure, conflicting with the run-time startup code's expectations. See questions 2.18 and 10.9.

2. If `setbuf` or `setvbuf` is called and if the supplied buffer is local to `main` (and automatic), the buffer may not exist any more by the time the stdio library tries to perform its final cleanup.

3. A cleanup function registered by `atexit` may have an error. Perhaps *it* is trying to reference data local to `main` or to another function that no longer exists.

(The second and third problems are closely related to question 7.5; see also question 11.16.)

Reference: CT&P §5.3 pp. 72–3

16.5

Question: **This program runs perfectly on one machine, but I get weird results on another. Stranger still, adding or removing debugging printouts changes the symptoms. What's wrong?**

Answer: Lots of things could be going wrong; here are a few of the more common things to check:

- uninitialized local variables* (see also question 7.1)
- integer overflow, especially on 16-bit machines, especially of an intermediate result when doing things like `a * b / c` (see also question 3.14)
- undefined evaluation order (see questions 3.1 through 3.4)
- omitted declaration of external functions, especially those that return something other than `int` (see questions 1.25 and 14.2)
- dereferenced null pointers (see Chapter 5)
- improper `malloc/free` use (assuming that freshly allocated memory contains 0, assuming that freed storage persists, freeing something twice; see also questions 7.19 and 7.20)

---

*On a stack-based machine, at least, the value that an uninitialized local variable happens to receive tends to depend on what is on the stack and hence what has been called recently. That's why inserting or removing debugging printouts can make a bug go away; `printf` is a large function, so calling it or not can make a large difference in what's left on the stack.

- pointer problems in general (see also questions 16.7 and 16.8)
- mismatch between `printf` format and arguments, especially trying to print `long ints` using `%d` (see questions 12.7 and 12.9)
- trying to call, for example, `malloc(256 * 256 * sizeof(double))`, especially on machines with limited memory (see also questions 7.16 and 19.23)
- array overflow problems, especially of small, temporary buffers, perhaps used for constructing strings with `sprintf`* (see also questions 7.1, 12.21, and 19.28)
- invalid assumptions about the mapping of typedefs, especially `size_t` (see question 7.15)
- floating-point problems (see questions 14.1 and 14.4)
- anything you thought was a clever exploitation of the way you believe code is generated for your specific system

Proper use of function prototypes can catch several of these problems; `lint` would catch several more. See also questions 16.3, 16.4, and 18.4.

16.6

Question: Why does this code crash?

```
char *p = "hello, world!";
p[0] = 'H';
```

Answer: String constants are in fact constant. The compiler may place them in nonwritable storage, and it is therefore not safe to modify them. When you need writable strings, you must allocate writable memory for them, either by declaring an array or by calling `malloc`. Try

```
char a[] = "hello, world!";
```

---

*A bug of this sort in the author's own formatting software delayed an already late manuscript of this book by another few days, nearly costing him the goodwill of his editor.

By the same argument, a typical invocation of the old UNIX `mktemp` function

```
char *tmpfile = mktemp("/tmp/tmpXXXXXX");
```

is nonportable. The proper usage is

```
char tmpfile[] = "/tmp/tmpXXXXXX";
mktemp(tmpfile);
```

See also question 1.32.

References: ANSI §3.1.4
            ISO §6.1.4
            H&S §2.7.4 pp. 31–2

16.7

Question: I've got some code that's trying to unpack external structures, but it's crashing with a message about an "unaligned access." What does this mean? The code looks like this:

```
struct mystruct {
        char c;
        long int i32;
        int i16;
};

char buf[7], *p;
fread(buf, 7, 1, fp);
p = buf;
s.c = *p++;
s.i32 = *(long int *)p;
p += 4;
s.i16 = *(int *)p;
```

Answer: The problem is that you're playing too fast and loose with your pointers. Some machines require that data values be stored at appropriately aligned addresses. For instance, 2-byte `short ints` might be constrained to sit at even addresses and 4-byte `long ints` at multiples of 4. (See also question 2.12.) By converting a `char *` (which can point to any byte) to an `int *` or `long int *` and then indirecting on it, you can end up asking the processor to fetch a multibyte value from an unaligned address, which it isn't willing to do.

A better way to unpack external structures is with code like this:

```
unsigned char *p = buf;

s.c = *p++;

s.i32 = (long)*p++ << 24;
s.i32 |= (long)*p++ << 16;
s.i32 |= (unsigned)(*p++ << 8);
s.i32 |= *p++;

s.i16 = *p++ << 8;
s.i16 |= *p++;
```

This code also gives you control over byte order. (This example, though, assumes that a char is 8 bits and that the long int and int being unpacked from the "external structure" are 32 and 16 bits, respectively.) See question 12.42 (which contains some similar code) for a few explanations and caveats.

See also question 4.5.

References: ANSI §3.3.3.2, §3.3.4
          ISO §6.3.3.2, §6.3.4
          H&S §6.1.3 pp. 164–5

16.8

Question: What do "segmentation violation" and "bus error" mean? What's a "core dump"?

Answer: These symptoms (and any similar messages having to do with memory-access violations or protection faults) generally mean that your program tried to access memory it shouldn't have, invariably as a result of improper pointer use. Likely causes are:

- inadvertent use of null pointers (see also questions 5.2 and 5.20)
- uninitialized, misaligned, or otherwise improperly allocated pointers (see questions 7.1, 7.2, and 16.7)
- stale aliases to memory that has been relocated (see question 7.29)

- corruption of the `malloc` arena (see question 7.19)
- attempts to modify read-only values (those declared `const`, and string literals—see question 1.32)
- mismatched function arguments, especially involving pointers; two possibilities are `scanf` (see question 12.12) and `fprintf` (make sure it receives its first `FILE *` argument)

Under UNIX, any of these problems almost invariably leads to a "core dump": a file named `core`,* created in the current directory, containing a memory image of the crashed process, for debugging.

The distinction between "bus error" and "segmentation violation" may or may not be significant; different versions of UNIX generate these signals under different sets of circumstances. Roughly speaking, a segmentation violation indicates an attempt to access memory that doesn't even exist; a bus error indicates an attempt to access memory in an illegal way (perhaps due to an unaligned pointer; see question 16.7).

See also questions 16.3 and 16.4.

---

*Yes, the name "core" derives ultimately from old ferrite core memories.

17 Style

Computer programs are written not only to be processed by computers, but also to be read by other programmers. In making programs readable (and maintainable, and less error prone), attention must be paid to considerations other than simple acceptability to the compiler. Style considerations are necessarily the least objective aspects of computer programming: Opinions on code style, like those on religion, can be debated endlessly. Good style is a worthy goal and can usually be recognized, but it cannot be rigorously codified. Nevertheless, the absence of objective standards, or even of any industrywide consensus on what constitutes good style, does not mean that programmers should abandon any attempt to write readable code.

17.1

Question: **What's the best style for code layout in C?**

Answer: Kernighan and Ritchie, while providing the example most often copied, also supply a good excuse for disregarding it:

The position of braces is less important, although people hold passionate beliefs. We have chosen one of several popular styles. Pick a style that suits you, then use it consistently.

It is more important that the layout chosen be consistent (with itself and with nearby or common code) than that it be "perfect." If your coding environment (i.e., local custom or company policy) does not suggest a style and you don't feel like inventing your own, just copy K&R.

Each of the various popular styles has its good and bad points. Putting the open brace on a line by itself wastes vertical space; combining it with the following line makes it cumbersome to edit; combining it with the previous line prevents it from lining up with the close brace and may make it more difficult to see.

Indenting by eight columns per level is most common but often gets you uncomfortably close to the right margin (which may be a hint that you should break up the function). If you indent by one tab but set tab stops at something other than eight columns, you're requiring other people to read your code with the same software setup that you used.

The elusive quality of "good style" involves much more than mere code layout details; don't spend time on formatting to the exclusion of more substantive code quality issues.

See also question 17.2.

References: K&R1 §1.2 p. 10
K&R2 §1.2 p. 10

17.2

Question: **How should functions be apportioned among source files?**

Answer: Usually, related functions are put together in one file. Sometimes (as when developing libraries), it is appropriate to have exactly one source file (and, consequently, one object module) per independent function. Other times, and especially for some programmers, numerous source files can be cumbersome, and it may be tempting (or even appropriate) to put most or all of a program in a few big source files. When the scope of certain functions or global variables is to be limited by using the `static` keyword, source file layout becomes more constrained: The static functions and variables and the functions sharing access to them must all be in the same file.

In other words, there are a number of tradeoffs, so it is difficult to give general rules. See also questions 1.7, 1.9, 10.6, and 10.7.

17.3

Question: Here's a neat trick for checking whether two strings are equal:

```
if(!strcmp(s1, s2))
```

Is this good style?

Answer: It is not particularly good style, although it is a popular idiom. The test succeeds if the two strings are equal, but the use of ! ("not") suggests that it tests for *in*equality.

A better option is to define a macro:

```
#define Streq(s1, s2) (strcmp((s1), (s2)) == 0)
```

which you can then use like this:

```
if(Streq(s1, s2))
```

Another possibility (which borders on preprocessor abuse; see question 10.2) is to define

```
#define StrRel(s1, op, s2) (strcmp(s1, s2) op 0)
```

after which you can say things like

```
if(StrRel(s1, ==, s2)) …
if(StrRel(s1, !=, s2)) …
if(StrRel(s1, >=, s2)) …
```

See also question 17.10.

17.4

Question: Why do some people write if(0 == x) instead of if(x == 0)?

Answer: It's a trick to guard against the common error of writing

```
if(x = 0)
```

If you're in the habit of writing the constant before the ==, the compiler will complain if you accidentally type

```
if(0 = x)
```

Evidently, it can be easier to remember to reverse the test than to remember to type the doubled = sign. (To be sure, accidentally using = instead of == is a typo that even the most experienced C programmer can make.)

On the other hand, some people find these reversed tests ugly or distracting,* and argue that a compiler should warn about if(x = 0). (In fact, many compilers do warn about assignments in conditionals, though you can always write if((x = expression)) or if((x = expression) != 0) if you really mean it.)

Reference: H&S §7.6.5 pp. 209–10

17.5

Question: **I came across some code that puts a (void) cast before each call to printf. Why?**

Answer: Although printf does return a value (the number of characters printed or an error code), few programs bother to check the return values from each call. Since some compilers (and lint) will warn about discarded return values, an explicit cast to (void) is a way of saying "Yes, I've decided to ignore the return value from this call, but please continue to warn me about other (perhaps inadvertently) ignored return values." It's also common to use void casts on calls to strcpy and strcat, since the return value is never surprising.

References: K&R2 §A6.7 p. 199
Rationale §3.3.4
H&S §6.2.9 p. 172, §7.13 pp. 229–30

17.6

Question: **If NULL and 0 are equivalent as null pointer constants, which should I use?**

Answer: See question 5.9.

---

*Note also that the reversed test convention is not sufficient, as it will not catch if(a = b) .

17.7

Question: Should I use symbolic names, such as TRUE and FALSE, for Boolean constants or plain 1 and 0?

Answer: See question 9.4.

17.8

Question: What is "Hungarian notation"? Is it worthwhile?

Answer: Hungarian notation is a naming convention, invented by Charles Simonyi, that encodes things about a variable's type (and perhaps its intended use) in its name. It is well loved in some circles and roundly castigated in others. Its chief advantage is that it makes a variable's type or intended use obvious from its name; its chief disadvantage is that type information is not necessarily a worthwhile thing to carry around in the name of a variable.

Reference: Simonyi and Heller, "The Hungarian Revolution"

17.9

Question: Where can I get the "Indian Hill Style Guide" and other coding standards?

Answer: Various documents are available for anonymous ftp from:

Site:	File or directory:
cs.washington.edu	pub/cstyle.tar.Z
	(the updated Indian Hill guide)
ftp.cs.toronto.edu	doc/programming
	(including Henry Spencer's
	"10 Commandments for C Programmers")
ftp.cs.umd.edu	pub/style-guide

(The Indian Hill guide is also available from SSC, P.O. Box 55549, Seattle, WA 98155, (206) 782-7733, sales@ssc.com .)

You may also be interested in the books *The Elements of Programming Style*, *Plum Hall Programming Guidelines*, and *C Style: Standards and Guidelines*; see the bibliography. (The *Standards and Guidelines* book is not in fact a style guide but rather a set of guidelines on selecting and creating style guides.)

17.10

Question: Some people say that `goto` statements are evil and that I should never use them. Isn't that a bit extreme?

Answer: Programming style, like writing style, is somewhat of an art and cannot be codified by inflexible rules, although discussions about style often seem to center exclusively on such rules.

In the case of the `goto` statement, it has long been observed that unfettered use of `goto`s quickly leads to unmaintainable spaghetti code. However, a simple, unthinking ban on the `goto` statement does not necessarily lead immediately to beautiful programming: An unstructured programmer is just as capable of constructing a Byzantine tangle without using any `goto`s (perhaps substituting oddly nested loops and Boolean control variables instead). Many programmers adopt the moderate stance that `goto`s are usually to be avoided but are acceptable in a few well-constrained situations, if necessary: as multilevel `break` statements, to coalesce common actions inside a `switch` statement, or to centralize cleanup tasks in a function with several error returns.

Most observations or "rules" about programming style (Structured Programming is Good, `goto`s are Bad, functions should fit on one page, etc.) usually work better as guidelines than as rules and work much better if programmers understand what the guidelines are trying to accomplish. Blindly avoiding certain constructs or following rules without understanding them can lead to just as many problems as the rules were supposed to avert.

Furthermore, many opinions on programming style are just that: opinions. They may be strongly argued and strongly felt, they may be backed up by solid-seeming evidence and arguments, but the opposing opinions may be just as strongly felt, supported, and argued. It's usually futile to get dragged into "style wars," because on certain issues (such as those referred to in questions 5.3, 5.9, 9.4, and 10.7), opponents can never seem to agree or agree to disagree or stop arguing.

Finally, as William Strunk has written (quoted in the introduction to Strunk and White's classic *Elements of Style*):

> It is an old observation that the best writers sometimes disregard the rules of rhetoric. When they do, however, the reader will usually find in the sentence some compensating merit, attained at the cost of the violation. Unless he is certain of doing as well, he will probably do best to follow the rules.

References: Dijkstra, "Go To Statement Considered Harmful"
Knuth, "Structured Programming with goto Statements"

17.11

Question: People always say that good style is important, but when they go out of their way to use clear techniques and make their programs readable, they seem to end up with less efficient programs. Since efficiency is so important, isn't it necessary to sacrifice some style and readability?

Answer: It's true that grossly inefficient programs are a problem, but the blind zeal with which many programmers often chase efficiency is also a problem. Cumbersome, obscure programming tricks not only destroy readability and maintainability but may also lead to slimmer long-term efficiency improvements than would more appropriate design or algorithm choices. With care, it is possible to design code that is both clean and efficient.

See also question 20.13.

18 Tools and Resources

You can't do too much practical programming in an armchair; you obviously need a compiler, and certain other tools can be extremely handy as well. This chapter discusses several tools, with a focus on `lint`, and also talks about some other resources.

Several of the tools and resources mentioned here can be found on the Internet. Be aware that site names and file locations can change; the addresses printed here, though correct at the time of this writing, may not work by the time you try them. (See question 18.16 for assistance.)

Tools

18.1

Question: Where can I find:

a C cross-reference generator?

a C beautifier/pretty-printer?

Answer: Look for programs (see also question 18.16) named:

cflow, cxref, calls, cscope, xscope, or ixfw.

cb, indent, GNU indent, or vgrind.

a revision control or configuration management tool?	RCS or SCCS.
a C source obfuscator (shrouder)?	obfus, shroud, or opqcp.
a "make" dependency generator?	makedepend, or try `cc -M` or `cpp -M`.
tools to compute code metrics?	ccount, Metre, lcount, or csize, or see URL http://www.qucis. queensu.ca:1999/ Software Engineering/Cmetrics.html; there is also a package sold by McCabe and Associates.
a C lines-of-source counter?	This can be done very crudely with the standard UNIX utility `wc` and considerably better with `grep -c ";"`.
a prototype generator?	See question 11.31.
a tool to track down `malloc` problems?	See question 18.2.
a "selective" C preprocessor?	See question 10.18.
language translation tools?	See questions 11.31 and 20.26.
C verifiers (`lint`)?	See question 18.7.
a C compiler?	See question 18.3.

(This list of tools is by no means complete; if you know of tools not mentioned, you're welcome to contact the author.)

Other lists of tools, and discussion about them, can be found in the Usenet newsgroups comp.compilers and comp.software-eng.

See also questions 18.3 and 18.16.

18.2

Question: How can I track down these pesky `malloc` problems?

Answer: A number of debugging packages exist to help track down `malloc` problems; one popular one is Conor P. Cahill's "dbmalloc," posted to comp.sources.misc in 1992, volume 32. Others are "leak," available in volume 27 of the comp.sources.unix archives; JMalloc.c and JMalloc.h in the "Snippets" collection; and MEMDEBUG from ftp.crpht.lu in pub/sources/memdebug/. See also question 18.16.

A number of commercial debugging tools exist and can be invaluable in tracking down `malloc`-related and other stubborn problems:

- Bounds-Checker for DOS, from Nu-Mega Technologies, P.O. Box 7780, Nashua, NH 03060-7780, (603) 889-2386.

- CodeCenter (formerly Saber-C), from Centerline Software (formerly Saber), 10 Fawcett Street, Cambridge, MA 02138-1110, (617) 498-3000.

- Insight, from ParaSoft Corporation, 2500 E. Foothill Blvd., Pasadena, CA 91107, (818) 792-9941, insight@parasoft.com.

- Purify, from Pure Software, 1309 S. Mary Ave., Sunnyvale, CA 94087, (800) 224-7873, info-home@pure.com.

- SENTINEL, from AIB Software, 46030 Manekin Plaza, Dulles, VA 20166, (703) 430-9247, (800) 296-3000, info@aib.com.

18.3

Question: What's a free or cheap C compiler I can use?

Answer: A popular and high-quality free C compiler is the FSF's GNU C compiler, or gcc, available by anonymous ftp from prep.ai.mit.edu in directory pub/gnu or at several other FSF archive sites. An MS-DOS port, djgpp, is also available; it can be found in the Simtel and Oakland archives and probably many others, usually in a directory such as pub/msdos/djgpp/ or simtel/msdos/djgpp/.

A shareware compiler, PCC, is available as PCC12C.ZIP .

A very inexpensive MS-DOS compiler is Power C, from Mix Software, 1132 Commerce Drive, Richardson, TX 75801 (214) 783-6001.

Another recently developed compiler is lcc, available for anonymous ftp from ftp.cs.princeton.edu in pub/lcc/.

Archives associated with the Usenet newsgroup comp.compilers contain a great deal of information about available compilers, interpreters, grammars, etc. (for many languages). The comp.compilers archives (including an FAQ list), maintained by the moderator, John R. Levine, are at iecc.com . A list of available compilers and related resources, maintained by Mark Hopkins,

Steven Robenalt, and David Muir Sharnoff, is at ftp.idiom.com in pub/compilers-list/.

See also question 18.16.

lint

C was developed along with the UNIX operating system and shares its philosophy of "each tool should do exactly one job and do it well." Traditionally, a C compiler's job was to generate machine code from source code, not to warn the programmer about every possibly incorrect or inadvisable technique. That task was reserved for a separate program, named lint (after the bits of fluff it supposedly picks from programs). Although lint has waned in significance over the years, newer compilers have not always picked up on the same diagnostic tasks in its stead, so there may still be a place for it in the wise programmer's arsenal.

18.4

Question: I just typed in this program, and it's acting strangely. What can be wrong with it?

Answer: See if you can run lint first (perhaps with the -a, -c, -h, -p or other options*). Many C compilers are really only half-compilers, taking the attitude that it's not *their* problem if you didn't say what you meant or if what you said is virtually guaranteed not to work. (But do also see whether your compiler has extra warning levels that can be optionally requested.)

See also questions 16.5 and 16.8.

Reference: Darwin, *Checking C Programs with lint*

---

*Beware that under some versions of lint, these options request additional checking and that on some others, they disable it.

18.5

Question: How can I shut off the "warning: possible pointer alignment problem" message that `lint` gives me for each call to `malloc`?

Answer: The problem is that traditional versions of `lint` do not know, and cannot be told, that `malloc` "returns a pointer to space suitably aligned for storage of any type of object." It is possible to provide a pseudoimplementation of `malloc`, using a `#define` inside of `#ifdef lint`, which effectively shuts this warning off, but a simpleminded definition will also suppress meaningful messages about truly incorrect invocations. It may be easier simply to ignore the message, perhaps in an automated way with `grep -v`. (But don't get in the habit of ignoring too many `lint` messages; otherwise, one day you'll overlook a significant one.)

18.6

Question: Can I declare `main` as `void` to shut off these annoying "main returns no value" messages?

Answer: See question 11.12.

18.7

Question: Where can I get an ANSI-compatible `lint`?

Answer: Products called PC-Lint and FlexeLint (in "shrouded source form," for compilation on almost any system) are available from Gimpel Software, 3207 Hogarth Ln., Collegeville, PA 19426 (610) 584-4261, or gimpel@netaxs.com.

The ANSI-compatible UNIX System V release 4 `lint` is available separately (bundled with other C tools) from UNIX Support Labs or from System V resellers.

A redistributable, ANSI-compatible `lint` may be available from ftp.eskimo.com in u/s/scs/ansilint/.

Another ANSI-compatible `lint` (which can also perform higher-level formal verification) is LCLint, available via anonymous ftp from larch.lcs.mit.edu in pub/Larch/lclint/.

In the absence of `lint`, many modern compilers do attempt to diagnose almost as many problems as `lint` does.

18.8

Question: **Don't ANSI function prototypes render `lint` obsolete?**

Answer: Not really. Prototypes work only if they are present and correct; an inadvertently incorrect prototype is worse than useless. Furthermore, `lint` checks consistency across multiple source files and checks both data declarations and functions. Finally, an independent program like `lint` will probably always be more scrupulous at enforcing compatible, portable coding practices than will any particular, implementation-specific, feature- and extension-laden compiler.

If you do want to use function prototypes instead of `lint` for cross-file consistency checking, make sure that you set the prototypes up correctly in header files. See questions 1.7 and 10.6.

Resources

Once again, remember that the Internet is always in a state of flux, so some of the network addresses listed in this section may have changed by the time you read this.

18.9

Question: **Are any C tutorials or other resources available on the Internet?**

Answer: Yes, several:

"Notes for C programmers," by Christopher Sawtell, is available from svrftp.eng.cam.ac.uk in misc/sawtell_C.shar and from garbo.uwasa.fi in /pc/c-lang/c-lesson.zip.

Tim Love's guide to "C for Programmers" is available by ftp from svr-ftp.eng.cam.ac.uk in the misc directory. A hypertext version is at http://club.eng.cam.ac.uk/help/tpl/languages/C/teaching_C/teaching_C.html.

The Coronado Enterprises C tutorials are available on Simtel mirrors in pub/msdos/c/.

Rick Rowe has a tutorial that is available from ftp.netcom.com as pub/rowe/tutorde.zip or ftp.wustl.edu as pub/MSDOS_UPLOADS/programming/c_language/ctutorde.zip.

There is evidently a web-based course at http://www.strath.ac.uk/CC/Courses/CCourse/CCourse.html.

Finally, on some UNIX machines, you can try typing `learn c` at the shell prompt.

(*Disclaimer:* I have not reviewed these tutorials; I have heard that at least one of them contains a number of errors. Also, this sort of information rapidly becomes out of date; these addresses may not work by the time you read this and try them.)

Several of these tutorials, along with pointers to a great deal of other information about C, are accessible via the web at http://www.lysator.liu.se/c/index.html.

Vinit Carpenter maintains a list of resources for learning C and C++; it is posted to comp.lang.c and comp.lang.c++ and archived where the on-line versions of this book are (see question 20.40). A hypertext version is at http://vinny.csd.mu.edu/.

See also question 18.10.

18.10

Question: **What's a good book for learning C?**

Answer: There are far too many books on C to list here; it's impossible to rate them all. Many people believe that the best one was also the first: *The C Programming Language*, by Brian Kernighan and Dennis Ritchie ("K&R," now in its second edition). Opinions vary on K&R's suitability as an initial programming text: Many of us did learn C from it and learned it well; some, however, feel that it is a bit too clinical as a first tutorial for those without much programming background.

An excellent reference manual is *C: A Reference Manual*, by Samuel P. Harbison and Guy L. Steele, now in its fourth edition.

Mitch Wright maintains an annotated bibliography of C and UNIX books; it is available for anonymous ftp from ftp.rahul.net in directory pub/mitch/ YABL/.

See also question 18.9.

18.11

Question: Where can I find answers to the exercises in K&R?

Answer: They have been written up in *The C Answer Book*; see the bibliography.

18.12

Question: Does anyone know where the source code from books like *Numerical Recipes in C,* Plauger's *The Standard C Library,* or Kernighan and Pike's *The UNIX Programming Environment* is available on line?

Answer: Books containing large quantities of potentially useful source code, including the ones mentioned in the question, usually make explicit mention of the availability of source code and policies for its use. Published source code is copyrighted and may generally not be used or, especially, redistributed without permission (and perhaps a few restrictions, though presumably the publisher doesn't mind your typing it in for personal use). Often a diskette is available from the publisher; also, many publishers are setting up ftp sites and web pages.

Some of the routines from *Numerical Recipes* have been released to the public domain; look on ftp.std.com in the directory vendors/ Numerical-Recipes/Public-Domain/.

The source code in *this* book, though copyrighted, is explicitly made available to use in your programs in any way that you wish. (Naturally, the author and publisher would appreciate it if you acknowledged this book as your source.) The larger code fragments, plus related material, can be found at aw.com in directory cseng/authors/summit/cfaq/.

18.13

Question: Where can I find the sources of the standard C libraries?

Answer: One source (though not public domain) is *The Standard C Library*, by P.J. Plauger (see the bibliography). Implementations of all or part of the C library have been written and are readily available as part of the netBSD and GNU (also Linux) projects. See also question 18.16.

18.14

Question: I need code to parse and evaluate expressions. Where can I find some?

Answer: Two available packages are "defunc," available via ftp from sunsite.unc. edu in pub/packages/development/libraries/defunc-1.3.tar.Z, and "parse," at lamont.ldgo.columbia.edu. Other options include the S-Lang interpreter, available from amy.tch.harvard.edu in pub/slang, and the shareware Cmm ("C-minus-minus" or "C minus the hard stuff"). See also question 18.16.

Some parsing/evaluation code can be found in *Software Solutions in C* (Chapter 12, pp. 235–55).

18.15

Question: Where can I get a BNF or YACC grammar for C?

Answer: The definitive grammar is, of course, the one in the ANSI standard; see question 11.2. Another grammar (along with one for C++) by Jim Roskind is in pub/c++grammar1.1.tar.Z at ics.uci.edu . A fleshed-out, working instance of the ANSI grammar (due to Jeff Lee) is on ftp.uu.net (see question 18.16) in usenet/net.sources/ansi.c.grammar.Z (including a companion lexer). The FSF's GNU C compiler contains a grammar, as does the appendix to K&R2.

The comp.compilers archives contain more information about grammars; see question 18.3.

References: K&R1 §A18 pp. 214–9
K&R2 §A13 pp. 234–9
ANSI §A.2
ISO §B.2
H&S pp. 423–35 Appendix B

18.16

Question: **Where and how can I get copies of all these freely distributable programs?**

Answer: As the number of available programs, the number of publicly accessible archive sites, and the number of people trying to access them all grow, this question becomes both easier and more difficult to answer.

Several large, public-spirited archive sites have been set up, such as ftp.uu.net, archive.umich.edu, oak.oakland.edu, sumex-aim.stanford.edu, and wuarchive.wustl.edu; these sites have huge amounts of software and other information all freely available. For the FSF's GNU project, the central distribution site is prep.ai.mit.edu. These well-known sites tend to be extremely busy and difficult to reach, but there are also numerous "mirror" sites that try to spread the load around.

On the connected Internet, the traditional way to retrieve files from an archive site is with anonymous ftp. For those without ftp access, there are also several ftp-by-mail servers in operation. More and more, the world-wide web (WWW) is being used to announce, index, and even transfer large data files. There are probably yet newer access methods, too.

Those are some of the easy parts of the question to answer. The hard part is in the details—this book cannot begin to list all of the available archive sites or all of the various ways of accessing them. If you have access to the Internet at all, you probably have access to more up-to-date information about active sites and useful access methods than this book does.

The other easy-and-hard aspect of the question, of course, is simply *finding* which site has what you're looking for. A tremendous amount of work is going on in this area, and new indexing services are probably springing up every day. One of the first was "archie": For any program or resource available on the Internet, if you know its name, an archie server can usually tell you which anonymous ftp sites have it. Your system may have an `archie` command, or you can send the mail message "help" to the address archie@archie. cs.mcgill.ca for information.

If you have access to Usenet, see the regular postings in newsgroups comp.sources.unix and comp.sources.misc, which describe the archiving policies for those groups and how to access their archives. The group comp.archives contains numerous announcements of anonymous ftp availability of various items. Finally, comp.sources.wanted has an FAQ list, "How to find sources," with more information.

See also question 14.12.

18.17

Question: Where are the on-line versions of this book?

Answer: See question 20.40.

19 System Dependencies

C is a programming language, not an operating system. No programming language specifies all of the details about every interaction a program might want to have with its environment, but it is natural for a programmer who is trying to perform a system-specific task to ask how to do it in the context of the particular language being used. Real programs frequently need to perform such tasks as character-at-a-time input, cursor-controlled full-screen output, window manager interfacing (including menus and dialogs), mouse input, graphics, serial port communication, printer support, interfacing to various peripheral I/O devices, networking, etc. C's definition, however, is silent on all of these.

The specific techniques required to perform these tasks vary widely across today's popular machines and operating systems, so complete answers for every combination cannot be given. The list of questions in this chapter is a laundry list of things you can't do in portable C: Most of the answers boil down to "It's system dependent." (When the brief answers in this chapter prove insufficient, you'll want to find some detailed documentation specific to the system you're using.)

The system-dependent questions in this chapter are divided into several categories:

Keyboard and Screen I/O

19.1

Question: **How can I read a single character from the keyboard without waiting for the Return key? How can I stop characters from being echoed on the screen as they're typed?**

Answer: Alas, there is no standard or portable way to do these things in C. Concepts such as screens and keyboards are not even mentioned in the standard, which deals only with simple I/O "streams" of characters.

Input to a computer program typically passes through several stages. At the lowest level, device-dependent routines within the operating system handle the details of interfacing with particular devices, such as keyboards, serial lines, disk drives, etc. Above that, modern operating systems tend to have a device-independent I/O layer, unifying access to any file or device. Finally, a C program is usually insulated from the operating system's I/O facilities by the portable functions of the stdio library.

At some level, interactive keyboard input is usually collected and presented to the requesting program a line at a time. This gives the operating system a chance to support input line editing (backspace/delete/rubout, etc.) in a consistent way, without requiring that it be built into every program. Only when the user is satisfied and presses the Return key (or equivalent) is the line made available to the calling program. Even if the calling program appears to be reading input a character at a time (with `getchar` or the like), the first call blocks until the user has typed an entire line, at which point potentially many characters become available and many character requests (e.g., `getchar` calls) are satisfied in quick succession.

When a program wants to read each character immediately as it arrives, its course of action will depend on where in the input stream the line collection is happening and how it can be disabled. Under some systems (e.g., MS-DOS, VMS in some modes), a program can use a different or modified set of OS-level input calls to bypass line-at-a-time input processing. Under other systems (e.g., UNIX, VMS in other modes), the part of the operating system responsible for serial input (often called the "terminal driver") must be placed in a mode that turns off line-at-a-time processing, after which all calls to the usual input routines (e.g., `read`, `getchar`, etc.) will return characters immediately. Finally, a few systems (particularly older, batch-oriented mainframes) perform input processing in peripheral processors that cannot be told to do anything other than line-at-a-time input.

Therefore, when you need to do character-at-a-time input (or disable keyboard echo, which is an analogous problem), you will have to use a technique specific to the system you're using, assuming it provides one. Here are brief answers for some common situations. Depending on which operating system you're using and what libraries you have available, you may be able to use one (or more!) of the following techniques:

- If you can use the "curses" library, you can call `cbreak`* (and perhaps `noecho`), after which calls to `getch` will return characters immediately.

- If all you're trying to do is read a short password without echo, you may be able to use a function called `getpass`, if it's available. (Another possibility for hiding typed passwords is to select black characters on a black background.)

- Under "classic" versions of UNIX, use `ioctl` and the TIOCGETP and TIOCSETP (or TIOCSETN) requests on file descriptor 0 to manipulate the sgttyb structure, defined in `<sgtty.h>` and documented in tty(4). In the `sg_flags` field, set the CBREAK (or RAW) bit, and perhaps clear the ECHO bit.

- Under System V UNIX, use `ioctl` and the TCGETAW and TCSETAW requests on file descriptor 0 to manipulate the termio structure, defined in `<termio.h>`. In the `c_lflag` field, clear the ICANON (and perhaps ECHO) bits. Also, set `c_cc[VMIN]` to 1 and `c_cc[VTIME]` to 0.

- Under any operating system (UNIX or otherwise) offering POSIX compatibility, use the `tcgetattr` and `tcsetattr` calls on file descriptor 0 to manipulate the termios structure, defined in `<termios.h>`. In the

---

*In some old versions of curses, the function to request character-at-a-time input is `crmode`, not `cbreak`.

c_lflag field, clear the ICANON (and perhaps ECHO) bits. Also, set c_cc[VMIN] to 1 and c_cc[VTIME] to 0.

- In a pinch, under UNIX, use system (see question 19.27) to invoke the stty command to set terminal driver modes (as in the preceding three items).

- Under MS-DOS, use getch or getche or the corresponding BIOS interrupts.

- Under VMS, try the Screen Management (SMG$) routines, or curses, or issue low-level $QIO's with the IO$_READVBLK function code (and perhaps IO$M_NOECHO, and others) to ask for one character at a time. (It's also possible to set character-at-a-time or "pass through" modes in the VMS terminal driver.)

- Under other operating systems, you're on your own.

(As an aside, note that simply using setbuf or setvbuf to set stdin to unbuffered will *not* generally serve to allow character-at-a-time input.)

If you change terminal modes, save a copy of the initial state and be sure to restore it no matter how your program terminates.

If you're trying to write a portable program, a good approach is to define your own suite of three functions to (1) set the terminal driver or input system into character-at-a-time mode (if necessary), (2) get characters, and (3) return the terminal driver to its initial state when the program is finished.

As an example, here is a tiny test program that prints the decimal values of the next 10 characters as they are typed, without waiting for Return. It is written in terms of three functions, as described, and is followed by implementations of the three functions for curses, classic UNIX, System V UNIX, and MS-DOS. (The on-line archives associated with this book contain a more complete set of functions.)

```
#include <stdio.h>

main()
{
        int i;
        if(tty_break() != 0)
              return 1;
        for(i = 0; i < 10; i++)
              printf(" = %d\n", tty_getchar());
        tty_fix();
        return 0;
}
```

This implementation of the three functions is for curses:

```
#include <curses.h>

int tty_break()
{
        initscr();
        cbreak();
        return 0;
}

int tty_getchar()
{
        return getch();
}

int tty_fix()
{
        endwin();
        return 0;
}
```

Here is the code for "classic" (V7, BSD) UNIX:

```
#include <stdio.h>
#include <sgtty.h>

static struct sgttyb savemodes;
static int havemodes = 0;

int tty_break()
{
        struct sgttyb modmodes;
        if(ioctl(fileno(stdin), TIOCGETP, &savemodes) < 0)
                return -1;
        havemodes = 1;
        modmodes = savemodes;
        modmodes.sg_flags |= CBREAK;
        return ioctl(fileno(stdin), TIOCSETN, &modmodes);
}
```

```
int tty_getchar()
{
      return getchar();
}

int tty_fix()
{
      if(!havemodes)
            return 0;
      return ioctl(fileno(stdin), TIOCSETN, &savemodes);
}
```

The code for System V UNIX is similar:

```
#include <stdio.h>
#include <termio.h>

static struct termio savemodes;
static int havemodes = 0;

int tty_break()
{
      struct termio modmodes;
      if(ioctl(fileno(stdin), TCGETA, &savemodes) < 0)
            return -1;
      havemodes = 1;
      modmodes = savemodes;
      modmodes.c_lflag &= ~ICANON;
      modmodes.c_cc[VMIN] = 1;
      modmodes.c_cc[VTIME] = 0;
      return ioctl(fileno(stdin), TCSETAW, &modmodes);
}

int tty_getchar()
{
      return getchar();
}

int tty_fix()
{
      if(!havemodes)
            return 0;
      return ioctl(fileno(stdin), TCSETAW, &savemodes);
}
```

Finally, here is an implementation for MS-DOS:

```
int tty_break() { return 0; }

int tty_getchar()
{
        return getche();
}

int tty_fix() { return 0; }
```

Turning off echo is left as an exercise for the reader.

For detailed information on terminal (keyboard and screen) I/O programming, see an FAQ list, book, or documentation set specific to your operating system. (Note that there can be many more details to take care of, e.g., special characters to disable as well as more mode bits to toggle, than were mentioned here.)

See also question 19.2.

References: PCS §10 pp. 128–9, §10.1 pp. 130–1
           POSIX §7

19.2

Question: **How can I find out whether characters are available for reading (and if so, how many)? Alternatively, how can I do a read that will not block if no characters are available?**

Answer: These, too, are entirely specific to the operating system. Some versions of curses have a `nodelay` function. Depending on your system, you may also be able to use "nonblocking I/O," a system call named `select` or `poll`, the FIONREAD ioctl, `c_cc[VTIME]`, `kbhit`, `rdchk`, or the O_NDELAY option to `open` or `fcntl`. You can also try setting an alarm to cause a blocking read to time out after a certain interval (under UNIX, look at `alarm`, `signal`, and maybe `setitimer`).

If what you're trying to do is read input from several sources without blocking, you will definitely want to use some kind of a "select" call, because a busy-wait, polling loop is terribly inefficient on a multitasking system.

See also question 19.1.

19.3

Question: How can I display a percentage-done indication that updates itself in place or show one of those "twirling baton" progress indicators?

Answer: These simple things, at least, you can do fairly portably. Printing the character '\r' will usually give you a carriage return without a line feed, so that you can overwrite the current line. The character '\b' is a backspace and will usually move the cursor one position to the left.

Using these characters, you can print a percentage-done indicator:

```
for(i = 0; i < lotsa; i++) {
        printf("\r%3d%%", (int)(100L * i / lotsa));
        fflush(stdout);
        do_timeconsuming_work();
}
printf("\ndone.\n");
```

or a baton:

```
printf("working: ");
for(i = 0; i < lotsa; i++) {
        printf("%c\b", "|/-\\"[i%4]);
        fflush(stdout);
        do_timeconsuming_work();
}
printf("done.\n");
```

See also question 12.4.

References: ANSI §2.2.2
            ISO §5.2.2

19.4

Question: How can I clear the screen? How can I print things in inverse video? How can I move the cursor to a specific *x, y* position?

Answer: Such things depend on the terminal type (or display) you're using. You will have to use a library such as termcap, terminfo, or curses, or some system-specific routines to perform these operations.

Functions in the curses library to look for are `clear`, `move`, `standout/standend`, and `attron/attroff/attrset`; the last three work with attribute codes such as A_REVERSE. MS-DOS libraries typically have functions named `gotoxy` and `clrscr` or `_clearscreen`; you can also use the ANSI.SYS driver or low-level interrupts. Under termcap or terminfo, use `tgetstr` to retrieve strings like `cl`, `so/se`, and `cm` for clear screen, standout mode, and cursor motion, respectively; then output the strings (using `cm` additionally requires calling `tgoto`). Some baroque terminals require attention to other "capabilities" as well; study the documentation carefully. Be aware that some older terminals may not support the desired capabilities at all.

For clearing the screen, a halfway portable solution is to print a form-feed character (`'\f'`), which will cause some displays to clear. Even more portable would be to print enough newlines to scroll everything away. As a last resort, you could use `system` (see question 19.27) to invoke an operating system clear-screen command.

References: PCS §5.1.4 pp. 54–60, §5.1.5 pp. 60–2
Strang, *Programming with curses*
Strang, Mui, and O'Reilly, *termcap & terminfo*

19.5

Question: **How do I read the arrow keys? What about function keys?**

Answer: Terminfo, some versions of termcap, and some versions of curses have support for these non-ASCII keys. Typically, a special key sends a multi-character sequence (usually beginning with ESC, `'\033'`); parsing these can be tricky. (The curses library will do the parsing for you, if you call `keypad` first.)

Under MS-DOS, if you receive a character with value 0 (*not* `'0'`!) while reading the keyboard, it's a flag indicating that the next character read will be a code indicating a special key. See any DOS programming guide for lists of keyboard codes. (Very briefly, the up, left, right, and down arrow keys are 72, 75, 77, and 80, and the function keys are 59 through 68.)

Reference: PCS §5.1.4 pp. 56–7

Other I/O

19.6

Question: How do I read the mouse?

Answer: Consult your system documentation. Mouse handling is completely different under the X window system, MS-DOS, the Macintosh, and probably every other system.

Reference: PCS §5.5 pp. 78–80

19.7

Question: How can I do serial ("comm") port I/O?

Answer: It's system dependent. Under UNIX, you typically open, read, and write a device file in /dev and use the facilities of the terminal driver to adjust its characteristics. (See also questions 19.1 and 19.2.) Under MS-DOS, you can use the predefined stream stdaux, a special file such as COM1, some primitive BIOS interrupts, or (if you require high performance) any number of interrupt-driven serial I/O packages.

19.8

Question: How can I direct output to the printer?

Answer: Under UNIX, either use popen (see question 19.30) to write to the lp or lpr program, or perhaps open a special file such as /dev/lp. Under MS-DOS, write to the (nonstandard) predefined stdio stream stdprn or open the special files PRN or LPT1.

Reference: PCS §5.3 pp. 72–4

19.9

Question: How do I send escape sequences to control a terminal or other device?

Answer: If you can figure out how to send characters to the device at all (see question 19.8), it's easy enough to send escape sequences. In ASCII, the ESC code is 033 (27 decimal), so code like

```
fprintf(ofp, "\033[J");
```

sends the sequence ESC [J .

Some programmers prefer to parameterize the ESC code, like this:

```
#define ESC 033

fprintf(ofp, "%c[J", ESC);
```

19.10

Question: How can I do graphics?

Answer: Once upon a time, UNIX had a fairly nice little set of device-independent plot routines described in plot(3) and plot(5), but they've largely fallen into disuse.

If you're programming for MS-DOS, you'll probably want to use libraries conforming to the VESA or BGI standards.

If you're trying to talk to a particular plotter, making it draw is usually a matter of sending it the appropriate escape sequences; see also question 19.9. The vendor may supply a C-callable library, or you may be able to find one on the Internet.

If you're programming for a particular window system (Macintosh, X windows, Microsoft Windows), you will use its facilities; see the relevant documentation or newsgroup or FAQ list.

Reference: PCS §5.4 pp. 75–7

Files and Directories

19.11

Question: How can I check whether a file exists? I want to warn the user if a requested input file is missing.

Answer: It's surprisingly difficult to make this determination reliably and portably. Any test you make can be invalidated if the file is created or deleted (i.e., by some other process) between the time you make the test and the time you try to open the file.

Three possible test routines are `stat`, `access`, and `fopen`. (To make an approximate test for file existence with `fopen`, just open for reading and close immediately.) Of these, only `fopen` is widely portable, and `access`, where it exists, must be used carefully if the program uses the UNIX set-UID feature.

Rather than trying to predict in advance whether an operation such as opening a file will succeed, it's often better to try it, check the return value, and complain if it fails. (Obviously, this approach won't work if you're trying to avoid overwriting an existing file, unless you've got something like the `O_EXCL` file opening option available, which does just what you want in this case.)

References: PCS §12 pp. 189, 213
          POSIX §5.3.1, §5.6.2, §5.6.3

19.12

Question: How can I find out the size of a file prior to reading it in?

Answer: If the "size of a file" is the number of characters you'll be able to read from it in C (or that were written to it by a previous program), it is difficult or impossible to determine this number exactly (other than by reading the whole file).

Under UNIX, the `stat` call (specifically, the `st_size` field of the stat structure) will give you an exact answer.* Several other systems supply a UNIX-like `stat` call, but the sizes reported for text files may be approximate

---

*Unless some other process is writing to the file, that is.

(due to differing end-of-line representations; see question 12.40). You can open the file and use `fstat`, or `fseek` to the end of the file and then use `ftell`, but these tend to have the same problems: `fstat` is not portable and generally tells you the same thing `stat` tells you; `ftell` is not guaranteed to return a byte count except for binary files. Some systems provide functions called `filesize` or `filelength`, but these are not portable, either.

Are you sure you have to determine the file's size in advance? Since the most accurate way of determining the size of a file as a C program will see it is to open the file and read it, perhaps you can rearrange the code to learn the size as it reads. (In general, your program should behave gracefully if the number of characters read does not match prior expectations, since any advance determination of the size might be approximate.) See also questions 7.29 and 20.2.

References: ANSI §4.9.9.4   PCS §12 p. 213
           ISO §7.9.9.4   POSIX §5.6.2
           H&S §15.5.1 pp. 352–3

19.13

Question: **How can a file be shortened in place without completely clearing or rewriting it?**

Answer: BSD systems provide `ftruncate`, several others supply `chsize`, and a few may provide a (possibly undocumented) `fcntl` option F_FREESP. Under MS-DOS, you can sometimes use `write(fd, "", 0)`. However, there is no portable solution, or a way to delete blocks at the beginning. See also question 19.14.

19.14

Question: **How can I insert or delete a line (or record) in the middle of a file?**

Answer: In general, there is no way to do this.* The usual solution is simply to rewrite the file.

---

*If your operating system provides nonsequential, record-oriented files, it probably has insert/delete operations, but C provides no particular support.

When you find yourself needing to insert data into an existing file, here are a few alternatives you can try:

- Rearrange the data file so that you can append the new information at the end.
- Put the information in a second file.
- Leave some blank space (e.g. a line of 80 spaces or a field like 0000000000) in the file when it is first written and overwrite it later with the final information (see also question 12.30).

Instead of deleting records, you might consider just marking them as "deleted" and having the code that reads the file ignore them. (You could run a separate coalescion program once in a while to rewrite the file, finally discarding the deleted records.)

See also questions 12.30 and 19.13.

19.15

Question: **How can I recover the file name given an open stream or file descriptor?**

Answer: This problem is generally insoluble. Under UNIX, for instance, a scan of the entire disk (perhaps involving special permissions) would theoretically be required and would fail if the descriptor were connected to a pipe or referred to a deleted file (and could give a misleading answer for a file with multiple links). It is best to remember the names of files yourself when you open them (perhaps with a wrapper function around `fopen`).

19.16

Question: **How can I delete a file?**

Answer: The standard C library function is `remove`. (This is therefore one of the few questions in this chapter for which the answer is *not* "It's system dependent.") On older, pre-ANSI UNIX systems, remove may not exist, in which case you can try unlink.*

References: K&R2 §B1.1 p. 242
ANSI §4.9.4.1
ISO §7.9.4.1
H&S §15.15 p. 382
PCS §12 pp. 208, 220–1
POSIX §5.5.1, §8.2.4

19.17

Question: Why can't I open a file by its explicit path? This call is failing:

```
fopen("c:\newdir\file.dat", "r")
```

Answer: The file you actually requested—with the characters \n and \f in its name—probably doesn't exist and isn't what you thought you were trying to open.

In character constants and string literals, the backslash \ is an escape character, giving special meaning to the character following it. In order for literal backslashes in a pathname to be passed through to fopen (or any other function) correctly, they have to be doubled, so that the first backslash in each pair quotes the second one:

```
fopen("c:\\newdir\\file.dat", "r");
```

Alternatively, under MS-DOS, it turns out that forward slashes are also accepted as directory separators, so you could use

```
fopen("c:/newdir/file.dat", "r");
```

(Note, by the way, that header file names mentioned in preprocessor #include directives are *not* string literals, so you may not have to worry about backslashes there.)

---

*There is a slight semantic difference between remove and unlink: unlink is guaranteed (on UNIX, anyway) to work even on open files; remove has no such guarantee.

19.18

Question: I'm getting an error: "Too many open files." How can I increase the allowable number of simultaneously open files?

Answer: There are at least two resource limitations on the number of simultaneously open files: the number of low-level "file descriptors" or "file handles" available in the operating system and the number of FILE structures available in the stdio library. Both must be sufficient. Under MS-DOS systems, you can control the number of operating system file handles with a line in CONFIG.SYS. Some compilers come with instructions (and perhaps a source file or two) for increasing the number of stdio FILE structures.

19.19

Question: How can I find out how much free space is available on disk?

Answer: There is no portable way. Under some versions of UNIX, you can call `statfs`. Under MS-DOS, use interrupt 0x21 subfunction 0x36 or perhaps a function such as `diskfree`. Another possibility is to use `popen` (see question 19.30) to invoke and read the output of a "disk free" command (e.g., `df` on UNIX).

(Note that the amount of free space apparently available on a disk may not match the size of the largest file you can store, for all sorts of reasons.)

19.20

Question: How can I read a directory in a C program?

Answer: See whether you can use the `opendir` and `readdir` functions, which are part of the POSIX standard and are available on most UNIX variants. Implementations also exist for MS-DOS, VMS, and other systems. (MS-DOS also has FINDFIRST and FINDNEXT routines, which do essentially the same thing.) The `readdir` function returns only file names; if you need more information about the file, try calling `stat`. To match filenames to some wildcard pattern, see question 13.7.

Here is a tiny example that lists the files in the current directory:

```
#include <stdio.h>
#include <sys/types.h>
#include <dirent.h>

main()
{
        struct dirent *dp;
        DIR *dfd = opendir(".");
        if(dfd != NULL) {
                while((dp = readdir(dfd)) != NULL)
                        printf("%s\n", dp->d_name);
                closedir(dfd);
        }
        return 0;
}
```

(On older systems, the header file to include may be <direct.h> or
<dir.h>, and the pointer returned by readdir may be a struct direct *.
This example assumes that "." is a synonym for the current directory.)

In a pinch, you could use popen (see question 19.30) to call an operating
system list-directory program and read its output. (If you need only the file
names displayed to the user, you could conceivably use system; see question
19.27.)

References: K&R2 §8.6 pp. 179–84
            PCS §13 pp. 230–1
            POSIX §5.1
            Schumacher, *Software Solutions in C* §8

19.21

Question: How do I create a directory? How do I remove a directory (and
its contents)?

Answer: If your operating system supports these services, they are likely to
be provided in C via functions named mkdir and rmdir. Removing a directory's contents as well will require listing them (see question 19.20) and calling remove (see also question 19.16). If you don't have these C functions

available, try `system` (see question 19.27) along with your operating system's delete command(s).

References: PCS §12 pp. 203–4
POSIX §§5.4.1, 5.5.2

Accessing Raw Memory

19.22

Question: How can I find out how much memory is available?

Answer: Your operating system may provide a function that returns this information, but it's quite system dependent. (Also, the number may vary over time.) If you're trying to predict whether you'll be able to allocate a certain amount of memory, just try it—call `malloc` (requesting that amount) and check the return value.

19.23

Question: How can I allocate arrays or structures bigger than 64K?

Answer: A reasonable computer ought to give you transparent access to all available memory. If you're not so lucky, you'll either have to rethink your program's use of memory or use various system-specific techniques.

Even so, 64K is (still) a pretty big chunk of memory. No matter how much memory your computer has available, it's asking a lot to be able to allocate huge amounts of it contiguously. (The C standard does not guarantee that a single object can be larger than 32K.) Often, it's a good idea to use data structures that don't require that all memory be contiguous. For dynamically allocated multidimensional arrays, you can use pointers to pointers, as illustrated in questions 6.16 and 20.2. Instead of a large array of structures, you can use a linked list or an array of pointers to structures.

If you're using a PC-compatible (8086-based) system and running up against a 640K limit, consider using "huge" memory model, expanded or extended memory, `malloc` variants such as `halloc` or `farmalloc`, a 32-bit "flat" compiler (e.g., djgpp; see question 18.3), some kind of a DOS extender, or another operating system.

References: ANSI §2.2.4.1
          ISO §5.2.4.1

19.24

Question: What does the error message "DGROUP data allocation exceeds 64K" mean, and what can I do about it? I thought that using large model meant that I could use more than 64K of data!

Answer: Even in large memory models, MS-DOS compilers apparently place certain data (strings, some initialized global or `static` variables) in a default data segment, and it's this segment that is overflowing. Either use less global data or, if you're already limiting yourself to reasonable amounts (and if the problem is due to something like the number of strings), you may be able to coax the compiler into not using the default data segment for so much. Some compilers place only "small" data objects in the default data segment and give you a way (e.g., the `/Gt` option under Microsoft compilers) to configure the threshold for "small."

19.25

Question: How can I access memory (a memory-mapped device or graphics memory) located at a certain address? How can I do PEEK and POKE in C?

Answer: Set a pointer, of the appropriate type, to the appropriate numeric address (using an explicit cast to assure the compiler that you really do intend this nonportable conversion):

```
unsigned int *magicloc = (unsigned int *)0x12345678;
```

Then, `*magicloc` refers to the location you want. (If you want to refer to a byte at a certain address rather than to a word, use `unsigned char *`.)

Under MS-DOS, you may find a macro like `MK_FP()` handy for working with segments and offsets. As suggested by Gary Blaine, you can also declare tricky array pointers that allow you to access screen memory using array notation. For example, on an MS-DOS machine in an 80×25 text mode, given the declaration

```
unsigned short (far * videomem)[80] =
            (unsigned short (far *)[80])0xb8000000;
```

you can access the character and attribute byte at row `i`, column `j` with `videomem[i][j]`.

Many operating systems execute user-mode programs in a protected mode where direct access to I/O devices (or to *any* address outside the running process) is simply not possible. In such cases, you will have to ask the operating system to carry out I/O operations for you.

See also questions 4.14 and 5.19.

References: K&R1 §A14.4 p. 210   ISO §6.3.4
            K&R2 §A6.6 p. 199   Rationale §3.3.4
            ANSI §3.3.4   H&S §6.2.7 pp. 171–2

19.26

Question: How can I access an interrupt vector located at the machine's location 0? If I set a pointer to 0, the compiler might translate it to a nonzero internal null pointer value.

Answer: See question 5.19.

"System" Commands

19.27

Question: How can I invoke another program (a standalone executable or an operating system command) from within a C program?

Answer: Use the library function `system`, which does exactly that.

Some systems also provide a family of `spawn` routines that accomplish approximately the same thing. These are not as portable as `system`, which is required under the ANSI C Standard, although in any case, the interpretation of the command string—its syntax and the set of commands accepted—will obviously vary tremendously.

The `system` function "calls" a command in the manner of a subroutine, and control eventually returns to the calling program. If you want to overlay the calling program with another program (that is, a "chain" operation), you'll need a system-specific routine, such as the `exec` family on UNIX.

Note that `system`'s return value is the command's exit status and usually has nothing to do with the output of the command. See also questions 19.28 and 19.30.

References: K&R1 §7.9 p. 157
K&R2 §7.8.4 p. 167, §B6 p. 253
ANSI §4.10.4.5
ISO §7.10.4.5
H&S §19.2 p. 407
PCS §11 p. 179

19.28

Question: How can I call `system` when parameters (filenames, etc.) of the executed command aren't known until run time?

Answer: Just use `sprintf` (or perhaps `strcpy` and `strcat`) to build the command string in a buffer; then call `system` with that buffer. (Make sure that the buffer is allocated with enough space; see also questions 7.2 and 12.21.)

Here is a contrived example suggesting how you might build a data file, then sort it (assuming the existence of a sort utility and UNIX- or MS-DOS-style input/output redirection):

```
char *datafile = "file.dat";
char *sortedfile = "file.sort";
char cmdbuf[50];
FILE *fp = fopen(datafile, "w");

/* ...write to fp to build data file... */

fclose(fp);

sprintf(cmdbuf, "sort < %s > %s", datafile, sortedfile);
system(cmdbuf);

fp = fopen(sortedfile, "r");
/* ...now read sorted data from fp... */
```

19.29

Question: How do I get an accurate error status return from **system** on MS-DOS?

Answer: You can't; COMMAND.COM doesn't tend to provide one. If you don't need COMMAND.COM's services (i.e., if you're just trying to invoke a simple program, without I/O redirection and such), try one of the **spawn** routines, instead.

19.30

Question: How can I invoke another program or command and trap its output?

Answer: UNIX and some other systems provide a **popen** function, which sets up a stdio stream on a pipe connected to the process running a command, so that the calling program can read the output (or alternatively supply the input). Using **popen**, the last example from question 19.28 would look like

```
extern FILE *popen();

sprintf(cmdbuf, "sort < %s", datafile);

fp = popen(cmdbuf, "r");

/* ...now read sorted data from fp... */

pclose(fp);
```

(Do be sure to call **pclose**, as shown; leaving it out will seem to work at first but may eventually run you out of processes.)

If you can't use **popen**, you may be able to use **system**, with the output going to a file that you then open and read, as the code in question 19.28 was doing already.*

If you're using UNIX and **popen** isn't sufficient, you can learn about **pipe, dup, fork,** and **exec.**

---

*Using **system** and a temporary file assumes that you don't need the called program to run concurrently with the main program.

(One thing that probably would *not* work, by the way, would be to use freopen.)

Reference: PCS §11 p. 169

Process Environment

19.31

Question: How can my program discover the complete pathname to the executable from which it was invoked?

Answer: The string in argv[0] may represent all or part of the pathname, or it may be empty. You may be able to duplicate the command language interpreter's search path logic to locate the executable if the name in argv[0] is present but incomplete. However, there is no guaranteed solution.

References: K&R1 §5.11 p. 111
         K&R2 §5.10 p. 115
         ANSI §2.1.2.2.1
         ISO §5.1.2.2.1
         H&S §20.1 p. 416

19.32

Question: How can I automatically locate a program's configuration files in the same directory as the executable?

Answer: It's difficult, in general; it's an equivalent problem to the one in question 19.31. Even if you can figure out a workable way to do it, you might want to consider making the program's auxiliary (library) directory configurable, perhaps with an environment variable. (It's especially important to allow variable placement of a program's configuration files when the program will be used by several people, e.g., on a multiuser system.)

19.33

Question: How can a process change an environment variable in its caller?

Answer: It may or may not be possible to do so at all. Different operating systems implement global name/value functionality in different ways. Whether the "environment" can be usefully altered by a running program—and if so, how—is system dependent.

Under UNIX, a process can modify its own environment (some systems provide `setenv` or `putenv` functions for the purpose), and the modified environment is generally passed on to child processes, but it is *not* propagated back to the parent process. (The environment of the parent process can be altered only if the parent is explicitly set up to listen for some kind of change requests.)

19.34

Question: How can I open files mentioned on the command line and parse option flags?

Answer: See question 20.3.

19.35

Question: Is `exit(status)` truly equivalent to returning the same `status` from `main`?

Answer: See question 11.16.

19.36

Question: How can I read in an object file and jump to functions in it?

Answer: You want a dynamic linker or loader. It may be possible to allocate some memory and read in object files, but you have to know an awful lot about object file formats, relocation, etc., and this approach can't work if code and data reside in separate address spaces or if code is otherwise privileged.

Under BSD UNIX, you could use `system` and `ld -A` to do the linking for you. Many versions of SunOS and System V have the -ldl library containing functions such as `dlopen` and `dlsym`, which allow object files to be dynamically loaded. Under VMS, use LIB$FIND_IMAGE_SYMBOL. The GNU project has a package called "dld".

Other System-Dependent Operations

Question: How can I implement a delay or time a user's response with subsecond resolution?

Answer: Unfortunately, there is no portable way. V7 UNIX and derived systems provided a fairly useful `ftime` routine with resolution up to a millisecond, but it has disappeared from System V and POSIX. Other routines you might look for on your system include `clock`, `delay`, `gettimeofday`, `msleep`, `nap`, `napms`, `setitimer`, `sleep`, `times`, and `usleep`. (A routine called `wait`, however, is—at least under UNIX—*not* what you want.) The `select` and `poll` calls (if available) can be pressed into service to implement simple delays. On MS-DOS machines, it is possible to reprogram the system timer and timer interrupts.

Of these, only `clock` is part of the ANSI standard. The difference between two calls to `clock` gives elapsed execution time, and if CLOCKS_PER_SEC is greater than 1, the difference will have subsecond resolution. However, `clock` gives elapsed processor time used by the current program, which on a multitasking system may differ considerably from real time.

If you're trying to implement a delay and all you have available is a time-reporting function, you can implement a CPU-intensive busy-wait, but this is an option only on a single-user, single-tasking machine, as it is terribly antisocial to any other processes. Under a multitasking operating system, be sure to use a call that puts your process to sleep for the duration, such as `sleep` or `select`, or `pause` in conjunction with `alarm` or `setitimer`.

For really brief delays, it's tempting to use a do-nothing loop like

```
long int i;
for(i = 0; i < 1000000; i++)
        ;
```

but resist this temptation if at all possible! For one thing, your carefully calculated delay loops will stop working next month when a faster processor comes out. Perhaps worse, a clever compiler may notice that the loop does nothing and optimize it away completely.

References: H&S §18.1 pp. 398–9
          PCS §12 pp. 197–8, 215–6
          POSIX §4.5.2

19.38

Question: How can I trap or ignore keyboard interrupts like control-C?

Answer: The basic step is to call `signal`, either as

```
#include <signal.h>
signal(SIGINT, SIG_IGN);
```

to ignore the interrupt signal, or as

```
extern void func(int);
signal(SIGINT, func);
```

to cause control to transfer to function `func` on receipt of an interrupt signal.*

On a multitasking system such as UNIX, it's best to use a slightly more involved technique:

```
extern void func(int);
if(signal(SIGINT, SIG_IGN) != SIG_IGN)
        signal(SIGINT, func);
```

---

*Actually, there may be several different keyboard interrupts. On many systems, the "interrupt signal" referred to as SIGINT is generated by control-C. UNIX systems also have SIGQUIT, usually generated by control-\ (although both SIGINT and SIGQUIT can in fact be bound to any key). MS-DOS systems also have control-Break, which usually results in SIGINT. On the Macintosh, SIGINT is sometimes generated by command-period.

The test and extra call ensure that a keyboard interrupt typed in the foreground won't inadvertently interrupt a program running in the background (and it doesn't hurt to code calls to `signal` this way on any system).*

On some systems, keyboard interrupt handling is also a function of the mode of the terminal-input subsystem; see question 19.1. On some systems, checking for keyboard interrupts is performed only when the program is reading input, and keyboard interrupt handling may therefore depend on which input routines are being called (and *whether* any input routines are active at all). On MS-DOS systems, `setcbrk` or `ctrlbrk` functions may also be involved.

References: ANSI §§4.7, 4.7.1
ISO §§7.7, 7.7.1
H&S §19.6 pp. 411–3
PCS §12 pp. 210–2
POSIX §§3.3.1, 3.3.4

19.39

Question: How can I handle floating-point exceptions gracefully?

Answer: On many systems, you can define a function `matherr`, which will be called when there are certain floating-point errors, such as errors in the math functions in `<math.h>`. You may also be able to use `signal` (see question 19.38) to catch SIGFPE. See also question 14.9.

Reference: Rationale §4.5.1

19.40

Question: How do I use sockets? Do networking? Write client/server applications?

Answers: All of these questions are outside of the scope of this book and have much more to do with the networking facilities you have available than they do with C. Good books on the subject are Douglas Comer's three-volume

---

*On modern UNIX systems using job control, background processes are in separate process groups and so don't receive keyboard interrupts, but it still doesn't hurt to code calls to `signal` this way, and any remaining users of non-job-control shells will thank you.

Internetworking with TCP/IP and W. R. Stevens's *UNIX Network Programming*. (There is also plenty of information out on the Internet.)

Retrospective

19.41

Question: But I can't use all these nonstandard, system-dependent functions, because my program has to be ANSI compatible!

Answer: You're out of luck. Either you misunderstood your requirement or it's an impossible one to meet. ANSI/ISO Standard C simply does not define ways of doing these things. (POSIX defines a few.) It is possible, and desirable, for *most* of a program to be ANSI compatible, deferring the system-dependent functionality to a few functions in a few files that are rewritten for each system ported to; see question 19.1 for an example. See also question 19.42.

19.42

Question: Why isn't any of this standardized in C? Any real program has to do some of these things.

Answer: In fact, some standardization has occurred along the way. In the beginning, C did not have a standard library at all; programmers always had to "roll their own" utility functions. After several abortive attempts, a certain set of library functions (including the `str*` and stdio families of functions) became a *de facto* standard, at least on UNIX systems, but the library was not yet a formal part of the language. Vendors could (and occasionally did) provide completely different functions along with their compilers.

In the ANSI/ISO C Standard, a library definition (based on the 1984 /usr/group standard and largely compatible with the traditional UNIX library) was adopted with as much standing as the language itself. The standard C library's treatment of file and device I/O is, however, rather minimal. It states how streams of characters are written to and read from files, and it provides a few suggestions about the display behavior of control characters, such as `\b`, `\r`, and `\t`, but beyond that it is silent.

If the standard were to attempt to define standard mechanisms for accessing things like keyboards and displays, it might seem to be a big convenience for programmers. But it would be a monumental task: There is already a huge variety of display devices and huge variation among the operating systems through which they are usually accessed. We cannot assume that the years to come will offer any less variety.

At one time, the common output device for C programs was a Teletype; later, it was a "dumb" terminal, and after that it was a "smart" VT100 or other ANSI X3.64-compatible terminal that today might be called "dumb." Today, it's likely to be a bitmapped color display screen. What will it be in five years? How will the operating systems of that time deal with its capabilities?

See also question 11.34.

Reference: Rationale §2.2.2, §4.9, §4.9.2

20 Miscellaneous

This chapter, as its name implies, covers a variety of topics that don't fit into any of the other chapters. The first two sections cover miscellaneous programming techniques and the manipulation of individual bits and bytes. Next come discussions of efficiency and C's `switch` statement. The section on "miscellaneous language features" is largely historical; it explains why a few of C's features are as they are and why C doesn't have a few features people sometimes wish for. It leads into some questions involving C and other languages.

Whole books have been written about algorithms, and this is not one of them, but the section on algorithms covers a few questions that seem to come up all the time among C programmers. Finally, the last section closes with some trivia and information about the on-line versions of this book.

The questions and sections in this chapter are broken down as follows:

Miscellaneous Techniques	20.1–20.6
Bits and Bytes	20.7–20.12
Efficiency	20.12–20.16
Switch Statements	20.16–20.18

Miscellaneous Techniques

20.1

Question: **How can I return multiple values from a function?**

Answer: There are several ways of doing this. (These examples show hypothetical polar-to-rectangular coordinate conversion functions, which must return both an x and a y coordinate.)

- Pass pointers to several locations that the function can fill in:

```
#include <math.h>

polar_to_rectangular(double rho, double theta,
        double *xp, double *yp)
{
    *xp = rho * cos(theta);
    *yp = rho * sin(theta);
}


...


    double x, y;
    polar_to_rectangular(1., 3.14, &x, &y);
```

- Have the function return a structure containing the desired values:

```
struct xycoord { double x, y; };

struct xycoord
polar_to_rectangular(double rho, double theta)
{
        struct xycoord ret;
        ret.x = rho * cos(theta);
        ret.y = rho * sin(theta);
        return ret;
}

...

        struct xycoord c = polar_to_rectangular(1., 3.14);
```

- Use a hybrid: Have the function accept a pointer to a structure, which it fills in:

```
polar_to_rectangular(double rho, double theta,
            struct xycoord *cp)
{
        cp->x = rho * cos(theta);
        cp->y = rho * sin(theta);
}

...

        struct xycoord c;
        polar_to_rectangular(1., 3.14, &c);
```

(Another example of this technique is the UNIX system call stat.)

- In a pinch, you can use global variables (though this is rarely a good idea).

See also questions 2.7, 4.8, and 7.5.

20.2

Question: What's a good data structure to use for storing lines of text? I started to use fixed-size arrays of arrays of char, but they're too restrictive.

Answer: One good way of doing this is with a pointer (simulating an array) to a set of pointers (each simulating an array) of char. This data structure is sometimes called a "ragged array" and looks something like this:

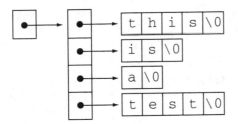

You could set up the tiny array in the figure with these simple declarations:

```
char *a[4] = {"this", "is", "a", "test"};
char **p = a;
```

(where p is the pointer to pointer to char and a is an intermediate array used to allocate the four pointers to char).

To really do dynamic allocation, you'd of course have to call malloc:

```
#include <stdlib.h>
char **p = malloc(4 * sizeof(char *));
if(p != NULL) {
        p[0] = malloc(5);
        p[1] = malloc(3);
        p[2] = malloc(2);
        p[3] = malloc(5);

        if(p[0] && p[1] && p[2] && p[3]) {
                strcpy(p[0], "this");
                strcpy(p[1], "is");
                strcpy(p[2], "a");
                strcpy(p[3], "test");
        }
}
```

(Some libraries have a strdup function that would streamline the inner malloc and strcpy calls. It's not standard, but it's obviously trivial to implement something like it.)

Here is a code fragment that reads an entire file into memory, using the same kind of ragged array. This code is written in terms of the `agetline` function from question 7.30.

```
#include <stdio.h>
#include <stdlib.h>
extern char *agetline(FILE *);
FILE *ifp;

/* assume ifp is open on input file */

char **lines = NULL;
size_t nalloc = 0;
size_t nlines = 0;
char *p;

while((p = agetline(ifp)) != NULL) {
    if(nlines >= nalloc) {
        nalloc += 50;
        lines = realloc(lines, nalloc * sizeof(char *));
        if(lines == NULL) {
            fprintf(stderr, "out of memory");
            exit(1);
        }
    }

    lines[nlines++] = p;
}
```

(See the comments on reallocation strategy in question 7.30.)
    See also question 6.16.

20.3

Question: How can I open files mentioned on the command line and parse option flags?

Answer: Here is a skeleton that implements a traditional UNIX-style `argv` parse, handling option flags beginning with - and optional filenames. (The two flags accepted by this example are -a and -b; -b takes an argument.)

```c
#include <stdio.h>
#include <string.h>
#include <errno.h>

main(int argc, char *argv[])
{
        int argi;
        int aflag = 0;
        char *bval = NULL;

        for(argi = 1; argi < argc && argv[argi][0] == '-';
                                                        argi++) {
                char *p;
                for(p = &argv[argi][1]; *p != '\0'; p++) {
                        switch(*p) {
                        case 'a':
                                aflag = 1;
                                printf("-a seen\n");
                                break;

                        case 'b':
                                bval = argv[++argi];
                                printf("-b seen (\"%s\")\n", bval);
                                break;

                        default:
                                fprintf(stderr,
                                    "unknown option -%c\n", *p);
                        }
                }
        }

        if(argi >= argc) {
                /* no filename arguments; process stdin */
                printf("processing standard input\n");
        } else {
                /* process filename arguments */
```

```
        for(; argi < argc; argi++) {
                FILE *ifp = fopen(argv[argi], "r");
                if(ifp == NULL) {
                        fprintf(stderr, "can't open %s: %s\n",
                                argv[argi], strerror(errno));
                        continue;
                }

                printf("processing %s\n", argv[argi]);

                fclose(ifp);
        }
    }

    return 0;
}
```

(This code assumes that fopen sets errno when it fails, which is not guaranteed but usually works and makes error messages much more useful. See also question 20.4.)

Several canned functions are available for doing command line parsing in a standard way; the most popular one is getopt (see also question 18.16). Here is the previous example, rewritten to use getopt:

```
extern char *optarg;
extern int optind;

main(int argc, char *argv[])
{
        int aflag = 0;
        char *bval = NULL;
        int c;

        while((c = getopt(argc, argv, "ab:")) != -1)
                switch(c) {
                case 'a':
                        aflag = 1;
                        printf("-a seen\n");
                        break;
```

```
        case 'b':
                bval = optarg;
                printf("-b seen (\"%s\")\n", bval);
                break;
    }

    if(optind >= argc) {
            /* no filename arguments; process stdin */
            printf("processing standard input\n");
    } else {
            /* process filename arguments */

            for(; optind < argc; optind++) {
                    FILE *ifp = fopen(argv[optind], "r");
                    if(ifp == NULL) {
                      fprintf(stderr, "can't open %s: %s\n",
                              argv[optind], strerror(errno));
                        continue;
                    }

                    printf("processing %s\n", argv[optind]);

                    fclose(ifp);
            }
    }

    return 0;
}
```

The preceding examples overlook a number of nuances: A lone "-" is often taken to mean "read standard input"; the marker "--" often signifies the end of the options (proper versions of getopt do handle this); it's traditional to print a usage message when a command is invoked with improper or missing arguments.

If you're wondering how argv is laid out in memory, it's a "ragged array"; see the picture in question 20.2.

References: K&R1 §5.11 pp. 110–4   H&S §20.1 p. 416
          K&R2 §5.10 pp. 114–8   PCS §5.6 pp. 81–2, §11 p. 159, pp. 339–40 Appendix F
          ANSI §2.1.2.2.1   Schumacher, *Software Solutions in C* §4 pp. 75–85
          ISO §5.1.2.2.1

20.4

Question: What's the right way to use `errno`?

Answer: In general, you should detect errors by checking return values and use `errno` only to distinguish among the various causes of an error, such as "File not found" or "Permission denied." (Typically, you use `perror` or `strerror` to print these discriminating error messages.) It's necessary to detect errors with `errno` only when a function does not have a unique, unambiguous, out-of-band error return (i.e., because all of its possible return values are valid; one example is `atoi`). In these cases (and in these cases only; check the documentation to be sure whether a function allows this), you can detect errors by setting `errno` to 0, calling the function, then testing `errno`. (Setting `errno` to 0 first is important, as no library function ever does that for you.)

To make error messages useful, they should include all relevant information. Besides the `strerror` text derived from `errno`, it may also be appropriate to print the name of the program, the operation that failed (preferably in terms that will be meaningful to the user), the name of the file for which the operation failed, and, if some input file (script or source file) is being read, the name and current line number of that file.

See also question 12.24.

References: ANSI §4.1.3, §4.9.10.4, §4.11.6.2
             ISO §7.1.4, §7.9.10.4, §7.11.6.2
             CT&P §5.4 p. 73
             PCS §11 p. 168, §14 p. 254

20.5

Question: How can I write data files that can be read on other machines with different word size, byte order, or floating-point formats?

Answer: The most portable solution is to use text files (usually ASCII), written with `fprintf` and read with `fscanf` or the like. (Similar advice also applies to network protocols.) Be skeptical of arguments that imply that text files are too big or that reading and writing them is too slow. Not only is their efficiency frequently acceptable in practice, but the advantages of being able to interchange them easily between machines and to manipulate them with standard tools can be overwhelming.

If you must use a binary format, you can improve portability, and perhaps take advantage of prewritten I/O libraries, by making use of standardized formats such as Sun's XDR (RFC 1014), OSI's ASN.1 (referenced in CCITT X.409 and ISO 8825 "Basic Encoding Rules"), CDF, netCDF, or HDF. See also questions 2.12, 12.38, and 12.42.

Reference: PCS §6 pp. 86, 88

20.6

Question: If I have a **char *** variable pointing to the name of a function, how can I call that function? Code like

```
extern int func();
char *funcname = "func";
int r = (*funcname)();
```

or

```
r = (*(int (*)())funcname)();
```

doesn't seem to work.

Answer: By the time a program is running, information about the names of its functions and variables (the "symbol table") is no longer needed and may therefore not be available. The most straightforward thing to do, therefore, is to maintain that information yourself, with a correspondence table of names and function pointers:

```
int func(), anotherfunc();

struct { char *name; int (*funcptr)(); } symtab[] = {
      "func",           func,
      "anotherfunc",    anotherfunc,
};
```

Then, search the table for the name and call via the associated function pointer with code like this:

```
#include <stddef.h>
#include <string.h>

int (*findfunc(char *name))()
{
        int i;

        for(i = 0; i < sizeof(symtab) / sizeof(symtab[0]); i++) {
                if(strcmp(name, symtab[i].name) == 0)
                        return symtab[i].funcptr;
        }

        return NULL;
}


        ...

        char *funcname = "func";
        int (*funcp)() = findfunc(funcname);
        if(funcp != NULL)
                (*funcp)();
```

The callable functions should all have compatible argument and return types. (Ideally, the function pointers would also specify the argument types.)

It is sometimes possible for a program to read its own symbol table if it is still present, but it must first be able to find its own executable (see question 19.31), and it must know how to interpret the symbol table (some UNIX C libraries provide an nlist function for this purpose). See also questions 2.15 and 19.36.

Reference: PCS §11 p. 168

Bits and Bytes

20.7

Question: How can I manipulate individual bits?

Answer: Bit manipulation is straightforward in C and commonly done. To extract (test) a bit, use the bitwise AND (&) operator, along with a bit mask representing the bit(s) you're interested in:

```
value & 0x04
```

To set a bit, use the bitwise OR ($|$ or $|=$) operator:

```
value |= 0x04
```

To clear a bit, use the bitwise complement (~) and the AND (& or &=) operators:

```
value &= ~0x04
```

(The preceding three examples all manipulate the third-least significant, or 2^2, bit, expressed as the constant bitmask 0x04.)

To manipulate an arbitrary bit, use the shift-left operator (<<) to generate the mask you need:

```
value & (1 << bitnumber)
value |= (1 << bitnumber)
value &= ~(1 << bitnumber)
```

Alternatively, you may wish to precompute an array of masks:

```
unsigned int masks[] =
    {0x01, 0x02, 0x04, 0x08, 0x10, 0x20, 0x40, 0x80};

value & masks[bitnumber]
value |= masks[bitnumber]
value &= ~masks[bitnumber]
```

To avoid surprises involving the sign bit, it is often a good idea to use unsigned integral types in code that manipulates bits and bytes.

See also questions 9.2 and 20.8.

References: K&R1 §2.9 pp. 44–5   ISO §6.3.3.3, §6.3.7, §6.3.10, §6.3.12
          K&R2 §2.9 pp. 48–9   H&S §7.5.5 p. 197, §7.6.3 pp. 205–6, §7.6.6 p. 210
          ANSI §3.3.3.3, §3.3.7, §3.3.10, §3.3.12

20.8

Question: How can I implement sets or arrays of bits?

Answer: Use arrays of char or int with a few macros to access the desired bit in the proper cell of the array. Here are some simple macros to use with arrays of char:

```
#include <limits.h>                /* for CHAR_BIT */

#define BITMASK(b) (1 << ((b) % CHAR_BIT))
#define BITSLOT(b) ((b) / CHAR_BIT)
#define BITSET(a, b) ((a)[BITSLOT(b)] |= BITMASK(b))
#define BITCLEAR(a, b) ((a)[BITSLOT(b)] &= ~BITMASK(b))
#define BITTEST(a, b) ((a)[BITSLOT(b)] & BITMASK(b))
#define BITNSLOTS(nb) ((nb + CHAR_BIT - 1) / CHAR_BIT)
```

(If you don't have <limits.h>, try using 8 for CHAR_BIT.)

Here are some usage examples:

• To declare an "array" of 47 bits:

```
char bitarray[BITNSLOTS(47)];
```

• To set the 23rd bit:

```
BITSET(bitarray, 23);
```

• To test the 35th bit:

```
if(BITTEST(bitarray, 35)) …
```

• To compute the union of two bit arrays and place it in a third array (with all three arrays as previously declared):

```
for(i = 0; i < BITNSLOTS(47); i++)
        array3[i] = array1[i] | array2[i];
```

• To compute the intersection, use & instead of |.

As a more realistic example, here is a quick implementation of the Sieve of Eratosthenes, for computing prime numbers:

```
#include <stdio.h>
#include <string.h>

#define MAX 100

main()
{
        char bitarray[BITNSLOTS(MAX)];
        int i, j;

        memset(bitarray, 0, BITNSLOTS(MAX));

        for(i = 2; i < MAX; i++) {
                if(!BITTEST(bitarray, i)) {
                        printf("%d\n", i);
                        for(j = i + i; j < MAX; j += i)
                                BITSET(bitarray, j);
                }
        }
        return 0;
}
```

See also question 20.7.

References: H&S §7.6.7 pp. 211–6

20.9

Question: How can I determine whether a machine's byte order is big-endian or little-endian?

Answer: The usual techniques are to use a pointer:

```
int x = 1;
if(*(char *)&x == 1)
        printf("little-endian\n");
else  printf("big-endian\n");
```

or a union:

```
union {
        int i;
        char c[sizeof(int)];
} x;
x.i = 1;
```

```
if(x.c[0] == 1)
        printf("little-endian\n");
else  printf("big-endian\n");
```

See also question 10.16.

Reference: H&S §6.1.2 pp. 163–4

20.10

Question: How can I convert integers to binary or hexadecimal?

Answer: Make sure that you really know what you're asking. Integers are stored internally in binary, although for most purposes, it is not incorrect to think of them as being in octal, decimal, or hexadecimal, whichever is convenient. The base in which a number is expressed matters only when that number is read in from or written out to the outside world, either in the form of a source code constant or in the form of I/O performed by a program.

In source code, a nondecimal base is indicated by a leading 0 or 0x (for octal or hexadecimal, respectively). During I/O, the base of a formatted number is controlled in the printf and scanf family of functions by the choice of format specifier (%d, %o, %x, etc.) and in the strtol and strtoul functions by the third argument. During *binary* I/O, however, the base again becomes immaterial: If numbers are being read or written as individual bytes (typically with getc or putc) or as multibyte words (typically with fread or fwrite), it is meaningless to ask what "base" they are in.

If what you need is formatted binary conversion, it's easy enough to do. Here is a little function for formatting a number in a requested base:

```
char *
baseconv(unsigned int num, int base)
{
        static char retbuf[33];
        char *p;

        if(base < 2 || base > 16)
                return NULL;

        p = &retbuf[sizeof(retbuf)-1];
        *p = '\0';
```

```
    do {
            *--p = "0123456789abcdef"[num % base];
            num /= base;
    } while(num != 0);


    return p;
}
```

(Note that this function, as written, returns a pointer to static data, such that only one of its return values can be used at a time; see question 7.5. A better size for the `retbuf` array would be `sizeof(int)*CHAR_BIT+1`; see question 12.21.)

For more information about "binary" I/O, see questions 2.11, 12.37, and 12.42. See also questions 8.6 and 13.1.

References: ANSI §§4.10.1.5, 4.10.1.6
            ISO §§7.10.1.5, 7.10.1.6

20.11

Question: Can I use base-2 constants (something like `0b101010`)? Is there a `printf` format for binary?

Answer: No, on both counts. You can convert base-2 string representations to integers with `strtol`. If you need to print numbers out in base 2, see the example code in question 20.10.

Efficiency

20.12

Question: What is the most efficient way to count the number of bits that are set in a value?

Answer: Many "bit-fiddling" problems like this one can be sped up and streamlined using lookup tables (but see question 20.13). On the next page is a little function that computes the number of bits in a value, 4 bits at a time.

```
static int bitcounts[] =
        {0, 1, 1, 2, 1, 2, 2, 3, 1, 2, 2, 3, 2, 3, 3, 4};

int bitcount(unsigned int u)
{
        int n = 0;

        for(; u != 0; u >>= 4)
                n += bitcounts[u & 0x0f];

        return n;
}
```

20.13

Question: How can I make my code more efficient?

Answer: Efficiency, though an enormously popular topic, is not important nearly as often as people tend to think it is. Most of the code in most programs is not time critical, and when it is not, it is far more important that it be written clearly and portably. (Remember that computers are very, very fast and that even "inefficient" code can run without apparent delay.)

It is notoriously difficult to predict what the "hot spots" in a program will be. When efficiency is a concern, it is important to use profiling software to determine which parts of the program deserve attention. Often, computation time is swamped by peripheral tasks, such as I/O and memory allocation, which can be sped up by using buffering and caching techniques.

Even for code that *is* time critical, it is not as important to "microoptimize" the coding details. Many of the frequently suggested "efficient coding tricks" are performed automatically by even simpleminded compilers. Heavy-handed optimization attempts can make code so bulky that performance is in fact degraded, by increasing the number of page faults or by overflowing instruction caches or pipelines. Furthermore, optimization tricks are rarely portable (i.e., they may speed things up on one machine but slow them down on another). In any case, tweaking the coding usually results in at best linear performance improvements; the big payoffs are in better algorithms.

If the performance of your code is so important that you are willing to invest programming time in source-level optimizations, make sure that you are using the best optimizing compiler you can afford. (Compilers, even mediocre ones, can perform optimizations that are impossible at the source level.)

When efficiency is truly important, the best algorithm has been chosen, and even the coding details matter, the following suggestions may be useful. (These are mentioned merely because the question is frequent; appearance here does *not* necessarily constitute endorsement by the author. Note that several of these techniques cut both ways and may make things worse.)

- Sprinkle the code liberally with `register` declarations for oft-used variables; place them in inner blocks, if applicable. (On the other hand, most modern compilers ignore `register` declarations, on the assumption that they can perform register analysis and assignment better than the programmer can.)

- Check the algorithm carefully. Exploit symmetries where possible to reduce the number of explicit cases.

- Examine the control flow: Make sure that common cases are checked for first and handled more easily. If one side of an expression involving `&&` or `||` will usually determine the outcome, make it the left-hand side, if possible. (See also question 3.6.)

- Use `memcpy` instead of `memmove`, if appropriate (see question 11.25).

- Use machine- and vendor-specific routines and `#pragmas`.

- Manually place common subexpressions in temporary variables. (Good compilers do this for you.)

- Move critical, inner-loop code out of functions and into macros or in-line functions (and out of the loop, if invariant). If the termination condition of a loop is a complex but loop-invariant expression, precompute it and place it in a temporary variable. (Good compilers do these for you.)

- Change recursion to iteration, if possible.

- Unroll small loops.

- Discover whether `while`, `for`, or `do/while` loops produce the best code under your compiler and whether incrementing or decrementing the loop control variable works best.

- Remove `goto` statements—some compilers can't optimize as well in their presence.

- Use pointers rather than array subscripts to step through arrays (but see question 20.14).

- Reduce precision. (Using `float` instead of `double` may result in faster, single-precision arithmetic under an ANSI compiler, although older compilers convert everything to `double`, so using `float` can also be slower.) Replace time-consuming trigonometric and logarithmic functions with your own, tailored to the range and precision you need, and perhaps using table lookup. (Be sure to give your versions *different* names; see question 1.29.)

- Cache or precompute tables of frequently needed values. (See also question 20.12.)

- Use standard library functions in preference to your own. (Sometimes, the compiler inlines or specially optimizes its own functions.) On the other hand, if your program's calling patterns are particularly regular, your own special-purpose implementation may be able to beat the library's general-purpose version. (Again, if you do write your own version, give it a different name.)

- As a last, *last* resort, hand code critical routines in assembly language (or hand tune the compiler's assembly language output). Use `asm` directives, if possible.

Here are some things *not* to worry about:

- whether `i++` is faster than `i = i + 1`
- whether `i << 1` (or `i >> 1`, or `i & 1`) is faster than `i * 2` (respectively `i / 2`, `i % 2`)

(These are examples of optimizations that compilers regularly perform for you; see questions 20.14 and 20.15.)

It is not the intent here to suggest that efficiency can be completely ignored. Most of the time, however, by simply paying attention to good algorithm choices, implementing them cleanly, and avoiding obviously inefficient blunders (i.e., make sure you don't end up with an $O(n^3)$ implementation of an $O(n^2)$ algorithm), perfectly acceptable results can be achieved.

For more discussion of efficiency tradeoffs, as well as good advice on how to improve efficiency when it is important, see Chapter 7 of Kernighan and Plauger's *The Elements of Programming Style* and Jon Bentley's *Writing Efficient Programs*.

See also question 17.11.

20.14

Question: Are pointers really faster than arrays? How much do function calls slow things down? Is ++i faster than i = i + 1?

Answer: Precise answers to these and many similar questions depend, of course, on the processor and compiler in use. If you simply must know, you'll have to time test programs carefully. (Often, the differences are so slight that hundreds of thousands of iterations are required even to see them.* Check the compiler's assembly language output, if available, to see whether two purported alternatives aren't compiled identically.)

It is "usually" faster to march through large arrays with pointers rather than array subscripts, but for some processors, the reverse is true. (Better compilers should generate good code regardless of which notation you use.)

Function calls, though obviously incrementally slower than in-line code, contribute so much to modularity and code clarity that there is rarely good reason to avoid them. (Actually, by reducing bulk, functions can improve performance.) Also, some compilers are able to expand small, critical-path functions in-line, either as an optimization or at the programmer's request.

Before rearranging expressions such as i = i + 1, remember that you are dealing with a compiler, not a keystroke-programmable calculator. Any decent compiler will generate identical code for ++i, i += 1, and i = i + 1. The reasons for using ++i or i += 1 over i = i + 1 have to do with style, not efficiency. (See also question 3.12.)

20.15

Question: Is it worthwhile to replace multiplications and divisions with shift operators?

Answer: This is an excellent example of a potentially risky and usually unnecessary optimization. Any compiler worthy of the name can replace a constant, power-of-two multiplication with a left shift or a similar division of an unsigned quantity with a right shift. (Ritchie's original PDP–11 compiler, though it ran in less than 64K of memory and omitted several features now considered mandatory, performed both of these optimizations, without even

---

*If it's difficult to measure, it may suggest that you don't have to worry about the difference after all.

turning on its optional optimization pass.) Furthermore, a compiler will make these optimizations only when they're correct; many programmers overlook the fact that shifting a negative value to the right is *not* equivalent to division. (Therefore, when you need to make sure that these optimizations are performed, you may have to declare relevant variables as unsigned.)

switch **Statements**

20.16

Question: Which is more efficient: a switch statement or an if/else chain?

Answer: The differences, if any, are likely to be slight. The switch statement was designed to be efficiently implementable, although the compiler may use the equivalent of an if/else chain (as opposed to a compact jump table) if the case labels are sparsely distributed.

Do use switch when you can: It's definitely cleaner and perhaps more efficient (and certainly should never be any *less* efficient).

See also questions 20.17 and 20.18.

20.17

Question: Is there a way to switch on strings?

Answer: Not directly. Sometimes, it's appropriate to use a separate function to map strings to integer codes and then switch on those:

```
#define CODE_APPLE      1
#define CODE_ORANGE     2
#define CODE_NONE 0
```

```
switch(classifyfunc(string)) {
     case CODE_APPLE:
          ...

     case CODE_ORANGE:
          ...

     case CODE_NONE:
          ...
}
```

The `classifyfunc` function would look something like this:

```
static struct lookuptab {
     char *string;
     int code;
} tab[] = {
     {"apple",    CODE_APPLE},
     {"orange",   CODE_ORANGE},
};

classifyfunc(char *string)
{
     int i;
     for(i = 0; i < sizeof(tab) / sizeof(tab[0]); i++)
          if(strcmp(tab[i].string, string) == 0)
               return tab[i].code;

     return CODE_NONE;
}
```

Otherwise, of course, you can fall back on a conventional if/else chain:

```
if(strcmp(string, "apple") == 0) {
     ...
} else if(strcmp(string, "orange") == 0) {
     ...
}
```

(A macro like `streq()` from question 17.3 can make these comparisons a bit more convenient.)

See also questions 10.12, 20.16, 20.18, and 20.29.

References: K&R1 §3.4 p. 55   ISO §6.6.4.2
           K&R2 §3.4 p. 58   H&S §8.7 p. 248
           ANSI §3.6.4.2

20.18

Question: Is there a way to have nonconstant **case** labels (i.e., ranges or arbitrary expressions)?

Answer: No. The **switch** statement was originally designed to be quite simple for the compiler to translate; therefore, case labels are limited to single, constant, integral expressions. You *can* attach several case labels to the same statement, which will let you cover a small range if you don't mind listing all cases explicitly. If you want to select on arbitrary ranges or nonconstant expressions, you'll have to use an if/else chain.

See also questions 20.16 and 20.17.

References: K&R1 §3.4 p. 55
K&R2 §3.4 p. 58
ANSI §3.6.4.2
ISO §6.6.4.2
Rationale §3.6.4.2
H&S §8.7 p. 248

Miscellaneous Language Features

20.19

Question: Are the outer parentheses in **return** statements really optional?

Answer: Yes.

Long ago, in the early days of C, they were required, and just enough people learned C then, and wrote code that is still in circulation, that the notion that they might still be required is widespread.

(As it happens, parentheses are optional with the **sizeof** operator, too, as long as its operand is a variable or a unary expression.)

References: K&R1 §A18.3 p. 218
ANSI §3.3.3, §3.6.6
ISO §6.3.3, §6.6.6
H&S §8.9 p. 254

20.20

Question: Why don't C comments nest? How am I supposed to comment out code containing comments? Are comments legal inside quoted strings?

Answer: C comments don't nest mostly because PL/I's comments, which C's are borrowed from, don't either. Therefore, it is usually better to "comment out" large sections of code, which might contain comments, with `#ifdef` or `#if  0` (but see question 11.19).

The character sequences `/*` and `*/` are not special within double-quoted strings and do not therefore introduce comments, because a program (particularly one generating C code as output) might want to print them. (It is difficult to imagine why anyone would want or need to place a comment inside a quoted string. It is easy to imagine a program needing to print `"/*"`.)

Note also that `//` comments, as in C++, are not currently legal in C, so it's not a good idea to use them in C programs (even if your compiler supports them as an extension).

References: K&R1 §A2.1 p. 179
  K&R2 §A2.2 p. 192
  ANSI §3.1.9 (esp. footnote 26), Appendix E
  ISO §6.1.9, Annex F
  Rationale §3.1.9
  H&S §2.2 pp. 18–9
  PCS §10 p. 130

20.21

Question: Why isn't C's set of operators more complete? A few operators, such as `^^`, `&&=`, and `->=`, seem to be missing.

Answer: A logical exclusive-or operator (hypothetically "`^^`") might be nice, but it couldn't possibly have short-circuiting behavior analogous to `&&` and `||` (see question 3.6). Similarly, it's not clear how short-circuiting would apply to hypothetical assignment operators `&&=` and `||=`. (It's also not clear how often `&&=` and `||=` would be needed.)

Although p = p->next is an extremely common idiom for traversing a linked list, -> is not a binary arithmetic operator. A hypothetical ->= operator therefore wouldn't really fit the pattern of the other assignment operators—it would save a few keystrokes without really contributing much to the cleanliness or completeness of the language.

You can write an exclusive-or macro in several ways:

```
#define XOR(a, b) ((a) && !(b) || !(a) && (b))   /* 1 */
#define XOR(a, b) (!!(a) ^ !!(b))                 /* 2 */
#define XOR(a, b) (!!(a) != !!(b))                /* 3 */
#define XOR(a, b) (!(a) ^ !(b))                   /* 4 */
#define XOR(a, b) (!(a) != !(b))                  /* 5 */
#define XOR(a, b) ((a) ? !(b) : !!(b))            /* 6 */
```

The first is straight from the definition but is poor because it may evaluate its arguments multiple times (see question 10.1). The second and third "normalize" their operands* to strict 0/1 by negating them twice—the second then applies bitwise exclusive or (to the single remaining bit); the third one implements exclusive-or as !=. The fourth and fifth are based on an elementary identity in Boolean algebra, namely, that

$$a \oplus b = \bar{a} \oplus \bar{b}$$

(where $\oplus$ is exclusive-or and an overbar indicates negation). Finally, the sixth one, suggested by Lawrence Kirby and Dan Pop, uses the ?: operator to guarantee a sequence point between the two operands, as for && and ||. (There is still no "short circuiting" behavior, though, nor can there be.)

20.22

Question: If the assignment operator were :=, wouldn't it then be harder to accidentally write things like if(a = b) ?

Answer: Yes, but it would also be just a little bit more cumbersome to type all of the assignment statements a typical program contains.

---

*Normalization is important if the XOR() macro is to mimic the operation of the other Boolean operators in C, namely, that the true/false interpretation of the operands is based on whether they are nonzero or zero (see question 9.2).

In any case, it's really too late to be worrying about this sort of thing now. The choices of = for assignment and == for comparison were made, rightly or wrongly, over two decades ago and are not likely to be changed. (With respect to the question, many compilers and versions of lint will warn about if(a = b) and similar expressions; see also question 17.4.)

As a point of historical interest, the choices were made based on the observation that assignment is more frequent than comparison and so deserves fewer keystrokes. In fact, using = for assignment in C and its predecessor B represented a change from B's own predecessor BCPL, which did use : = as its assignment operator. (See also question 20.38.)

20.23

Question: Does C have an equivalent to Pascal's with statement?

Answer: No. The way in C to get quick and easy access to the fields of a structure is to declare a little local structure pointer variable (which, it must be admitted, is not quite as notationally convenient as a with statement and doesn't save quite as many keystrokes, though it is probably safer). That is, if you have something unwieldy like

```
structarray[complex_expression].a =
        structarray[complex_expression].b +
                structarray[complex_expression].c;
```

you can replace it with

```
struct whatever *p = &structarray[complex_expression];
p->a = p->b + p->c;
```

20.24

Question: Why doesn't C have nested functions?

Answer: It's not trivial to implement nested functions such that they have the proper access to local variables in the containing function(s), so they were deliberately left out of C as a simplification. (However, gcc does allow them, as an extension.) For many potential uses of nested functions (e.g., qsort comparison functions), an adequate if slightly cumbersome solution is to use an adjacent function with `static` declaration, communicating if necessary via a few `static` variables. (A cleaner solution when such functions must communicate is to pass around a pointer to a structure containing the necessary context.)

Other Languages

20.25

Question: How can I call FORTRAN (C++, BASIC, Pascal, Ada, LISP) functions from C? (And vice versa?)

Answer: The answer is entirely dependent on the machine and the specific calling sequences of the various compilers in use and may not be possible at all. Read your compiler documentation very carefully; sometimes, there is a "mixed-language programming guide," although the techniques for passing arguments and ensuring correct run-time startup are often arcane. The on-line versions of this book (see question 20.40) contain pointers to some more information about interlanguage calling.

In C++, a `"C"` modifier in an external function declaration indicates that the function is to be called using C calling conventions.

Reference: H&S §4.9.8 pp. 106–7

20.26

Question: Are there programs for converting Pascal or FORTRAN to C?

Answer: Yes. A number of programs for translating from FORTRAN and Pascal to C are available on the Internet, and several commercial companies provide translation utilities and services for these languages and others as well. It is difficult to provide a comprehensive, up-to-date list of all of the various translations available; the three most commonly mentioned are `p2c`, `ptoc`, and `f2c`. The electronic FAQ list associated with this book contains a bit more information. See questions 18.16 and 20.40.

20.27

Question: Is C++ a superset of C? What are the differences between C and C++? Can I use a C++ compiler to compile C code?

Answer: C++ was derived from C and is largely based on it, but some legal C constructs are not legal C++. Conversely, ANSI C inherited several features from C++, including prototypes and `const`, so neither language is really a subset or superset of the other.

The most important feature of C++ not found in C is, of course, the extended structure known as a `class`, which, along with operator overloading, makes object-oriented programming convenient. There are several other differences and new features: Variables may be declared anywhere in a block; `const` variables may be true compile-time constants; structure tags are implicitly typedeffed; an `&` in a parameter declaration requests pass by reference; and the `new` and `delete` operators, along with per-object constructors and destructors, simplify dynamic data structure management. Classes and object-oriented programming introduce a host of new mechanisms: inheritance, `friends`, virtual functions, templates, etc. (This list of C++ features is not intended to be complete; C++ programmers will notice many omissions.)

Some features of C that keep it from being a strict subset of C++ (that is, that keep C programs from necessarily being acceptable to C++ compilers) are that `main` may be called recursively, character constants are of type `int`, prototypes are not required, and `void *` implicitly converts to other pointer types. Also, every keyword in C++ that is not a keyword in C is available in C as an identifier; C programs that use words such as `class` and `friend` as ordinary identifiers will be rejected by C++ compilers.

In spite of the differences, many C programs will compile correctly in a C++ environment, and many recent compilers offer both C and C++ compilation modes.

Reference: H&S p. xviii, §1.1.5 p. 6, §2.8 pp. 36–7, §4.9 pp. 104–7

Algorithms

20.28

Question: I need a sort of an "approximate" strcmp routine for comparing two strings for close, but not necessarily exact, equality. What's a good way to do that?

Answer: Some nice information and algorithms having to do with approximate string matching, as well as a useful bibliography, can be found in Sun Wu and Udi Manber's paper "AGREP—A Fast Approximate Pattern-Matching Tool."

Another approach involves the "soundex" algorithm, which maps similar-sounding words to the same codes. Soundex was designed for discovering similar-sounding names (for telephone directory assistance, as it happens), but it can be pressed into service for processing arbitrary words.

References: Knuth Vol 3 §6 pp. 391–2
   Wu and Manber, "AGREP—A Fast Approximate Pattern-Matching Tool"

20.29

Question: What is hashing?

Answer: Hashing is the process of mapping strings to integers, usually in a relatively small range. A "hash function" maps a string (or other data structure) to a bounded number (the "hash bucket") that can more easily be used as an index in an array or for performing repeated comparisons. (Obviously, a mapping from a potentially huge set of strings to a small set of integers will not be unique. Any algorithm using hashing therefore has to deal with the possibility of "collisions.")

Many hashing functions and related algorithms have been developed; a full treatment is beyond the scope of this book. An extremely simple hash function for strings is simply to add up the values of all the characters:

```
unsigned hash(char *str)
{
        unsigned int h = 0;
```

```
        while(*str != '\0')
              h += *str++;
        return h % NBUCKETS;
}
```

A somewhat better hash function is

```
unsigned hash(char *str)
{
        unsigned int h = 0;
        while(*str != '\0')
              h = (256 * h + *str++) % NBUCKETS;
        return h;
}
```

Here the input string is treated as a large binary number (8 * `strlen(str)` bits long, assuming characters are 8 bits) and computes that number modulo NBUCKETS, by Horner's rule. (Here it is important that NBUCKETS be prime, among other things. To remove the assumption that characters are 8 bits, use UCHAR_MAX+1 instead of 256; the "large binary number" will then be CHAR_BIT * `strlen(str)` bits long. UCHAR_MAX and CHAR_BIT are defined in `<limits.h>`.)

When the set of strings is known in advance, it is also possible to devise "perfect" hashing functions that guarantee a collisionless, dense mapping.

References: K&R2 §6.6 pp. 143–5
Knuth Vol. 3 §6.4 pp. 506–49
Sedgewick §16 pp. 231–44

20.30

Question: How can I generate random numbers with a normal, or Gaussian, distribution?

Answer: See question 13.20.

20.31

Question: How can I find the day of the week given the date?

Answer: Here are three methods:

1. Use `mktime` or `localtime` (see question 13.13). Here is a code fragment that computes the day of the week for February 29, 2000:

```c
#include <stdio.h>
#include <time.h>

char *wday[] = {"Sunday", "Monday", "Tuesday", "Wednesday",
                "Thursday", "Friday", "Saturday"};

struct tm tm;

tm.tm_mon = 2 - 1;
tm.tm_mday = 29;
tm.tm_year = 2000 - 1900;
tm.tm_hour = tm.tm_min = tm.tm_sec = 0;
tm.tm_isdst = -1;

if(mktime(&tm) != -1)
        printf("%s\n", wday[tm.tm_wday]);
```

When using `mktime` like this, it's usually important to set **tm_isdst** to −1, as shown (especially if **tm_hour** is 0); otherwise, a daylight saving time correction could push the time past midnight into another day.

2. Use Zeller's congruence, which says that if

> *J* is the number of the century (i.e., the year / 100),
> *K* the year within the century (i.e., the year % 100),
> *m* the month,
> *q* the day of the month,
> *h* the day of the week (where 1 is Sunday),

and if January and February are taken as months 13 and 14 of the previous year (affecting both *J* and *K*), *h* for the Gregorian calendar is the remainder when the sum

$$q + 26(m + 1) / 10 + K + K/4 + J/4 - 2J$$

is divided by 7, and where all intermediate remainders are discarded.* The translation into C is straightforward:

```c
h = (q + 26 * (m + 1) / 10 + K + K/4 + J/4 + 5*J) % 7;
```

---

*At least one slightly modified form of Zeller's congruence has been widely circulated; the formulation shown here is the original.

(where we use +5*J instead of -2*J to make sure that both operands of the modulus operator % are positive; this bias totaling 7*J will obviously not change the final value of h, modulo 7).

3. Use this elegant code by Tomohiko Sakamoto:

```
dayofweek(y, m, d)        /* 0 = Sunday */
int y, m, d;              /* 1 <= m <= 12,  y > 1752 or so */
{
        static int t[] = {0, 3, 2, 5, 0, 3, 5, 1, 4, 6, 2, 4};
        y -= m < 3;
        return (y + y/4 - y/100 + y/400 + t[m-1] + d) % 7;
}
```

See also questions 13.14 and 20.32.

References: ANSI §4.12.2.3
           ISO §7.12.2.3
           Zeller, "Kalender-Formeln"

20.32

Question: Will 2000 be a leap year? Is (**year % 4 == 0**) an accurate test for leap years?

Answer: Yes and no, respectively. The rules for the present Gregorian calendar are that leap years occur every four years but not every 100 years, *except* that they do occur every 400 years, after all. In C, these rules can be expressed as:

```
year % 4 == 0 && (year % 100 != 0 || year % 400 == 0)
```

See a good astronomical almanac or other reference* for details.

Actually, if the domain of interest is limited (perhaps by the range of a time_t) such that the only century year it encompasses is 2000, the expression

```
(year % 4 == 0)                /* 1901-2099 only */
```

is accurate, if less than robust.

---

*Make sure that you check a *good* reference; some are wrong when it comes to calendar rules or mention the existence of a 4000-year rule that has not been adopted and won't be needed for another 2000 years, anyway.

If you trust the implementor of the C library, you can use mktime to determine whether a given year is a leap year; see the code fragments in questions 13.14 or 20.31 for hints.

Note also that the transition from the Julian to the Gregorian calendar involved deleting several days to make up for accumulated errors. (The transition was first made in Catholic countries under Pope Gregory XIII in October 1582 and involved deleting 10 days. In the British Empire, 11 days were deleted when the Gregorian calendar was adopted in September 1752. A few countries didn't switch until the 20th century.) Calendar code that has to work for historical dates must therefore be especially careful.

20.33

Question: Why can tm_sec in the tm structure range from 0 to 61, suggesting that there can be 62 seconds in a minute?

Answer: That's actually a buglet in the standard. There can be 61 seconds in a minute during a leap second. It's possible for there to be two leap seconds in a year, but it turns out that it's guaranteed that they'll never both occur in the same day (let alone the same minute).

Trivia

20.34

Question: Here's a good puzzle: How do you write a program that produces its own source code as its output?

Answer: It is quite difficult to write a self-reproducing program that is truly portable, due particularly to quoting and character set difficulties.

Here is a classic example (which is normally presented on one line, although it will "fix" itself the first time it's run):

```
char*s="char*s=%c%s%c;main(){printf(s,34,s,34);}";
main(){printf(s,34,s,34);}
```

(This program, like many of the genre, assumes that the double-quote character " has the value 34, as it does in ASCII.)

Question: What is "Duff's Device"?

Answer: It's a devastatingly deviously unrolled byte-copying loop, devised by Tom Duff while he was at Lucasfilm. In its "classic" form, it looks like:

```
register n = (count + 7) / 8;   /* count > 0 assumed */
switch (count % 8)
{
case 0:   do { *to = *from++;
case 7:        *to = *from++;
case 6:        *to = *from++;
case 5:        *to = *from++;
case 4:        *to = *from++;
case 3:        *to = *from++;
case 2:        *to = *from++;
case 1:        *to = *from++;
             } while (--n > 0);
}
```

In this loop, count bytes are to be copied from the array pointed to by from to the memory location pointed to by to (which is a memory-mapped device output register, which is why to isn't incremented). It solves the problem of handling the leftover bytes (when count isn't a multiple of 8) by interleaving a switch statement with the loop, which copies bytes 8 at a time. (Believe it or not, it *is* legal to have case labels buried within blocks nested in a switch statement like this. In his announcement of the technique to C's developers and the world, Duff noted that C's switch syntax, in particular its "fall through" behavior, had long been controversial and that "this code forms some sort of argument in that debate, but I'm not sure whether it's for or against.")

20.36

Question: When will the next International Obfuscated C Code Contest (IOCCC) be held? How do I submit contest entries? Who won this year's IOCCC? How can I get a copy of the current and previous winning entries?

Answer: The contest schedule is tied to the dates of the USENIX conferences at which the winners are announced. At the time of this writing, it is expected that the yearly contest will open in October. To obtain a current copy of the rules and guidelines, send e-mail with the Subject: line "send rules" to judges@toad.com. (Note that this is *not* the addresses for submitting entries.)

The rules, guidelines, and timetables tend to change from year to year. Make sure that you have the current contest's announcement prior to submitting entries.

Contest winners should be announced at the winter USENIX conference in January and are posted to the Internet sometime thereafter. Winning entries from previous years (back to 1984) are archived at ftp.uu.net (see question 18.16) under the directory pub/ioccc/.

As a last resort, previous winners may be obtained by sending e-mail to the judges address with the string "send *year* winners" in the Subject: line, where *year* is a single four-digit year, a year range, or the word "all."

Reference: Libes, *Obfuscated C and Other Mysteries*

20.37

Question: What was the `entry` keyword mentioned in K&R1?

Answer: It was reserved to allow the possibility of having functions with multiple, differently named entry points, as in FORTRAN. It was not, to anyone's knowledge, ever implemented (nor does anyone remember what sort of syntax might have been imagined for it). It has been withdrawn and is not a keyword in ANSI C. (See also question 1.12.)

Reference: K&R2 p. 259 Appendix C

20.38

Question: Where does the name "C" come from, anyway?

Answer: C was derived from Ken Thompson's experimental language B, which was inspired by Martin Richards's BCPL (Basic Combined Programming Language), which was a simplification of CPL (Cambridge Programming Language). For a while, there was speculation that C's successor might be named P (the third letter in BCPL) instead of D, but of course the most visible descendant language today is C++.

Reference: Ritchie, "The Development of the C Language"

20.39

Question: How do you pronounce "`char`"?

Answer: You can pronounce the C keyword "`char`" in at least three ways: like the English words "char," "care," or "car"; the choice is arbitrary.

20.40

Question: Where are the on-line versions of this book?

Answer: This book is an expanded version of the FAQ list from the Usenet newsgroup comp.lang.c. A copy of the on-line list may be obtained from aw.com in directory cseng/authors/summit/cfaq or ftp.eskimo.com in directory u/s/scs/C-faq/. You can also retrieve it from Usenet; it is normally posted to comp.lang.c on the first of each month, with an Expires: line that should keep it around all month. A parallel, abridged version is available (and posted), as is a list of changes accompanying each significantly updated version. (These on-line versions, though, do not contain nearly as much material as this book does.)

The various versions of the on-line list are also posted to the newsgroups comp.answers and news.answers . Several sites archive news.answers postings and other FAQ lists, including comp.lang.c's; two sites are rtfm.mit.edu (directories pub/usenet/news.answers/C-faq/ and pub/usenet/comp.lang.c/) and ftp.uu.net (directory usenet/news.answers/C-faq/). An archie server (see question 18.16) should help you find others; the command "find C-faq" should list some of them. If you don't have ftp access, a mailserver at rtfm.mit.edu can mail you FAQ lists: Send a message containing the single word `help` to mail-server@rtfm.mit.edu for more information.

Finally, a hypertext version of this book is available on the World-wide Web. The hypertext version will be updated to correct any errors and may expand to include even more questions and answers. The URL of the hypertext version is http://www.aw.com/cseng/authors/summit/cfaq/cfaq.html.

Glossary

These definitions are of terms as they are used in this book. Some of these terms have more formal, slightly different definitions; this glossary is not an authoritative dictionary. Many of these terms are from the ANSI/ISO C Standard; see ANSI §1.6 or ISO §3.

aggregate *n.* An array, structure, or union type. *adj.* Refers to such a type.

actual argument See *argument*.

alias *n.* A reference (usually in the form of a pointer) to an object that is also known via other references (i.e., its own name or other pointers). *vt.* To create such a reference.

ANSI *n.* The American National Standards Institute. *adj.* Used informally to refer to standard C; see question 11.1.

argument *n.* A value passed in an argument list during a function call or function-like macro invocation. Often emphasized "actual argument." Compare *parameter*.

argv *n.* The traditional name for the array ("vector") of command-line arguments that is passed to `main()` when a C program is invoked; see questions 11.12 and 20.3.

arithmetic *adj.* Refers to a type or value on which conventional arithmetic can be performed. The arithmetic types in C are the *integral* types and the floating types (`float`, `double`, and `long double`).

ASCII *n., adj.* The American Standard Code for Information Interchange, ANSI X3.4-86.

assignment context *n.* An expression context that is recognizably the source of an assignment or conversion to a destination of known type. The assignment contexts in C are initializations, the right-hand side of assignment expressions, casts, return statements, and function arguments in the presence of a prototype.

automatic *adj.* (Often as "automatic duration.") Refers to an object that has its storage automatically allocated on entry to a function (or a nested block) and deallocated on return from the function (or exit from the block). In other words, refers to local, nonstatic variables (as opposed to global variables or static variables whether inside or outside of a function). Compare *static*, sense 1. See question 1.30.

big-endian *adj.* Refers to storage of a multibyte quantity with the most-significant byte at the lowest address. See also *byte order*.

binary *adj.* 1. Base two. 2. Refers to I/O done in a byte-for-byte or bit-for-bit way, without formatting or interpretation, i.e., a direct copy operation between internal memory and external storage. 3. Refers to a file that is to be interpreted as a sequence of raw bytes, in which any byte values may appear. Compare *text*. See questions 12.38, 12.40, and 20.5. 4. Refers to an operator taking two operands. Compare *unary*.

bind *vt, vi.* Informally, to "stick to" or "stick together"; usually used to indicate which operand(s) are associated with which operator, based on precedence rules.

bitmask *n.* A *mask*, sense 1.

byte *n.* A unit of storage suitable for holding one character. Compare *octet*. See question 8.10. See ANSI §1.6 or ISO §3.4.

byte order *n.* The characteristic ordering of multibyte quantities (usually integral) in memory, on disk, or in a network or other bytewise I/O stream. The two common byte orders (most-significant-first and least-significant-first) are often called *big-endian* and *little-endian*.

canonical mode *n.* The mode of a *terminal driver* in which input is collected a line at a time, allowing the user to correct mistakes with the backspace/delete/rubout or other keys. See question 19.1.

.c file *n.* A *source file*, sense 2. (See questions 1.7 and 10.6.)

cast *n.* The syntax

(*type-name*)

where *type-name* is a type name such as int or char * ; used to indicate an explicit conversion of a value to another type. *vt.* To convert a value using a cast.

conforming *adj.* 1. Refers to an implementation (a compiler or other language processor) that will accept any *strictly conforming* program. 2. Refers to a program that is acceptable to a conforming implementation. (See ANSI §1.7 or ISO §4.)

cpp *n.* The traditional name for a standalone program implementing the features of the C preprocessor.

decay *vi.* To undergo an implicit transformation to a value of slightly reduced type. Informally, arrays and functions tend to decay into pointers in C. See questions 1.34 and 6.3.

declaration *n.* 1. In general, a syntactical element that describes the name(s) and type of one or more variables, functions, structures, unions, or enumerations. 2. More specifically, such a description that refers to a variable or function that has its *definition* elsewhere. See question 1.7.

declarator *n.* The "second half" of a C declaration, consisting of an identifier name along with optional *, [], or () syntax indicating (if present) that the identifier is a pointer, array, function, or some combination. See question 1.21.

definition *n.* 1. A *declaration* of a variable or function that allocates and optionally initializes storage (in the case of a variable) or provides the function body (in the case of a function). A definition in this sense is the opposite of *declaration*, sense 2. See question 1.7. 2. A declaration of a structure, union, or enumeration type that describes the type (and usually assigns a *tag*) without necessarily defining any variables of that type. 3. A preprocessor #define directive.

dereference *vt.* To look up a value referred to. Usually, the "value referred to" is the value pointed to by a pointer, so to "dereference a pointer" simply means to see what it points to (in C, either with the unary * operator or the "array subscripting" operator [ ]). Occasionally, may refer to the fetching of the value of *any* variable. See also *indirect*.

dope vector *n.* An array (or pointer-simulated array) that consists merely of pointers to other arrays (or other pointer-simulated arrays). See also *ragged array*. See questions 6.16 and 20.2.

endianness *n.* byte order.

external *n.* A function or variable that is referred to but not defined by a source file (or object module). Often shows up in the error message "undefined external" printed by a linker when a definition cannot be found.

field *n.* 1. Loosely, a member of a structure or union. (An unambiguous term is *member*.) 2. Specifically, a bitfield (see question 2.25).

formal parameter *n.* See *parameter*.

freestanding environment *n.* A C environment that does not support the C libraries; one intended for embedded applications and the like. Compare *hosted environment*. (See ANSI §1.7 or ISO §4.)

FSF *n.* The Free Software Foundation.

FTP 1. *n.* The Internet File Transfer Protocol. 2. *vt.* To transfer a file by FTP.

full expression *n.* The complete expression that forms an expression statement; one of the controlling expressions of an if, switch, while, for, or do/while statement; or the expression in an initializer or a return statement. A full expression is not part of a larger expression. (See ANSI §3.6 or ISO §6.6.)

function pointer *n.* A pointer to any function type. Compare *object pointer*.

gcc *n.* The FSF's GNU C compiler.

GNU *n.* The FSF's "GNU's Not UNIX!" project.

.h file   *n.* A *header file*.

header file *n.* A file containing declarations and certain definitions but not function bodies or global variable definitions, incorporated into a translation unit during preprocessing via the #include directive. Compare *source file*. See question 10.6.

H&S The book *C: A Reference Manual* by Samuel P. Harbison and Guy L. Steele, Jr. (see the bibliography for a complete citation).

hosted environment *n.* A C environment that also supports the C libraries. Compare *freestanding environment*. (See ANSI §1.7 or ISO §4.)

idempotent *adj.* Acting exactly once; innocuous if reapplied. In C, usually refers to header files; see questions 10.7 and 11.21.

identifier *n.* A name, usually having meaning in a particular *namespace* and *scope*. See question 1.29.

implementation *n.* A compiler or other language translator, together with its run-time libraries. Used in constructions such as "Whether plain `char` is signed or unsigned is implementation-defined" and "These identifiers are reserved to the implementation."

implementation-defined *adj.* Refers to behavior that is not fully specified by the standard but that is required to be defined, and documented, by any particular implementation. Example: whether plain `char` is signed or unsigned. See question 11.33.

#include file *n.* A *header file.*

incomplete type *n.* A type that is not completely specified but that may nevertheless be used in some contexts. Examples: dimensionless arrays; structure or union types with tags but without member information. (See ANSI §3.1.2.5 or ISO §6.1.2.5.)

in-band *adj.* Refers to a sentinel value that is not always unique within the set of values where it appears. Compare *out-of-band.* Example: CP/M or MS-DOS control-Z end-of-file markers. See question 12.40.

indirect *vi.* To apply a level of indirection. For example, to "indirect on a pointer" means to chase where the pointer points to (as opposed to merely discovering the pointer's value). See also *dereference.*

int *n.* The integral type, usually matching a machine's natural word size, which is most often used (and in some cases is used by default) to represent integers in C.

integer *n.* An integer of some size (perhaps `short` or `long`), not necessarily plain `int`.

integral *adj.* Refers to a type that can represent integers. The integral types in C are `char`, three sizes of `int` (`short`, plain, and `long`), `signed` and `unsigned` variants of all of these, and enumerations.

ISO *n.* The International Organization for Standardization or Organisation Internationale de Normalisation.

K&R *n.* 1. The book *The C Programming Language* (see the bibliography for a complete citation). 2. That book's authors, Brian Kernighan and Dennis Ritchie. *adj.* Refers to the early version of C described in the first edition ("K&R1") of the book.

lhs *n.* The left-hand side, usually of an assignment, or more generally, of any binary operator.

lint *n.* A program written by Steve Johnson as companion to his `pcc`, for performing cross-file and other error checking not normally performed by C compilers. The name supposedly derives from the bits of fluff it picks from programs. *vt.* To check a program with `lint`.

little-endian *adj.* Refers to storage of a multibyte quantity with the least-significant byte at the lowest address. See also *byte order.*

lvalue *n.* Originally, an expression that could appear on the left-hand sign of an assignment operator; hence, something that can perhaps be assigned to. More precisely, something that has a location, as opposed to a transient value. In the assignment

```
a = b;
```

a is an lvalue and is not fetched but is written to. Compare *rvalue*. See also question 6.7. See ANSI §3.2.2.1 (especially footnote 31) or ISO §6.2.2.1.

mask 1. *n.* An integer value interpreted specifically as a pattern of 1s and 0s with which to perform bitwise operations (&, |, etc.). 2. *vt.* To select certain bits using a mask (sense 1) and a bitwise operator. See question 20.7.

member *n.* One of the typed components of a structure or a union.

namespace *n.* A context within which names (identifiers) may be defined. There are several namespaces in C; for example, an ordinary identifier can have the same name as a structure tag, without ambiguity. See question 1.29.

narrow *adj.* Refers to a type that is widened under the default argument promotions: char, short, or float. See questions 11.3 and 15.2.

nonreentrant *adj.* Refers to a piece of code that makes use of static memory or temporarily leaves global data structures in an inconsistent state, such that it cannot safely be called while another instance of itself is already active. (That is, it cannot be called from an interrupt handler, because it might have been the code interrupted.)

"notreached" *interj.* A directive indicating to lint or some other program checker that control flow cannot reach a particular point and that certain warnings (e.g., "control falls off end of function without return") should therefore be suppressed. See question 11.12.

null pointer *n.* A distinguished pointer value that is not the address of any object or function. See question 5.1.

null pointer constant *n.* An integral constant expression with value 0 (or such an expression cast to void *), used to request a *null pointer*. See question 5.2.

O(n) *adj.* A notation referring to the "order" or computational complexity of an algorithm. O(n) algorithms take time roughly proportional to the number of items operated on. $O(n^2)$ algorithms take time proportional to the square of the number of items, etc.

object *n.* Any piece of data that can be manipulated by a C program: a simple variable, an array, a structure, a piece of malloc'ed memory, etc. See also *object pointer*.

object pointer *n.* A pointer to any object or incomplete type. Compare *function pointer*.

octet *n.* An 8-bit quantity. Compare *byte*.

opaque *adj.* Refers to a data type intended to be abstract: code using the type is not supposed to know how the type is implemented (whether it is a simple type or a structure and if a structure, what fields it contains). See question 2.4.

order of evaluation *n.* The order in which the operations implied by an expression are actually carried out by the processor. Compare *precedence*. See question 3.4.

out-of-band *adj.* Refers to a sentinel or otherwise exceptional value that is distinct from all normal values that can appear in some context (e.g., in a set of function return values, etc.). Compare *in-band*. Example: EOF (see question 12.1).

parameter *n.* The identifier in a function definition, function-like macro definition, or function prototype declaration that stands for the actual argument that will be passed. Often emphasized "formal parameter." Compare *argument*.
In the code

```
main()
{
    f(5);
    return 0;
}

f(int i);
{
}
```

the formal parameter of f is i and the actual argument is 5.
In the fragment

```
extern int g(int apple);
int orange = 5;
g(orange);
```

the formal parameter of g is apple and the actual argument is orange.

pass by reference *n.* An argument-passing mechanism in which a function receives a reference to the actual argument such that if it modifies it, it modifies the value in the caller. Not available in C (see question 4.11).

pass by value *n.* An argument-passing mechanism in which a function receives a copy of the actual argument such that if it modifies it, it modifies only its own copy (and does not affect the value in the caller). Always used in C. See questions 4.8, 4.11, and 7.21.

pcc *n.* Steve Johnson's Portable C Compiler, first written for the PDP–11 (as an alternative to Dennis Ritchie's cc) circa 1978. Retargeted to the VAX during the UNIX 32V and BSD projects, pcc saw *very* wide distribution and served as the base for a large number of C compilers. As much as K&R1, it served as the *de facto* definition of C for many years, until X3J11 began its work. (Note that the PCC mentioned in question 18.3 is probably no relation.)

precedence *n.* The "strength" of an operator, indicating how tightly it binds to its operands during parsing, especially as compared to other nearby operators. Along with associativity and explicit parentheses, precedence determines how an expression is parsed: which operators are applied to which operands and which subexpressions are the operands of which operators. Precedence does not necessarily say anything about *order of evaluation*; see question 3.4.

preprocessor *n.* The part of a compiler (traditionally, a separate program; hence the name) that handles the `#include`, `#define`, `#ifdef`, and related directives and performs substitution of defined macros in the rest of the program source.

pointer context *n.* An expression context in which it can be recognized that a pointer value is required. The pointer contexts in C are:

- any *assignment context* in which the destination (left-hand side) has pointer type;
- an `==` or `!=` comparison in which one side has pointer type;
- the second and third operands of the `?:` operator, when one of them has pointer type; and
- the operand of a pointer cast, such as `(char *)` or `(void *)`.

See question 5.2.

pun *vt.* To contrive to treat an object as if it had a different type, usually by using a union or an expression of the form `*(othertype *)&object`.

ragged array *n.* An array, usually simulated with pointers, in which the rows are not necessarily of the same length. See also *dope vector*. See questions 6.16 and 20.2.

reentrant *adj.* Refers to code that can safely be called from interrupts or in other circumstances in which it is possible that another instance of the code is simultaneously active. Reentrant code has to be very careful of the way it manipulates data: All data must either be local or else protected by semaphores or the like.

RFC *n.* An Internet Request For Comments document, available by anonymous ftp from ds.internic.net and many other sites.

rhs *n.* The right-hand side, usually of an assignment, or more generally, of any binary operator.

rvalue *n.* Originally, an expression that could appear on the right-hand sign of an assignment operator. More generally, any value that can participate in an expression or be assigned to some other variable. In the assignment

```
a = b;
```

b is an rvalue and has its value fetched. Compare *lvalue*. See ANSI §3.2.2.1 (especially footnote 31) or ISO §6.2.2.1. See also questions 3.16 and 4.5.

scope *n.* The region over which a declaration is active. *adj.* "In scope": visible. See question 1.29.

semantics *n.* The meaning behind a program: the interpretation that the compiler (or other translator) places on the various source code constructs. Compare *syntax*.

short circuit *v.* To prematurely terminate the evaluation of an expression when the outcome is determined. The short-circuiting operators in C are &&, ||, and ?:. In the case of && and ||, the second (right-hand) operand is not evaluated if the first one determines the outcome (is zero in the case of && or nonzero in the case of ||). In the case of ?:, only one of the second and third operands is evaluated, depending on the value of the first operand. See question 3.6.

side effect *n.* Something permanent that happens when an expression or subexpression is evaluated, beyond simply yielding a value. Typical side effects are: modifying a variable, printing something. See ANSI §2.1.2.3 or ISO §5.1.2.3.

sign preserving *adj.* Another name for the *unsigned preserving* rules.

source file *n.* 1. Any file containing C source. 2. More specifically, a file with a name ending in .c, containing function bodies and global variable definitions (and perhaps declarations and definitions of other kinds). Compare *header file, translation unit.* See questions 1.7 and 10.6.

static *adj.* 1. (Often as "static duration.") Refers to an object that persists throughout the lifetime of a program, being allocated and initialized just once, at program startup. Compare *automatic.* See question 1.30. 2. Local to a source file, i.e., not of global scope.

strictly conforming *adj.* Refers to a program that uses only the features described in the ANSI/ISO C Standard and does not depend on any unspecified, undefined, or implementation-defined behavior. (See ANSI §1.7 or ISO §4.)

string *n.* An array of char, or any allocated region of memory, containing a sequence of characters terminated with '\0'.

stringize *vt.* To convert a source token into a string literal. See questions 11.17 and 11.18.

string literal *n.* A sequence of characters between double quotes in source code. Used to initialize an array of char or to request an anonymous array containing a constant string (which will generally be accessed by the pointer the anonymous array decays to). See question 1.32.

syntax *n.* The text of a program: the series of tokens in which it is expressed. Compare *semantics.*

tag *n.* The (optional) name for a particular structure, union, or enumeration. See question 2.1.

token *n.* 1. The smallest syntactic unit generally seen by a compiler or other translator: a keyword, identifier, binary operator (including multicharacter operators such as += and &&), etc. 2. A whitespace-separated word within a string (see question 13.6).

translation unit *n.* The set of source files seen by the compiler and translated as a unit: generally one .c file (that is, *source file*, sense 2), plus all header files mentioned in #include directives.

undefined *adj.* Refers to behavior that is not specified by the standard, for which an implementation is *not* required to do anything reasonable. Example: the behavior of the expression i = i++. See questions 3.3 and 11.33.

terminal driver *n.* That portion of the system software responsible for character-based input and output, usually interactive; originally from and to a serially connected terminal, now more generally any virtual terminal, such as a window or network login session. See question 19.1.

text *adj.* Refers to a file or I/O mode intended for handling human-readable text, specifically, printable characters arranged into lines. Compare *binary*, sense 3. See question 12.40.

translator *n.* A program (compiler, interpreter, `lint`, etc.) that parses and interprets semantic meaning in C syntax.

unary *adj.* Refers to an operator taking one operand. Compare *binary*, sense 4.

unroll *vt.* To replicate the body of a loop one or more times (while correspondingly reducing the number of iterations) to improve efficiency by reducing loop control overhead (but at the expense of increased code size).

unsigned preserving *adj.* Refers to a set of rules, common in pre-ANSI implementations, for promoting signed and unsigned types that meet across binary operators and for promoting narrow unsigned types in general. Under the unsigned preserving rules, promotion is always to an unsigned type. Compare *value preserving*. See question 3.19.

unspecified *adj.* Refers to behavior that is not fully specified by the standard, for which each implementation must choose some behavior, though it need not be documented or even consistent. Example: the order of evaluation of function arguments and other subexpressions. See question 11.33.

value preserving *adj.* Refers to a set of rules, mandated by the ANSI C Standard and also present in some pre-ANSI implementations, for promoting signed and unsigned types that meet across binary operators and for promoting narrow unsigned types in general. Under the value preserving rules, promotion is to a signed type if it is large enough to preserve all values; otherwise to an unsigned type. Compare *unsigned preserving*. See question 3.19.

varargs *adj.* 1. Refers to a function that accepts a variable number of arguments, e.g., `printf`. (A synonym for *variadic*.) 2. Refers to one of the arguments in the variable-length part of a variable-length argument list.

variadic *adj.* Refers to a function that accepts a variable number of arguments, e.g., `printf`. (A synonym for *varargs*, sense 1.)

wrapper *n.* A function (or macro) that is "wrapped around" another, providing a bit of added functionality. For example, a wrapper around `malloc` might check `malloc`'s return value.

X3.159 *n.* The original ANSI C Standard, ANSI X3.159-1989. See question 11.1.

X3J11 *n.* The committee charged by ANSI with the task of drafting the C Standard. X3J11 now functions as the U.S. Technical Advisory Group to the ISO C standardization working group WG14. See question 11.1.

Bibliography

In the references sections in the individual questions, the following abbreviations are used:

ANSI   American National Standards Institute, American National Standard for Information Systems—Programming Language—C
CT&P   Andrew Koenig, *C Traps and Pitfalls*
H&S   Harbison and Steele, *C: A Reference Manual*
ISO   International Organization for Standardization, ISO 9899:1990
K&R1   Kernighan and Ritchie, *The C Programming Language*, First Edition
K&R2   Kernighan and Ritchie, *The C Programming Language*, Second Edition
PCS   Mark Horton, *Portable C Software*
Rationale Americal National Standards Institute, Rationale for American National Standard for Information Systems—Programming Language—C

Abramowitz, Milton, and Irene A. Stegun, eds. *Handbook of Mathematical Functions, with Formulas, Graphs, and Mathematical Tables*, Tenth Edition, U.S. Government Printing Office, 1972, ISBN 0-16-000202-8. (Also reprinted by Dover, 1964, ISBN 0-486-61272-4.)
Americal National Standards Institute. *American National Standard for Information Systems—Programming Language—C*, ANSI X3.159-1989 (see question 11.2). [ANSI]
———. *Rationale for American National Standard for Information Systems—Programming Language—C* (see question 11.2). [Rationale]

Bentley, Jon. *Programming Pearls*, Addison-Wesley, 1986, ISBN 0-201-10331-1.
———. *More Programming Pearls*, Addison-Wesley, 1988, ISBN 0-201-11889-0.

————. *Writing Efficient Programs*, Prentice-Hall, 1982, ISBN 0-13-970244-X.

Box, G.E.P., and Mervin E. Muller. "A Note on the Generation of Random Normal Deviates," *Annals of Mathematical Statistics*, Vol. 29 #2, June 1958, pp. 610–1.

Burki, David. "Date Conversions," *The C Users Journal*, February 1993, pp. 29–34.

Carroll, Lewis. *Through the Looking-Glass.*

————. "What the Tortoise Said to Achilles," *Mind*, n.s., Vol. 4, 1895, pp. 278–80. (Appears in Hofstadter, *Gödel, Escher, Bach*, 1979, pp. 43–5.)

Cline, Marshall P., and Greg A. Lomow. *C++ FAQs: Frequently Asked Questions*, Addison-Wesley, 1995, ISBN 0-201-58958-3.

Clinger, William D. "How to Read Floating-Point Numbers Accurately," *SIGPLAN Notices*, Vol. 25 #6, June 1990.

Darwin, Ian F. *Checking C Programs with lint*, O'Reilly, 1988, ISBN 0-937175-30-7.

Dijkstra, E. "Go To Statement Considered Harmful," *Communications of the ACM*, Vol. 11 #3, March 1968, pp. 147–8.

Goldberg, David. "What Every Computer Scientist Should Know about Floating-Point Arithmetic," *ACM Computing Surveys*, Vol. 23 #1, March 1991, pp. 5–48.

Harbison, Samuel P., and Guy L. Steele, Jr. *C: A Reference Manual*, Fourth Edition, Prentice-Hall, 1995, ISBN 0-13-326224-3. [H&S]

Horton, Mark R. *Portable C Software*, Prentice-Hall, 1990, ISBN 0-13-868050-7. [PCS]

Institute of Electrical and Electronics Engineers. *Portable Operating System Interface (POSIX)—Part 1: System Application Program Interface (API) [C Language]*, IEEE Std. 1003.1, ISO/IEC 9945-1.

International Organization for Standardization. *Programming Languages—C*, ISO/IEC 9899:1990 (see question 11.2). [ISO]

Kernighan, Brian W., and P.J. Plauger. *The Elements of Programming Style*, Second Edition, McGraw-Hill, 1978, ISBN 0-07-034207-5.

Kernighan, Brian W., and Dennis M. Ritchie. *The C Programming Language*, Prentice-Hall, 1978, ISBN 0-13-110163-3. [K&R1]

————. *The C Programming Language*, Second Edition, Prentice Hall, 1988, ISBN 0-13-110362-8, 0-13-110370-9. [K&R2]

Knuth, Donald E. *The Art of Computer Programming*. Volume 1: *Fundamental Algorithms*, Second Edition, Addison-Wesley, 1973, ISBN 0-201-03809-9. Volume 2: *Seminumerical Algorithms*, Second Edition, Addison-Wesley, 1981, ISBN 0-201-03822-6. Volume 3: *Sorting and Searching*, Addison-Wesley, 1973, ISBN 0-201-03803-X. [Knuth]

————. "Structured Programming with goto Statements," ACM *Computing Surveys*, Vol. 6 #4, December 1975, pp. 261–301.

Koenig, Andrew. C *Traps and Pitfalls*, Addison-Wesley, 1989, ISBN 0-201-17928-8. [CT&P]

Libes, Don. *Obfuscated C and Other Mysteries*, Wiley, 1993, ISBN 0-471-57805-3.

Marsaglia, G., and T.A. Bray. "A Convenient Method for Generating Normal Variables," *SIAM Review*, Vol. 6 #3, July 1964.

Park, Stephen K., and Keith W. Miller. "Random Number Generators: Good Ones are Hard to Find," *Communications of the ACM*, Vol. 31 #10, October 1988, pp. 1192–1201 (also technical correspondence August 1989, pp. 1020–4, and July 1993, pp. 108–10).

Plauger, P.J. *The Standard C Library*, Prentice-Hall, 1992, ISBN 0-13-131509-9.

Plum, Thomas. C *Programming Guidelines*, Second Edition, Plum Hall, 1989, ISBN 0-911537-07-4.

Press, William H., Saul A. Teukolsky, William T. Vetterling, and Brian P. Flannery. *Numerical Recipes in C*, Second Edition, Cambridge University Press, 1992, ISBN 0-521-43108-5.

Ritchie, Dennis M. "The Development of the C Language," 2nd ACM HOPL Conference, April 1993.

Schumacher, Dale. ed. *Software Solutions in C*, AP Professional, 1994, ISBN 0-12-632360-7.

Sedgewick, Robert. *Algorithms in C*, Addison-Wesley, 1990, ISBN 0-201-51425-7.

Simonyi, Charles, and Martin Heller. "The Hungarian Revolution," *Byte*, August, 1991, pp.131–8.

Steele, Guy L. Jr., and Jon L. White. "How to Print Floating-Point Numbers Accurately," *SIGPLAN Notices*, Vol. 25 #6, June 1990.

Straker, David. C *Style: Standards and Guidelines*, Prentice-Hall, ISBN 0-13-116898-3.

Strang, John. *Programming with curses*, O'Reilly, 1986, ISBN 0-937175-02-1.

Strang, John, Linda Mui, and Tim O'Reilly. *termcap & terminfo*, O'Reilly, 1988, ISBN 0-937175-22-6.

Strunk, William Jr., and E.B. White. *The Elements of Style*, Third Edition, Macmillan, 1979, ISBN 0-02-418220-6.

Sun Microsystems, Inc., "XDR: External Data Representation standard," Internet RFC 1014, 1987.

Tondo, Clovis L., and Scott E. Gimpel. *The C Answer Book*, Second Edition, Prentice-Hall, 1989, ISBN 0-13-109653-2.

U.S. Naval Observatory Nautical Almanac Office, *The Astronomical Almanac for the year 1994.*

Wu, Sun, and Udi Manber. "AGREP—A Fast Approximate Pattern-Matching Tool," USENIX Conference Proceedings, Winter 1992, pp. 153–62.

Zeller, Chr. "Kalender-Formeln," *Acta Mathematica*, Vol. 9, November 1886.

There is another bibliography in the revised Indian Hill style guide (see question 17.9). See also question 18.10.

Index

Related Titles
from Addison-Wesley

Barton/Nackman, *Scientific and Engineering C++: An Introduction to Advanced Techniques and Examples*, © 1994

Brooks, *The Mythical Man-Month: Essays on Software Engineering Anniversary Edition*, © 1996

Carroll/Ellis, *Designing and Coding Reusable C++*, © 1995

Cline/Lomow, *C++ FAQs: Frequently Asked Questions*, © 1994

Ellis/Stroustrup, *The Annotated C++ Reference Manual*, © 1990

Kelley/Pohl, *A Book on C, Third Edition*, © 1995

Kelley/Pohl, *C by Dissection: The Essentials of C Programming, Second Edition*, © 1992

Koenig, *C Traps and Pitfalls*, © 1989

Lippman, *C++ Primer, Second Edition*, © 1991

Sedgewick, *Algorithms in C*, © 1990

Stroustrup, *The C++ Programming Language, Second Edition*, © 1991

Stroustrup, *The Design and Evolution of C++*, © 1994

Teale, *C++ IOStreams Handbook*, © 1993

Winston, *On to C*, © 1994